Although the opinions of whites on issues of race and inequality have been examined in depth, the perceptions of blacks about these issues have been largely ignored. This book is a pathbreaking analysis of black opinions about the sources of their inequality in American society and the appropriate means for redressing this imbalance.

Using the results of a variety of national surveys of blacks conducted during the past decade, Sigelman and Welch describe the range of opinion within the black population and account for different views by identifying key influences on opinion formation. They examine correlations between various personal characteristics, such as gender, age, socioeconomic status, and educational attainment, and different explanations of inequality, focusing either on conditions within the black community or on exogenous factors, such as discrimination.

The perception of the prevalence of discrimination is determined to be a central factor in explanations of inequality as well as in opinions about the appropriate policies for promoting racial parity, such as busing and affirmative action. The findings indicate that blacks perceive a good deal more discrimination than whites think occurs, that blacks by and large have different explanations for inequality than have most whites, and that blacks favor more activist strategies to overcome racial inequality. The authors find, however, that blacks vary widely in their opinions and are in most instances no more homogenous in their attitudes than are whites. Among both blacks and whites, different explanations for inequality lead to different stances on the appropriate strategies for combating black inequality.

Black Americans' views of racial inequality

Black Americans' views of racial inequality

The dream deferred

Lee Sigelman
University of Arizona

Susan Welch
University of Nebraska

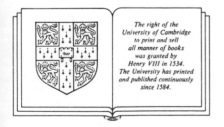

The right of the
University of Cambridge
to print and sell
all manner of books
was granted by
Henry VIII in 1534.
The University has printed
and published continuously
since 1584.

CAMBRIDGE UNIVERSITY PRESS
Cambridge
New York   Port Chester   Melbourne   Sydney

Published by the Press Syndicate of the University of Cambridge
The Pitt Building, Trumpington Street, Cambridge CB2 1RP
40 West 20th Street, New York, NY 10011, USA
10 Stamford Road, Oakleigh, Melbourne 3166, Australia

First published 1991

Printed in the United States of America

Library of Congress Cataloging-in-Publication Data
Sigelman, Lee.
    Black Americans' views of racial inequality : the dream deferred /
.Lee Sigelman and Susan Welch.
        p.   cm
    Includes bibliographical references.
    ISBN 0–521–40015–5
    1. Racism – United States – Public opinion.   2. United States – Race
relations – Public opinion. 3. Afro-Americans – Civil rights – Public
opinion.   4. Afro–Americans – Attitudes. 5. Public opinion – United
States.   I. Welch, Susan.   II. Title.
E185.615.S55 1991
305.896'073 – dc20   90-41558
                                                                       CIP

British Library Cataloging in Publication Data
Sigelman, Lee
    Black Americans' views of racial inequality : the dream
    deferred.
    1. United States. Racism. Attitudes of black persons
    I. Title   II. Welch, Susan
    305.800973

ISBN 0–521–40015–5 hardback

Contents

Tables and figures

Tables

Figures

Preface

This is a book about what and how black Americans think about racial inequality in the United States. Throughout this book, we employ the terms "blacks" and "black Americans" in preference to "African-American," even though the latter usage is becoming much more common and, in many quarters, much more acceptable. In a book that focuses on survey data concerning blacks' attitudes and opinions, it seems peculiarly appropriate that our usage be guided by a September–October 1989 ABC News/ *Washington Post* poll (which we discuss in considerable detail later in the book) indicating that blacks prefer "black" over "African-American" by a margin of 66 percent to 22 percent, as do whites, by an even wider margin.

We are grateful to numerous colleagues who have stimulated our thinking about the issues examined here. Among these are Lucius Barker, Lawrence Bobo, Ronald Brown, Michael Combs, Michael Dawson, Stanley Feldman, Paula McClain, Dianne Pinderhughes, Carol Sigelman, and Paul Sniderman. Richard Morin of the *Washington Post* graciously made some unpublished findings available to us. Gerhard Arminger provided wise methodological counsel, and Ken Girodias, Dennis Glover, Bill Lockwood, and Fuchang Wang all helped prepare the data sets for analysis. Emily Loose handled the manuscript professionally and offered numerous valuable suggestions for revision. Alan Booth and Andrew Welch Booth won Susan Welch's gratitude by taking everything in stride.

We dedicate this book to our parents, Doris W. Sigelman and Delbert F. and Marie S. Welch.

Introduction

Racial prejudice and discrimination have, in the finest social science tradition, long been considered worthy research topics, both for the ameliorative purposes to which research can be put and for the theoretical advances that careful analysis of these issues can produce. But for reasons both simple and complex, such research has ultimately told us distressingly little about what and how black Americans think about racial inequality.

Over the years, social scientists have written uncounted thousands of pages about values, attitudes, opinions, and behavior involving relations between blacks and whites. Classics like Gunnar Myrdal's *An American Dilemma,* published in 1944, and Gordon Allport's *The Nature of Prejudice,* published a decade later, established the basic research agenda to which many other works, such as Adorno, Frenkel-Brunswik, Levinson, and Sanford's *The Authoritarian Personality* (1950) and Selznick and Steinberg's *The Tenacity of Prejudice* (1969) also contributed. The unprecedented racial strife of the 1960s and 1970s sparked a doubling and redoubling of scholarly interest in prejudice and discrimination, leading to a new outpouring of research and an improved understanding of many vital issues. Since then, the focus on racism and racial attitudes has, if anything, become even more intense: In the last decade alone, several truly important works have been published, including Apostle, Glock, Piazza, and Suezele's *The Anatomy of Racial Attitudes* (1983), Kluegel and Smith's *Beliefs about Inequality* (1986), Schuman, Steeh, and Bobo's *Racial Attitudes in America* (1985), and Sniderman with Hagen's *Race and Inequality* (1985).

It is impossible to understand black-white relations in this country without consulting these books. Even so, in these leading works on racial attitudes in the United States, black people are conspicuous largely by their absence. These are books about white people, with only a passing glance toward blacks (a single chapter in *Racial Attitudes in America,* some scattered charts in *Beliefs about Inequality*), who inhabit their pages largely as

1

images in the minds of whites rather than *people* in their own right. One whose understanding of racial issues was based purely on these studies might thus be forgiven for having inferred that in contrast to living, breathing white people, blacks are mere mental constructs. Or perhaps one might infer that racial inequality is a matter of surpassing concern to whites but is of only incidental interest to blacks.

There are exceptions, of course. Matthews and Prothro's (1966) groundbreaking study of the political attitudes and behavior of black and white Southerners was, as far as we know, the first major survey of American blacks. It was followed two years later by a *Newsweek*-commissioned national survey of blacks (Brink and Harris, 1964, 1966). Thereafter, no national surveys of blacks were conducted for fifteen years, although a variety of local studies tapped attitudes of black urban residents in the wake of the protest and riots of the 1960s. Aberbach and Walker's (1973) Detroit study, Campbell and Schuman's (1968) fifteen-city study, and Sears and McConahay's (1973) Los Angeles study were among the most prominent of these (see also Caplan and Paige, 1968; Cataldo, Johnson, and Kellstedt, 1970; Farley, Hatchett, and Schumann, 1979; Marx, 1967; Orbell, 1967; Schuman and Hatchett, 1974). These local studies are quite revealing, but because they focus on issues relating directly to the riots and, in some cases, to black reactions to various protest tactics, they miss the broader issues with which we are concerned in this book. More recent analyses of black attitudes and behavior have drawn primarily upon the National Opinion Research Center's (NORC) General Social Survey (GSS) or the quadrennial American National Election Study (see, e.g., Herring, 1989; Parent and Stekler, 1985; Seltzer and Smith, 1985; Welch and Combs, 1985; for recent exceptions, see Allen, Dawson, and Brown, 1989; Woodrum and Bell, 1989), but, as we will discuss below, these worthwhile data bases have their own limitations. In the last several years, a few national surveys of blacks have been conducted, but little research based on these surveys has yet been published.

Thus, when we consider almost any controversial issue relating to race, we find that a great deal is known about whites' attitudes but little is known about blacks'. Take, for example, the issue of busing. Reams have been written about where whites stand on busing, and why (see, e.g., Bobo, 1983; Kelley, 1974; McClendon, 1985; McConahay, 1982; Sears and Allen, 1984; Sears, Hensler, and Speer, 1979; Sears and Kinder, 1985), but we know remarkably little about the attitudes of blacks, the ostensible beneficiaries of the policy. The same can be said of affirmative action, welfare programs, and virtually every other policy issue that bears on race relations and the social, economic, and political advancement of blacks. Even less is known about how blacks view racial inequality itself (exceptions are Bobo, 1989; Jaynes and Williams, 1989; Parent, 1985).

Clearly, much has been learned and much more remains to be learned from studies of the racial perceptions, beliefs, attitudes, and opinions of white people. But if we are to understand racial attitudes in the United States, we cannot be content to probe into the minds of whites while ignoring blacks.[1]

Why do we know so little?

Compared to what we know about whites, our understanding of blacks' attitudes remains rudimentary. How has this come to pass? We can think of many answers, but two stand out.

The matter of conscious priorities

The first answer is simply that it has long been considered more important to understand whites' attitudes than blacks'. In part, this priority may reflect a conscious or unconscious denigration of blacks by social scientists, though we doubt that this has been the primary problem in recent decades. It may also stem from an assumption that blacks' views on most racial issues are so transparent that research is largely superfluous (A. W. Smith, 1987: 443). This attitude ignores, among other things, the vast differences that exist among blacks in socioeconomic standing and policy views, for example, as well as in such basic racial views as insulation versus integration, passivity versus militancy, avoidance versus "whiteward" mobility, and self-hatred versus racial pride (Johnson, 1957). The priority placed on understanding white rather than black views about race may also stem from the relative scarcity of black social scientists. Much, though certainly not all, of the recent research on black attitudes has been done by black political scientists, psychologists, and sociologists. Finally, the exclusion of blacks as subjects in research on racial attitudes may be a product of the natural reluctance of survey researchers to ask sensitive, or even painful, personal questions. For any or all of these reasons, until recently it has been standard practice for survey researchers to skip race-related questions in interviews with black respondents.[2]

A propensity to take blacks' attitudes for granted and a reluctance to ask sensitive questions undoubtedly help explain why we know so little about what and how blacks think about racial inequality. But far more influential, in our view, has been the basic intellectual and political assumption motivating research on racial attitudes. Myrdal's (1944) characterization of the

American racial dilemma as fundamentally "a white man's problem" set the agenda for research on race relations. Thereafter, researchers, following Myrdal's lead, devoted primary attention to "what goes on in the minds of white Americans."[3] This view was well expressed by Paul Sheatsley, a pioneer in the study of whites' attitudes on race issues, who, looking back on early survey research efforts, noted that "It never occurred to us when we wrote questions in the Forties and Fifties to ask them of blacks because Myrdal's dilemma was a white dilemma and it was white attitudes that demanded study" (quoted by Schuman et al., 1985: 139). In this sense, the single-minded concentration on whites that has so dominated the research literature reflects more than anything else a widespread acceptance of Myrdal's conviction that the solution to the American dilemma is largely a matter of changing the negative attitudes white people hold toward blacks. This assumption stirred great controversy when the Kerner Commission articulated it in the late 1960s, but by then it had long since achieved paradigmatic status in social science.

Nor does the fault lie exclusively within the research community. Large survey projects, especially those focusing on relatively small subpopulations, require large-scale funding. Research on blacks has not always been a high priority for funding agencies. For example, though early proposals for funding NORC's GSS advocated facilitating the analysis of blacks' attitudes by drawing larger samples of blacks than their small percentage of the population would warrant, the black oversample was deleted from the initial GSS budget. Only sporadically, and later in the GSS's history, have black oversamples been carried out.

The matter of sheer numbers

The second reason why researchers have been so inattentive to the racial perceptions and attitudes of blacks has to do with the fact that blacks comprise only about 12 percent of the population of the United States. Like many other social, cultural, economic, and political minorities, black Americans pose a difficult target for survey research precisely because they are a minority. A researcher interested in the voting habits of, say, American Jews must somehow overcome the simple demographic fact that only about three or four of every hundred Americans are Jewish. To be sure, this leaves millions of Jews to study, but on a national basis Jews are, if not exactly needles in a haystack, relatively scarce. By chance, a random sample of 1,500 Americans, which is roughly the size of the samples drawn for many nationwide surveys, will include only fifty or sixty Jews – not nearly enough to provide a reliable basis for generalization, let alone to permit one to control for the other factors that have to be taken into account in analyzing political behavior (but see Welch and Ullrich, 1984). Of course, blacks outnumber Jews in the United States, but the basic problem remains. A random sample of 1,500 Americans will contain only about 180 blacks, not enough to sustain systematic analysis.

One solution is to sample from concentrated minority populations; for example, to look for Jews in New York City, where they are relatively numerous, rather than nationwide, where they are relatively rare. This strategy has much to recommend it, but it has a great drawback as well. Although the researcher presumably wants to say something about American Jews in general, Jews in New York may differ in important ways from their national counterparts. New York Jews are obviously unrepresentative geographically, and probably unrepresentative in income, education, cosmopolitan attitudes, and a host of other factors. Indeed, living close to a high proportion of other Jews may have its own contextual effects on social and political attitudes.

If the concentrated minority from which one has sampled is unrepresentative of its "parent" group in terms of its central tendencies or the diversity it encompasses, then sampling from it will confer an advantage in numbers without any corresponding advantage in generalizability. By the same token, sampling blacks in, say, Detroit provides much useful information, but does not allow one to address questions about the attitudes of black Americans in general, let alone to probe the attitudinal impacts of factors that might not be important in Detroit.

Thus, although general population surveys facilitate comparative research on men and women, Southerners and non-Southerners, urbanites and suburbanites, and so on, researchers interested in the attitudes and behavior of relatively small minorities like blacks cannot rely on general population surveys. The alternative of a specially targeted survey – in this case, a national survey of blacks – must overcome numerous conceptual, methodological, and technical problems of its own, such as defining the black population, devising a cost-effective sampling strategy, constructing valid, reliable questions that are comparable to items used in surveys of whites, and recruiting large numbers of trained black interviewers (see, e.g., Anderson, Silver, and Abramson, 1988; Jackson, Tucker, and Bowman, 1982; Morin, 1989). Due to the combined weight of these problems, survey research on blacks is still in its infancy.

Research goals and strategy

Because understanding blacks' attitudes toward racial inequality has traditionally been viewed as a low-priority, high-difficulty task, most researchers and funding agencies have turned their attention to projects thought to be of higher priority or lesser difficulty. This is our answer to the question of why we currently know so little about what and how black Americans think about black-white inequality.

We have no quarrel with the view that in the United States, racial prejudice and discrimination are mainly products of "what goes on in the minds of white Americans." But much can be learned by broadening the focus to include the minority side of the relationship. Most social scientists would consider it ludicrous to study sex role attitudes by focusing exclusively on men, but just such an asymmetry has occurred in research on racial attitudes.

The basic problem, then, is that the research literature, though worthwhile, is too narrow. Because it concentrates on white people's attitudes toward racial inequality, it does not, for the most part, permit us to speak *generically* about attitudes toward racial inequality, let alone about the attitudes of blacks. Whites' attitudes are obviously well worth trying to unravel, but if the purpose is to develop an understanding of attitudes toward racial inequality that transcends or clarifies racial differences, a broadening of the research agenda is clearly in order.

Questions to be addressed

Three aspects of blacks' attitudes toward racial inequality are at the center of our inquiry. The first are *perceptions*. To what extent do blacks themselves see themselves as targets of racial prejudice and discrimination, and do they perceive these problems as diminishing or increasing? The second are *explanations*. Drawing heavily on attribution theory and research and on recent studies of whites' explanations of inequality, we explore the ways blacks account for racial inequality in American society. Finally, we focus on *preferences* concerning various means of reducing racial inequality. We cast our net widely to include such disparate policies as busing to achieve racial balance in the schools, affirmative action, and public welfare programs.

On each of these topics, we initially explore two major issues of a descriptive nature. First, what are the broad outlines of black attitudes on each topic, and how have these attitudes changed over time? Second, at what points do the opinions of the majority of blacks converge with those of the majority of whites, and at what points do they diverge? Although this is a book about blacks' attitudes, we believe that the attitudes of whites illuminate those of blacks, and vice versa. We are interested, then, in determining where common ground exists between the two races and where it does not.

Beyond describing what blacks believe, we hope to gain a better under-

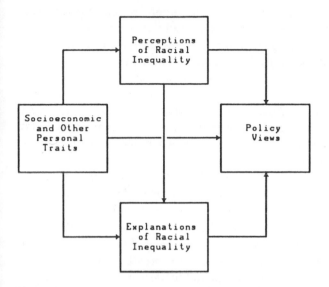

Figure 1.1. Model of blacks' views of racial inequality

standing of how blacks think about these issues and to account for attitudinal differentiation among blacks. A simple outline of our explanatory model is shown in Figure 1.1, which begins with differences among blacks in socioeconomic and other *personal characteristics*. These characteristics include gender, age, interracial friendship, and various aspects of socioeconomic status, including family income, educational attainment, home ownership, subjective class identification, perceived economic pressure, unemployment, and receipt of government assistance.

Our model suggests that these personal characteristics can be used to predict blacks' perceptions of racial discrimination. That is, we expect that these perceptions are shaped by individual characteristics such as age and social status. Living and working in a variety of conditions, different people experience different realities and come to perceive discrimination differently. Although it would be foolish to assume that all these personal experiences can be fully captured by a few variables, we do believe that these experiences are related to one's position in society, as defined by such categories as education, age, income, and gender. These characteristics affect the reality of discrimination that a black person faces; we expect more discrimination to be directed against the weaker, more vulnerable members of a minority group. But status in society also affects perceptions by helping shape the expectations people have about the amount of discrimination they will face. This expectation, along with the amount of discrimination one "really" faces, in turn affects perceptions of discrimination, though in rather complex ways. For example, older blacks who grew up in an era of enforced segregation may early in life have internalized an expectation of rampant racial discrimination. In today's racial climate, they may actually experience the same amount of discrimination as younger blacks do, but in the case of older blacks there would be a much larger gap between what they expect and what they experience. If this is so, then older blacks might logically be expected to perceive less discrimination today than younger blacks do, reflecting the gap between deeply-held expectations and recent experience.

Both personal characteristics and perceptions of discrimination affect explanations of racial inequality, the central component of our study. These explanations, or attributions, can conveniently be classified as those that blame discrimination and other external factors for racial inequality and those that blame blacks themselves for racial inequality. Our premise is that people, black or white, who perceive widespread discrimination are more likely than others to be sympathetic to the idea that discrimination is a primary cause of racial inequality.

We also examine the impact of personal characteristics on attributions. In particular, we test two competing hypotheses, one that argues that those at the bottom of the social ladder are more likely to blame themselves for their low social status, and another that posits that those at the bottom are more likely to blame others. Each is plausible, and prior researchers have not tested these alternatives in interpreting black explanations for inequality.

The final step in our model explores the impact of personal characteristics, perceptions of discrimination, and explanations of inequality upon blacks' policy preferences, the stopgaps or solutions that are favored for dealing with racial inequality. Here again, we are interested in accounting for differences among blacks, and, for the third time, our account begins with differences in personal characteristics. We expect that those at the bottom of the social ladder will be the most likely to favor government action to improve the condition of blacks. We also expect that those who view racial inequality as pervasive and as a product of blatant white discrimination will favor more government action than those who view racial inequality as less widespread or as a product of the shortcomings of blacks themselves. These expectations are based on the idea that those who believe that little discrimination exists or that inequality is attributable to weaknesses of blacks themselves would see no point to government action to ameliorate racial inequality. Thus we expect to observe a very strong tie between explaining inequality largely by discrimination and favoring government aid to help blacks generally and poor blacks particularly.

In general, then, we foresee a link between perceiving large amounts of discrimination, explaining black inequality by reference to such discrimination, and supporting government programs designed to aid blacks. And all along the way, we expect perceptions, attributions, and policy preferences to be shaped by socioeconomic and other personal characteristics.

Data

Fortunately, it is considerably easier for us to pursue this line of analysis than it would have been only a few years ago, since it is now possible to employ a secondary analysis strategy rather than undertaking a brand-new national survey of blacks.[4]

A recent inventory of problems and progress in measuring black public opinion lists only three national surveys of blacks, all conducted by the University of Michigan's Institute for Social Research (ISR): the National Survey of Black Americans, the Three Generation Family Study, and the 1984 National Black Election Study (A. W. Smith, 1987; see also Jackson, Tucker, and Bowman, 1982). Although these surveys all bear on the issue of racial inequality, none attacks the issue in anything approaching the depth necessary to sustain intensive analysis. As for the so-called Black GSS, an augmentation of the 1982 and 1987 GSS that increased the number of black interviewees to more than three times the one hundred and fifty or so in a regular cross-sectional sample, Smith discounts it because it "offers little to investigators interested specifically in blacks, *unless their subjects are ones covered in the regular GSS*" (1987: 451).

This may make a secondary analysis strategy seem hopeless. However, even though we are by no means operating in a data-rich area, surveys of black attitudes are now more abundant than Smith's bleak assessment would seem to indicate – abundant enough to make it feasible for us to analyze existing data rather than launching a major new data collection effort.

In the descriptive portions of our analysis (Chapters, 3, 5, and 7), we draw upon national survey data – some of it on whites' perceptions and attitudes – already catalogued by others (e.g., Kluegel and Smith, 1986; Schuman et al., 1985). We also employ data from the 1984 National Black Election Study (NBES) and from two national surveys by Louis Harris and Associates. The NBES was a telephone survey of a national sample of black Americans conducted by ISR. Before the election, ISR completed interviews with 1,151 respondents, 873 of whom were reinterviewed after the election. These interviews focused largely on the election, but delved into an array of other topics as well, including several of concern to us here.

In the first of the Harris surveys, conducted in October 1978 for the National Conference of Christians and Jews, national cross sections of 1,673 whites and 732 blacks were asked about their attitudes on issues pertaining to women and racial and religious minorities (blacks, Hispanics, Catholics, and Jews). In the second, conducted from June to September 1988 for the NAACP Legal Defense and Educational Fund, interviews were held with 2,008 whites, 1,005 blacks, and 110 Asian Americans.[5]

In the analytic portions of the book, and especially in Chapter 8, in which we analyze blacks' public policy preferences, we make use of data from the 1985 and 1986 GSS. Unfortunately, these were years when the GSS black sample was not augmented, but they were years in which several pertinent questions were asked. Combining the 1985 and 1986 samples yields a black sample size that, although modest, will serve for our purposes.[6]

Unfortunately, though we make frequent references to the NBES in the descriptive chapters of this book, it is not especially suitable for our analytic purposes. The basic problem is one that will be all too familiar to those experienced in secondary data analysis (see, e.g., Hyman, 1972; Kiecolt and Nathan, 1985): although the questions asked in the NBES made sense in light of the purposes for which they were intended (see, e.g., Gurin, Hatchett, and Jackson, 1988), they do not serve *our* analytic needs very well. For one thing, we are interested in making explicit comparisons between the ways racial inequality is viewed by black and white Americans, but the NBES surveyed only blacks. Even more importantly, although the NBES covered certain topics in considerable depth (indeed, in greater depth than the surveys upon which we rely most heavily here), it gave only the most fleeting attention to the central variable in our explanatory model. The NBES asked only a single question calling for an explanation of racial inequality, and did so using a format that undermined the validity of the answers (see Chapter 5 for more on measuring attributions). Because the NBES contained no satisfactory indicators of the key variable in our model, we were forced to look elsewhere for data with which to test the model.

We found what we were looking for in two national telephone polls conducted by Chilton Research Services for ABC News and the *Washington Post,* the first in February–March 1981 and the second in January 1986. In 1981, 1,358 whites and 446 blacks were interviewed concerning their racial attitudes. Some of the same items were repeated, and many new ones were added, in 1986, when 1,022 black men and women were interviewed about their views on issues of special interest to the black community. The 1986 ABC News/*Washington Post* poll is by far the most comprehensive survey of blacks' attitudes toward racial inequality, and it, supplemented by the 1981 ABC News/*Washington Post* poll, constitutes the major data source for our analyses.[7]

Based primarily upon the 1981 and 1986 ABC News/*Washington Post* surveys, then, we will test the explanatory model outlined in Figure 1.1 of both blacks' and whites' views of racial inequality. We noted above that we cannot place our main reliance upon the NBES because it contains no satisfactory measure of the central concept in our model, explanations of racial inequality. The ABC News/*Washington Post* surveys have some limitations of their own, though these are less critical than those imposed by the NBES. We are unable, using the ABC News/*Washington Post* surveys, to include either region or religiosity in the model. The latter omission is especially regrettable in light of the importance of the church as an influence on blacks' social and political attitudes and behavior (see, e.g., Brown and Jackson, 1986; Corbett, 1990; Frazier, 1974; Gurin et al., 1988; Harris, 1989; Hunt and Hunt, 1977; Marx 1971; Woodrum and Bell, 1989). Nor, on the basis of the ABC News/*Washington Post* surveys, can we incorporate in our model the concept of racial consciousness or identification, even though it has been shown to be strongly related to socioeconomic and other personal characteristics and political behavior (see, e.g., Allen, Dawson, and Brown, 1989; Brady and Sniderman, 1985; Broman, Neighbors, and Jackson, 1988; Gurin et al., 1988; Miller, Gurin, Gurin, and Malanchuk, 1981; Shingles, 1981).

However, rather than permitting these limitations to immobilize us, we proceed, recognizing that issues concerning model specification are an inescapable part of social science research. From this recognition stems our determination to treat our findings as more of a first word than the final word on the subject. At the same time, we remain reasonably confident that the model outlined above and tested below captures many of the most important components of, and influences upon, blacks' views of racial inequality.

The plan of the analysis

Our analysis proceeds in a simple progression. It is not our purpose to compose a detailed portrait of the changing socioeconomic condition of blacks in the United States, but we begin in Chapter 2 with an overview of the current status of blacks, designed to provide a context for the subsequent analyses of perceptual and attitudinal data. Here we explore where blacks actually stand vis-à-vis whites in terms of education, income, occupation, housing, and other badges of socioeconomic status, and whether their standing has improved or worsened in recent years. In Chapter 2 we also review a far-flung literature on the impact of personal characteristics upon perceptual, attributional, and policy differences among blacks. We outline our expectations – some quite precise, others rather cloudy – concerning the impact of age, gender, interracial friendship, and various components of socioeconomic status on the views of both blacks and whites.

Our analysis of what and how blacks think about racial inequality begins in Chapter 3 and continues through Chapter 8. In Chapter 3 we explore how blacks perceive their own personal situation and that of blacks in general. How widespread do they think prejudice and discrimination are? Do they perceive progress or retrogression in recent years? Are they optimistic or pessimistic about the future? Drawing primarily on data from the 1986 and 1989 ABC News/*Washington Post* surveys, we describe and interpret blacks' perceptions of black-white inequality. Wherever possible, we also compare blacks' perceptions with those of whites, relying on the 1981 and 1989 ABC News/*Washington Post* surveys.

There is, we shall see, no singular black perception concerning levels of and trends in racial prejudice and discrimination. Few blacks view racial prejudice and discrimination entirely as problems of a bygone era, but there is considerable disagreement about the scope and seriousness of these problems today. In Chapter 4, we probe the first set of linkages in our explanatory model, those tying blacks' personal characteristics to their perceptions of the extent and trend of prejudice and discrimination.

It is one thing for someone to perceive prejudice and discrimination as common or rare, to see these problems as waxing or waning, and to be optimistic or pessimistic about their future course. It is something else for someone to understand the sources of prejudice and discrimination and the reasons why progress in race relations is proceeding at a certain pace. People with identical perceptions of the extent of racial prejudice and discrimination may nonetheless disagree fundamentally about why blacks as a group continue to lag behind whites socioeconomically and about why blacks as a group have made some gains in recent years. Accordingly, in Chapter 5 we turn to blacks' explanations of racial inequality and black progress, again basing our analysis on data from the ABC News/*Washington Post* surveys.

Having described in Chapter 5 the basic patterns that characterize blacks' explanations of racial inequality and black progress and having compared these patterns to those that crop up in whites' thinking about the same subjects, we go on in Chapter 6 to see whether distinctive attributions are associated with the personal characteristics in our model, including perceptual differences. Do those who perceive discrimination as being widespread tend to offer different explanations of black-white inequality than those who see it as relatively rare? Finally, are the factors that tend to produce certain attributions among blacks the same as the factors that produce the same attributions among whites?

In Chapter 7 we proceed to blacks' views concerning some potential remedies for black-white inequality. Because relatively few policy questions have been asked in the ABC News/*Washington Post* surveys, we examine data from a wide range of sources, making Chapter 7 somewhat more eclectic than Chapters 3 through 6.

In Chapter 8 we explore the determinants of blacks' assessments of various policy alternatives, drawing on the ABC News/*Washington Post* and GSS polls. The perceptions and explanations that served as dependent variables in Chapters 4 and 6, respectively, play the role of independent variables in Chapter 8, along with the socioeconomic and other personal factors in our model.

Finally, in Chapter 9 we review our major findings and offer concluding commentary concerning what we know and what we do not know about what and how Americans, black and white, think about racial inequality, how these attitudes are changing, and how they help to shape American society.

Notes

1. For a parallel argument concerning Jews, who have often been ignored in research on antisemitism, see Tobin with Sassler (1988). On the tendency to ignore Hispanics in survey research, see de la Garza (1987).
2. A good case in point is a battery of questions in the 1977 NORC General Social Survey: "On the average, (Negroes/blacks) have worse jobs, income, and housing than white people. Do you think these differences are . . . Mainly due to discrimination? . . . Because most (Negroes/blacks) have less in-born ability to learn? . . . Because most (Negroes/blacks) don't have the chance for education it takes to rise out of poverty? . . . Because most (Negroes/blacks) just don't have the motivation or will power to pull themselves up out of poverty?" The answers to these questions say a great deal about how people understand racial inequality; indeed, these four GSS items are the precursors of the attribution questions on which we focus in Chapters 5 and 6. However, in 1977 the GSS interviewers skipped over these questions when blacks were the respondents. So nothing at all was learned about blacks' explanations for black-white inequality. Even in 1982 and 1987, when the GSS oversampled blacks in order to provide researchers with a more reliable data base on blacks' attitudes, this and several related questions that had routinely been asked of whites in earlier versions of the GSS were not used. These four items were, however, asked of GSS respondents in 1985 and 1986, and we employ these items in Chapter 8 below.
3. For a similar argument couched in similar language, see Jaynes and Williams (1989:115–16); see also Jackman and Senter (1983: 312).
4. For a different approach to understanding blacks' views, see Gwaltney (1981), who reports in-depth interviews with ordinary blacks.
5. For information on the NBES, see Survey Research Center (1984). The figures from this source referred to in later chapters are based on our analyses of the machine-readable data set, which we obtained from the Inter-University Consortium for Political and Social Research. As is also the case for the other data sets analyzed here, neither the collectors nor the distributors of these data bear any responsibility for our analyses and interpretations.

Detailed information about the Harris surveys can be found in Louis Harris and Associates (1978, 1989). We obtained the 1978 data set from the Institute for Social Research, University of North Carolina; the 1988 data set was not yet in the public domain when this manuscript was completed, so we have relied on the marginals provided in the Harris document itself. The 1978 surveys have attracted little attention in the scholarly community; insofar as we are aware, Jacobson's (1983) analyses of support for affirmative action among black Americans is the only secondary analyses of these data to date.

6. For details concerning the 1985 and 1986 GSS samples, see Davis and Smith (1987). We obtained a machine-readable version of the cumulative GSS data file through the Inter-University Consortium for Political and Social Research.

7. In September–October 1989, some of these questions were asked for the third time in a new ABC News/*Washington Post* race relations survey, this one of a random sample of 1,620 that included a special oversample of 371 blacks. Drawing upon published accounts of key findings (Morin and Balz, 1989a, 1989b) and upon breakdowns kindly made available to us by Richard Morin of the *Washington Post,* we report some descriptive findings from the 1989 ABC News/*Washington Post* survey. However, because the data set itself was not yet available for secondary analysis by the time we completed the manuscript for this book, the data analyses in Chapters 4, 6, and 8 are exclusively for the 1981 and 1986 versions of these surveys.

Our analysis relies primarily upon the ABC News/*Washington Post* surveys simply because these are by far the most comprehensive sources of data on the specific issues of concern to us. Other recent surveys, including the NBES, national polls conducted in 1984 and 1986 by the Joint Center for Political Studies, and the 1988 poll Louis Harris and Associates conducted for the NAACP Legal Defense and Educational Fund, touch on many of these issues, but in far less depth than the ABC News/*Washington Post* polls.

We obtained a machine-readable version of the 1981 survey from the Inter-University Consortium for Political and Social Research, and acquired the 1986 data set from the Roper Center for Public Opinion Research. The 1986 data set also contains a supplementary sample of 619 black residents of the Washington, D.C. area, but we have disregarded this supplementary sample.

In light of our heavy reliance on the ABC News/*Washington Post* data sets, a point of special clarification is in order concerning the weighting of the samples. Each of these data sets contains a weight variable designed to make the sample nationally representative in terms of education, sex, and age. The weight variable in the 1981 data set also corrects the sample's racial composition, an irrelevant consideration for the all-black 1986 sample. In both cases, weighting the sample increases the total number of cases. Although 1,358 whites and 446 blacks were actually interviewed in 1981, the weight variable inflates these numbers to 12,767 and 1,542, respectively. Case inflation is much less dramatic in the 1986 data set, for which the sample size increases only from 1,022 unweighted cases to 1,120 weighted ones.

If we intended to undertake only simple percentage comparisons and other descriptive analyses, case inflation would be inconsequential. However, it poses a problem here since we are testing relationships for statistical significance, which, *ceteris paribus,* is a function of sample size. Obviously, analyzing a subsample that has been multiplied roughly three-fold, such as blacks in 1981, or almost tenfold, such as whites in 1981, would greatly, but artificially, enhance our chances of uncovering statistically significant relationships. Disregarding the weight variable altogether would solve this problem, but would also render the samples demographically unrepresentative; for example, two-thirds of the respondents in the unweighted 1981 black sample were women and only one-third were men. Presumably to avoid such unrepresentativeness, Parent (1985) employed the weight variable in his analysis of the 1988 data, but in so doing he unintentionally biased his analysis toward uncovering significant relationships.

So neither employing nor not employing the weight variable is a wholly satisfactory alternative. Fortunately, there are other options. A simple solution that works nicely for the 1986 data set is to multiply the weight variable by a constant that lowers the total number of weighted cases to the actual number of interviewees while still correcting for education, sex, and age. Following this tack, we multiplied the 1986 weight by .9125 (that is, 1,022/1,120, the ratio of unweighted to weighted cases). This yielded a total of 1,022 weighted, demographically representative cases.

This simple reweighting strategy would introduce new problems into the 1981 data set, however, since both blacks and whites were sampled. Because blacks were oversampled relative to their actual population share, one function of weighting was to reduce them to their proper share of the total sample. The simple reweighting solution used for the 1986 data set would be unsatisfactory for 1981, since reweighting to a total of 1,804 blacks and whites – the original, unweighted number of respondents – would leave a reweighted total of only 194 blacks, less than half the number of blacks (446) in the original, unweighted sample. In short, by sidestepping the case inflation problem, such reweighting would err in the opposite direction by creating a black deflation problem.

Our solution for the 1981 data set involved a two-step reweighting designed to (a) make both the black and white subsamples demographically representative, and (b) avoid inflating or deflating the size of either subsample. Since we planned to analyze the responses of black and white respondents separately, it was easy, if cumbersome, to accomplish our two purposes. First, we multiplied the weight variable by a constant (.106) that corrected the education, sex, age, and race characteristics of the sample and produced a total of 1,358 whites, exactly the number of whites in the original, unweighted sample; we selected only the whites from this reweighted sample, disregarding the blacks. For the black sample, we multiplied the original weight variable by a constant (.289) that produced 446 blacks, the same number as in the unweighted sample; we selected only the blacks from this reweighted sample, disregarding the whites. In this way we retained the original, unweighted numbers of black and white respondents, and also achieved subsamples of whites and blacks that were representative in terms of education, sex, and age.

2

Socioeconomic status and differentiation among black Americans

Our major purposes in this chapter are to sketch a realistic picture of the social and economic status of black Americans and then to consider the likely perceptual and attitudinal effects of socioeconomic diversity among blacks. Such a picture must be painted in shades of gray. Over the last three decades, many bonds of racism have been loosened and blacks as a group have raised their standard of living and assumed a place in American society more equal to that of whites. But enduring residues of racism and legacies of segregation, coupled with structural changes in the American economy, have conspired to leave many blacks in poverty, to deter blacks as a group from achieving equal status with whites, and to imperil the gains blacks have fought so hard to achieve.

It is impossible in a single chapter and unnecessary in a book about attitudes to detail every significant aspect of blacks' current social and economic standing. Our more modest purpose is to point out some of the most important strides blacks have made toward achieving a fuller share of the material rewards American society has to offer and some of the barriers they continue to face.

Readers in search of comprehensive analysis of these issues would do well to consult Reynolds Farley and Walter Allen's (1987) *The Color Line and the Quality of Life in America,* Farley's (1984) earlier *Blacks and Whites: Narrowing the Gap,* or *A Common Destiny: Blacks and American Society,* the report of the blue-ribbon Committee on the Status of Black Americans (Jaynes and Williams, 1989). We draw freely upon these sources, though in most cases we use recent census documents to update them. Updating is especially important, because changes in the economic welfare of blacks during the Reagan years are matters of heated controversy.[1] Even more importantly, since the core of our analysis of blacks' perceptions and attitudes is based on survey data gathered in 1986 and 1989, an overview of the "objective" face of racial inequality at mid-decade sets the stage for understanding the perceptions and attitudes in which we are centrally interested.

Those who approach an analysis of the socioeconomic situation of blacks expecting to come away with a simple, uncomplicated picture are slated for disappointment. For many racial and ethnic groups, if we can understand the progress that has been made on a particular socioeconomic dimension – say, education – we will have a fairly reliable guide to progress on other dimensions – say, income, occupation, or wealth. This, as we shall see, is not true for blacks, and for this reason the broad concept of social class seems to us to have little utility for understanding the situation of blacks. Class is at best a murky concept – one analyst calls it an "intellectual jellyfish" (Pryor, 1981: 369; see also Jackman and Jackman, 1983) – and its meaning in the black community is even more nebulous than in the white. The difficulties of defining class in the black community stem from several social and economic realities of black life: education traditionally has not produced the same income gains for blacks as it has for other racial and ethnic groups (Boston, 1988; Duncan, Featherman, and Duncan, 1972); occupational status is not as readily passed from black parent to child (Oliver and Glick, 1982); moderate and high income are less tied to real wealth for blacks than others (Oliver and Shapiro, 1989); and income and education are almost entirely unrelated to blacks' subjective class identifications (Jackman and Jackman, 1983: 83).[2] Thus, the cluster of characteristics that collectively define class (education, income, occupation, wealth, subjective class identification, and so on) are less closely intertwined for blacks than they are for others. Hoping to avoid terminological problems associated with the class concept, we will speak primarily of "socioeconomic status" rather than "social class," using the former term simply as a shorthand for characteristics that are only loosely connected among blacks.[3]

The past as prologue

The status of black Americans has been transformed over the past fifty years. These dramatic changes encompass new legal rights, attitudinal transformations, and economic and social improvements.

Fifty years ago, nearly eight blacks in ten lived in the South, where their status had improved relatively little since the end of the Reconstruction era. In the South, law and custom segregated blacks from whites in virtually every aspect of life: The races were not to intermingle in schools, restaurants, theaters, buses or trains, hospitals or funeral parlors, swimming pools or restrooms, let alone to socialize, date, or marry (Woodward,

1974). The separation of the races was licensed locally under the *Plessy v. Ferguson* doctrine of "separate but equal," which in practice meant separate and unequal. Moreover, a strict code of social behavior mandated black deference to whites. These segregationist codes were enforced, when necessary, by economic sanctions and violence (Key, 1949; Myrdal, 1944; Woodward, 1974).

Blacks were barred from voting in most places, and black organizational activity was suspect. In the South in 1940, only three black adults in a hundred were registered to vote (Myrdal, 1944: 475; see also Matthews and Prothro, 1966), and even as late as 1964 black registration had risen to only 23 percent throughout the South and 7 percent in Mississippi, the "buckle" of the black belt.

The concentration of blacks in the South began to disperse after World War I.[4] Seeking economic advancement and greater personal freedom, many blacks made their way to the North. The first wave of the "great migration" occurred between 1918 and 1920. It grew larger in the 1920s, declined during the Depression years, and flowed even more rapidly during and after World War II. Between 1910 and 1930, 1.3 million blacks moved North, and by 1960, 3.7 million more. In the North, blacks were freer politically and had greater opportunities economically. Even so, they still found themselves at the bottom of the ladder in jobs and living conditions, and continued to be targets of racial prejudice and hostility.

Of course, many blacks remained in the South, but plummeting cotton prices during the Depression drove hundreds of thousands of black subsistence farmers into the cities. The proportion of black Southerners living in cities doubled between 1930 and 1960, when it reached 58 percent (McAdam, 1982).

The changing configuration of the black population posed new opportunities for blacks to participate politically (see McAdam, 1982: Chapter 5). The move northward led to the enfranchisement of millions of black voters, dramatically increasing the size of the black electorate. Urbanization within the South sometimes brought enfranchisement, too, and it usually meant better access to education and greater organizational resources. Urban black churches, the center of the black community, were larger, better financed, and more capably led than their rural counterparts (Mays and Nicholson, 1969). Especially outside the Deep South, codes of segregation were often less rigid in cities, and the impersonality of urban life made it somewhat easier for blacks to organize and protest without fear of violent retribution.

These changing black demographics also spawned protest organizations (see Jaynes and Williams, 1989: Chapter 4). Indeed, as early as 1909, black and white intellectuals and philanthropists had joined to form the National

Association for the Advancement of Colored People (NAACP). Initially, W. E. B. DuBois was the new organization's only black officer, but gradually other blacks assumed leadership roles. The NAACP concentrated largely on education and legal action aimed at bringing about greater racial equality. But even in its early years it also used direct action, boycotting and picketing to protest the 1915 film *Birth of a Nation,* which defamed blacks and glorified the Ku Klux Klan (Altschuler, 1982; Franklin, 1969; McAdam, 1982; Sitkoff, 1981).[5] The major focus of the NAACP's early years, however, was its crusade against lynchings, which were occurring at the rate of about eighty per year during the first decade of the century.

Even though it was seen by most whites as quite radical, the NAACP, founded by highly educated blacks and wealthy, educated whites, remained primarily middle class in orientation (Eisenberg, 1982; Wolters, 1970). Still, though its membership was less than one hundred thousand by 1930, it had dozens of chapters across the South as well as in the North. By 1950, the number of chapters neared one thousand in the South alone (McAdam, 1982; Morris, 1984).

Working-class blacks were drawn to the United Negro Improvement Association, a separatist movement led by Marcus Garvey. Garvey enrolled between one and six million blacks (estimates vary widely) into the organization, stressing black pride and unity in America, on the one hand, and the opportunity for blacks to return to Africa and found a new nation, on the other (see, e.g., Cronon, 1955; Essien-Udom, 1970; Franklin, 1967). The organization collapsed when Garvey was jailed in 1925 for mail fraud (for which he was later pardoned by President Coolidge), but as an eminent historian has commented, Garvey's was "the first and only real mass movement among Negroes in the history of the United States" (Franklin, 1967: 492).

Slowly, black protest began to score some successes. Lynching declined, especially after the mid-1920s, partly as a consequence of the NAACP's anti-lynching campaign.[6] In the 1930s the U.S. Supreme Court began to broaden its interpretation of the rights embedded in the Fourteenth and Fifteenth amendments (McAdam, 1982: 84).[7] Blacks picketed retail stores in the 1930s to encourage hiring of blacks (Meier and Rudwick, 1976: Chapter 14). During World War II, the threat of a massive black march on Washington, organized by A. Philip Randolph, led President Roosevelt to establish a Fair Employment Practices Committee and to ban discrimination in war industries (Sitkoff, 1981).

But it was not until the 1950s that the great battles that culminated in the demise of legally imposed segregation really began. The Supreme Court's 1954 *Brown v. Board of Education* decision, which held that separate public education could not be equal, and the success of the Montgomery, Alabama bus boycott, which showed that blacks could successfully challenge segregation through organized protest, sparked new organizational efforts in the black community (Branch, 1988; Garrow, 1986; Kluger, 1975; Morris, 1984; Sitkoff, 1982; J. Williams, 1987). During the late 1950s and early 1960s, these efforts mobilized blacks against almost every aspect of legal segregation.

Attacks on legal segregation were based on its inconsistency with the democratic beliefs espoused by most Americans. By turning a spotlight on the violence directed at peaceful blacks who were trying to register to vote, to eat at lunch counters, to attend public schools, or to sit wherever they wished on buses or trains, the civil rights movement raised the consciousness and touched the conscience of much of white America (Branch, 1988; Garrow, 1986).

The increased success of protest activities in the 1950s was partly a result of changing white attitudes. Part of this change stemmed from the increasing education and urbanization of whites, and part from World War II itself, when the American propaganda offensive against Germany heightened public revulsion toward the violent racism of the Nazis.[8] The war also profoundly affected those black soldiers who, having fought abroad under the banner of freedom, returned home to rediscover racism.

But the success of the protest movement also flowed from the continually shifting demography and increasing educational and organizational resources of the black community. These resources spawned a new generation of aggressive, articulate black leaders, tied together largely through a network of black churches that in due course was formalized in the Southern Christian Leadership Conference (Jaynes and Williams, 1989: ch. 4; Garrow, 1986; Morris, 1984).[9] The most visible of the new leaders, Martin Luther King, Jr., was able not only to mobilize a diverse coalition of black organizations, but also to appeal to whites through both the content of his message and the eloquence and nonviolence with which he delivered it.

The civil rights protest movement greatly enhanced the salience of the "race issue" in American politics, forcing the national parties (especially the Democrats) and the federal government (especially the Johnson administration) to begin grappling in earnest with the problems of blacks. The priority accorded to racial concerns by the two parties surged dramatically upward in 1964 (Carmines and Stimson, 1989: 56). Nor was this just empty talk, since the passage of two laws in the mid-1960s made many forms of segregation illegal. The Civil Rights Act of 1964 opened up public accommodations to blacks, overturning the doctrine of "separate but equal" in public facilities and barring discrimination in employment and education. The Voting Rights

\ct of 1965 made it a crime to interfere with anyone's right to vote and
uthorized federal officials to register voters in areas of low voter registra-
.on, primarily in the South. These laws, coupled with 1968 legislation out-
awing discrimination in housing, revolutionized the legal rights of blacks
nd seemed to fulfill the initial goals of the civil rights movement.

The elimination of legally imposed segregation ended the second-class
egal status of blacks, but it did not terminate their second-class social and
conomic status. The landmark legislation of the 1960s changed the lives of
nany blacks little, if at all. A legal right to dine in any restaurant or stay in
.ny hotel is of little avail if one has no money to pay the bill. The right to be
onsidered for good jobs without reference to one's race is cold comfort for
hose who lack the experience or education they need to get the jobs.

Other 1960s legislation tried to respond to these unresolved economic
)roblems. President Johnson's Great Society programs provided Medicare
ind Medicaid for the elderly and poor; the public schools received new
issistance targeted for the disadvantaged; and programs like Model Cities
ind Head Start were mounted as part of the War on Poverty.

All these programs provided some economic boosts for blacks, but the
Great Society was short-lived. As white America turned its attention away
'rom domestic problems and toward the conflict raging in Southeast Asia,
)lacks' growing frustration with their lack of economic and social progress
.riggered anger, alienation, and ultimately riots, first in Watts in 1965, then
n many other cities during the remainder of the decade.

Since the 1960s, no major new civil rights legislation has been enacted,
1or have new federal antipoverty programs been initiated. Civil rights and
:acial issues have fallen from the top to near the bottom of the American
)ublic's concern. In fact, the proportion of the public perceiving civil rights
is the most important problem facing the nation declined from a high of
nore than 30 percent in 1964–5 to practically nothing after 1970 (Smith,
1980). But the problems black Americans faced in the 1960s have not gone
away. Some argue that they have increased; others disagree, pointing to
progress made in solving them. It is to the question of how the status of
blacks has changed since the 1960s that we now turn.

Measuring black progress

Although we are primarily concerned with changes in the socioeconomic
standing of blacks over the last three decades, these changes cannot be
fully understood without reference to the changing situation of whites. In
assessing its own status, any group naturally compares itself with other
groups in the same society, especially the dominant group. Black Ameri-

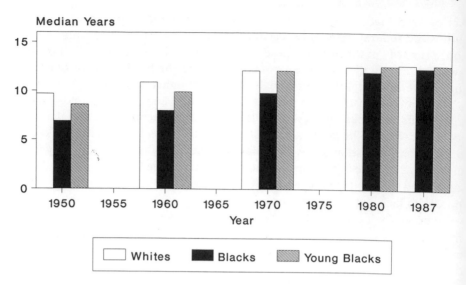

Figure 2.1. Median years of education, blacks and whites, 1950–1987
Sources: U.S. Bureau of the Census (1955: Table 127; 1989: Tables 211–12).

cans cannot be expected to celebrate simply because they are better off than they used to be or because they are better off than most people in most nations of the world.[10] Rather, they naturally tend to assess where they stand relative to the majority standard of living in their own country.

Psychologically, then, prosperity is, to a considerable degree, relative prosperity, and deprivation is, to a considerable degree, relative deprivation. For example, no one disputes that the real income of blacks has risen dramatically since 1960. The controversial question is whether black income has risen relative to white income, and thus whether blacks are coming any closer to attaining socioeconomic parity with whites.[11]

Education

Since World War II, great strides have been made toward educational equality between blacks and whites (see Smith and Welch, 1989, for example). In 1950, the average black had not completed seventh grade, and even in 1960, only eighth grade. But by 1980, the typical black was a high school graduate, and the trend has continued upward since then (see Figure 2.1). Of course, levels of educational attainment have soared in American society as a whole, as Figure 2.1 also reveals. In 1950, most whites, as well as most blacks, did not have a high school diploma. But what stands out in

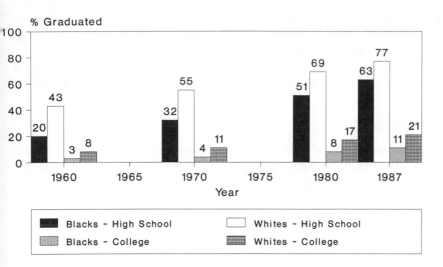

Figure 2.2. High school and college graduates, blacks and whites, 1960–1987
Source: U.S. Bureau of the Census (1989: Table 212).

Figure 2.1 is the diminution of the educational gap between blacks and whites. In 1950, the gap was nearly three full years of schooling. By 1970, it had declined to 2.3 years, and by 1987 it had fallen dramatically, to only three-tenths of a year. Young blacks (those between 25 and 29 years of age) have closed the gap even more rapidly, to the point that their median 12.7 years of schooling equals the figure for all whites, and is only slightly lower than that of whites in their own age bracket (12.8).

Blacks still lag in rates of high school and college graduation, but the racial gap in high school graduation has narrowed considerably (see Figure 2.2). In 1960, 43 percent of whites, but only 20 percent of blacks, were high school graduates. In 1987, the counterpart figures were 77 percent and 63 percent. Among those aged 25 to 29, the percentage of high school graduates is almost as high among blacks (83 percent) as it is among whites (86 percent) (U.S. Bureau of the Census, 1989: Table 211).

The picture is quite different for college degrees. In 1987, almost twice as high a proportion of whites (21 percent) as blacks (11 percent) had completed college. Even more discouragingly, unlike the other trends in education, this gap did not close during the early and middle 1980s, nor is the gap among young adults substantially different than it is among all adults ("Black and Hispanic College Enrollments Continue to Decline," 1990; Wingert, 1990).[12] In an era when white college attendance reached new heights, blacks' entry rates did not rise correspondingly (Hauser, 1990).

However, between 1986 and 1988, black enrollment did begin to rise again, and in 1988 it stood at an all-time high (Marriott, 1990). Only if this trend continues will blacks begin to catch up with whites at the highest levels of the educational pyramid, those that open the door to the best and most remunerative jobs (Hall, Mays, and Allen, 1984; Welch and Gruhl, 1990).

Employment

In a prophetic analysis written just before the passage of the Civil Rights Act of 1964, Thomas Pettigrew argued that legislation was only part of the solution: "If all racial prejudice and discrimination miraculously vanished," Pettigrew reminded his readers, "the Negro's problems would not be solved. Most white people would still be comfortably prosperous; most Negroes still precariously close to the ragged edge of poverty. The fundamental bottleneck to Negro economic progress [is] employment" (1964: 169).

Unemployment. Blacks have traditionally experienced unusually high rates of unemployment. For much of the past forty years the black unemployment rate has been about twice that of whites, and in recent years the gap has grown even wider (Cotton, 1989b; Farley, 1984), largely because of the growing deficit among blacks in the 16–24 age range (Farley and Allen, 1987: 214).

As unemployment spreads throughout the entire economy, so does black unemployment, but to higher levels. Booms and busts affect black unemployment more than white unemployment (Farley and Allen, 1987: 218). During the 1950s and 1960s, the black-white difference in unemployment rates hovered between four and six percentage points (Figure 2.3), but since the mid-1970s the gap has usually been between 8 and 11 points. Reaganomics was cruel to black employment prospects in the early 1980s. By the end of 1982, fully 20 percent of the black labor force was unemployed. Although unemployment in both races has greatly subsided since 1983, in 1988 it was still about five percentage points higher among blacks than whites. (For a more radical analysis, see Willhelm, 1986.)

Of course, those who are better educated have an easier time finding and keeping a job. It follows that black unemployment is attributable, in part, to the lower proportion of high school and college graduates among blacks. Indeed, Figure 2.4 shows that while the unemployment penalty for being black persists throughout all educational categories, it is minimal among college graduates and most severe among those who lack a high school diploma.[13] For example, in 1988, a time of over 10 percent black unemployment overall, the unemployment rate for black college graduates was only

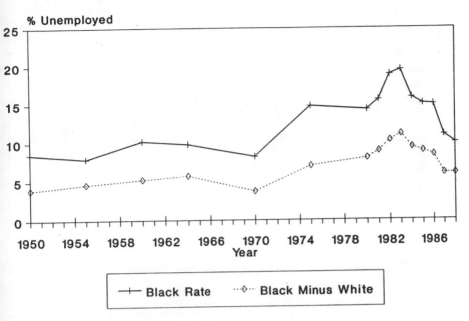

Figure 2.3. Black unemployment, 1950–1988
Sources: U.S. Bureau of the Census (1973: Table 358; 1989: Table 649); Ross (1967: 30). Data before 1975 are for nonwhites, most of whom were black.

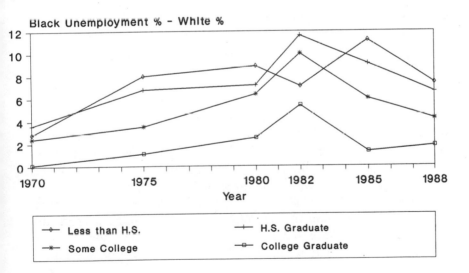

Figure 2.4. Black-white unemployment gap by education, 1970–1988
Sources: U.S. Bureau of the Census (1989: Table 649). Data before 1975 are for nonwhites, most of whom were black.

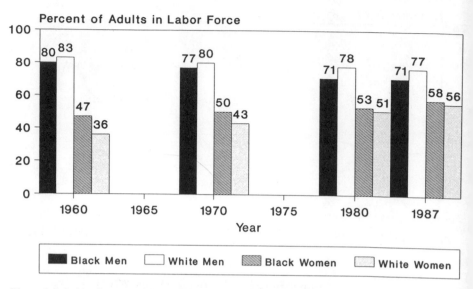

Figure 2.5. Labor force participation, blacks and whites, 1960–1987
Sources: Simms (1987); U.S. Bureau of the Census (1973: Table 348; 1989: Table 621). Data include those aged sixteen and over.

3.3 percent. Granted, this was 1.8 points higher than the rate for white college graduates; still, the black-white unemployment differential for college graduates was small compared to the more than seven percentage point gap between blacks and whites with less than a high school diploma (U.S. Bureau of Census, 1989: Table 649). In times of higher overall unemployment, the racial gap at the lower end of the educational spectrum is even wider.

Overall, blacks as a group are still operating at a greater disadvantage in the job market than would be predicted on the basis of black and white educational attainments (Cotton, 1989b). At higher levels of education, the racial gap diminishes, but at every level except that of college graduates the racial gap in unemployment has increased significantly since 1970.

Labor Force Participation. Another important piece of the employment picture is the proportion of each race in the labor force, a figure that indicates how many have quit looking for work as well as how many are unemployed.[14] According to Figure 2.5, about 29 percent of working-age black males are not in the labor force, as compared to about 23 percent of white males. Although not all the nonparticipants are discouraged workers, because some chose to retire early or are in ill health, Farley (1984: 42) reports that between 1970 and 1982 the proportion of adult black males under fifty-five who were not in the labor force for reasons other than being in school or ill increased by about three percent. This does not suggest a mass exodus from the labor force, but it does suggest that in addition to increasing unemployment, there is a trend for black males simply to drop out.[15] Between 1979 and 1986, the proportion of those between twenty and twenty-four not working for an entire year rose from 24 percent to 40 percent (*National Journal*, 1988: 1994; see also Smith and Welch, 1989).

The situation is different for black women (Figure 2.5). Like white women, black women have increased their participation in the labor force over the past two decades. In the past, higher proportions of black women than white women worked outside the home, but now this gap is almost closed as more white women enter the workforce.

Occupational Distributions. A third crucial aspect of employment is the distribution of occupations. Traditionally, blacks were relegated to the most menial jobs. In 1940, for example, 41 percent of black males were laborers and 60 percent of black working women were in domestic service. Discrimination by both labor unions and employers, reinforced by blacks' low levels of educational attainment, blocked blacks from higher paying and more prestigious jobs. Since 1960, though, blacks have made considerable occupational progress, aided by the Civil Rights Act of 1964.

In discussing black occupational progress, we shall first refer to the index of occupational dissimilarity, which ranges from 0 when blacks and whites are occupationally identical, to 100, when all occupations are segregated by race. Between 1960 and 1982, this index fell from 37 to 23 for men, indicating growing occupational racial integration among males (Farley, 1984: 48–9). For women, the index fell even faster, from about 43 in 1960 to less than 20 in 1982. Well over 50 percent of black women now hold white collar jobs.

This occupational convergence, as well as the remaining racial dissimilarities, can be seen in Table 2.1. Compared to their white counterparts, black men and women are disproportionately clustered in service occupations and as laborers and operatives. However, while in 1950 blacks were five times as likely as whites to work in service jobs, and in 1960 four times, by 1986 they were less than twice as likely to be service workers. And only about three percent of all black workers are now in private household service, a striking contrast to the pattern that prevailed as recently as 1960, when more than a third of all employed black women held such jobs.

Blacks are still substantially underrepresented in managerial and professional occupations. Black men occupy proportionately about half as many of these positions as white men, and black women about two-thirds as many as white women. Again, this represents substantial progress since

Table 2.1. *Occupational distributions, blacks and whites, 1950–1986* (in %)

Occupation	Percentages		Ratio		
	Blacks	Whites	1986	1960	1950
	A. Men				
Managerial and professional	13	26	.50		
Professional and technical				.49	.40
Managerial				.23	.22
Technical, sales, and administrative support	16	21	.78		
Sales				.23	.18
Clerical				.46	.29
Service, including private	18	9	2.10	5.20	4.00
Precision, craft, and repair	16	21	.78	.49	.38
Operatives and laborers	33	20	1.70	2.59	2.56
Farming	3	4	.80	2.00	2.00
Total	99	101			
	B. Women				
Managerial and professional	19	25	.69		
Professional and technical				.54	.42
Managerial				.25	.30
Technical, sales, and administrative support	38	46	.83		
Sales				.22	.15
Clerical				.23	.13
Service, including private	28	17	1.71	3.56	3.92
Precision, craft, and repair	3	2	1.04	1.00	.44
Operatives and laborers	13	8	1.57	1.00	1.03
Farming	a	1	.33	1.42	2.83
Total	101	99			

Notes: aLess than one-half of one percent. All figures are rounded to the nearest whole percent.
Sources: Ratios for males in 1950 and 1960 are from Glenn (1963: 110). Female ratios for 1950 are from Farley and Allen (1987: 265) and for 1960 are from U.S. Bureau of the Census (1965). Data for 1986 are from Simms (1987).

1960, when blacks were only one-fourth as likely as whites to be in managerial positions and half as likely to hold professional jobs.

These racial differences in professional and managerial occupations reflect the black-white educational gap, but only to some extent. Among men, whites are more likely to find managerial and professional positions than blacks with the same amount of education (Figure 2.6). Thus, even though three-fifths of black men with college degrees are in managerial or professional occupations, black men have been less able than whites to parlay their

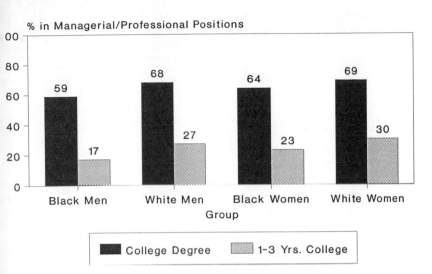

Figure 2.6. Managerial / professional employment, blacks and whites, 1988
Source: U.S. Bureau of the Census (1989: Table 643).

college degrees into managerial and professional jobs. Black women with college degrees, on the other hand, are only slightly less likely than their white counterparts to hold professional and managerial positions.[16]

Overall, the employment picture is mixed. On the positive side, blacks have broken down many occupational barriers, and the occupational distribution of blacks and whites is much more similar than it was a quarter of a century ago. On the other hand, blacks have not reached top jobs in proportion to their numbers, and as a group they bear a staggering share of the burden of unemployment. During the 1960s, black unemployment was thought to have reached crisis proportions (U.S. National Advisory Commission on Civil Disorders, 1968), but by every measure the situation is worse now than it was then. A higher proportion of blacks than whites is unemployed, and when blacks are unemployed they remain out of work longer (Simms, 1987). There is also evidence that some black males are dropping out of the labor force altogether, exacerbating the problem. Although there have been some positive trends during the post-1983 economic recovery, black unemployment is higher than it was in 1980, and much higher than it was in the 1950s and 1960s.

The only silver lining in this cloud is that the racial gap in unemployment narrows among those with more education. Thus, if the educational level of blacks continues to improve, there is some hope for the longer term. However, some major caveats must be registered. First, while the average

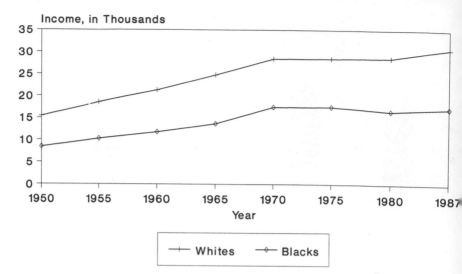

Figure 2.7. Median family income, blacks and whites, 1950–1985
Source: U.S. Bureau of the Census (1989: Table 724).

number of years of school completed continues to increase among blacks, many less educated blacks will continue to have little prospect of finding a job. Indeed, the employment and income pictures are dim for those of any race who do not go on after high school, as the premium for a college education becomes larger. Moreover, even though the mean level of black education has risen dramatically over the past quarter-century, black unemployment has risen just as dramatically. The black-white gap in unemployment is huge even among those with a high school diploma and some college. Finally, the American economy continues to change in ways that offer relatively little opportunity for those with few job-related skills and little education (Cotton, 1989b; Wilson, 1987).

Income and poverty

The average black is better off financially today than ever before (see Landry, 1987, for an analysis of black consumption patterns). In 1987, the average black family income was $16,800, twice what it had been, in constant dollars, in 1950 (see Figure 2.7). Because the size of the black family has shrunk (by 13 percent since 1970), the average black family is more than twice as well off financially today as 1950. Consistent with these figures, Smith and Welch (1987) classify fully 59 percent of black families as middle class and another 11 percent as affluent, compared to only 26 percent and 3 percent, respectively, in 1940.

However, Figure 2.7 also contains some disturbing news about black family income. For one thing, it declined during the late 1970s and early 1980s, and it is now just inching back toward its mid-1970s level. Moreover, while black income was doubling, white income, which started from a much larger base, was nearly doubling, too. Accordingly, the ratio of black to white family income has remained virtually constant, increasing only from .55 to .58. That is, on average, black families now have 58 percent as much income as white families do. However, families spend dollars, not relative dollars, and in this sense the trend in the black-white income gap is even more problematic than percentage comparisons suggest. In constant dollars, the income gap between black and white families grew from $7,000 in 1950 to more than $12,000 by 1985 (see also Cotton, 1989a).

So are blacks making progress on the income front? Figure 2.7 shows why there is no simple answer to this question. Blacks are clearly better off than they used to be in absolute terms, and the ratio of black to white income is inching upward. But in absolute dollars of income, they are falling farther and farther behind whites. Thus, depending on the measure used, it is accurate to allege that blacks are worse off in income relative to whites than was the case twenty-five years ago, or that they are better off.

To understand these trends, it is helpful to decompose family income into its constituent elements, which include the average wages earned by black and white workers and the composition of black and white families (which affects the number of earners per family). According to Figure 2.8, in 1985 the average hourly wage for black men was $6.25, 81 percent of the $7.69 earned by the average white male. There was no appreciable wage gap between black and white women, but each earned a third less than white men. The wage gap between white and black men declined between 1959 and 1979, while that between white and black women essentially disappeared (Farley, 1984: 67; see also Smith and Welch, 1989). This decline in the wage gap continued through the 1980s (Farley, 1988). When hours worked and salient labor force characteristics such as education, experience, and region are held constant, black women actually earn more than white women, though both earn substantially less than black males, who in turn earn only about 88 percent as much as white males. The 12 percent wage penalty for being black is somewhat lower than the 18 percent difference in real wages.

Another important factor in determining family income is family composition. Figure 2.9 reveals that the proportion of female-headed families has grown in both the black and white communities, but the growth has been

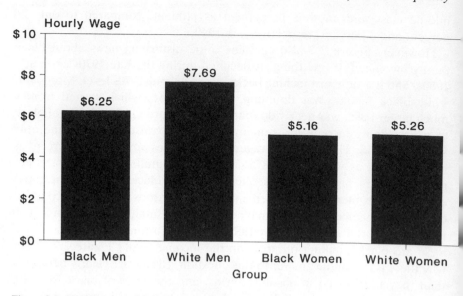

Figure 2.8. Hourly wages, blacks and whites, 1987
Source: U.S. Bureau of the Census (1987: Table 683).

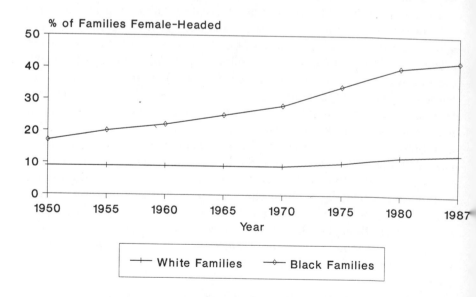

Figure 2.9. Female-headed families, blacks and whites, 1950–1987
Sources: U.S. Bureau of the Census (1989: Table 44). Data for 1950 and 1960 from U.S. National Advisory Commission on Civil Disorders (1968: 261).

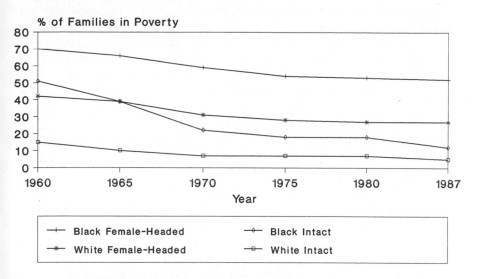

Figure 2.10. Poverty by family type, blacks and whites, 1960–1987
Sources: U.S. Bureau of the Census (1986a: Table 1; 1987: Table 746).

much faster among blacks. As of 1987, fully 42 percent of black families were headed by women, compared to 13 percent of white families. Female-headed black families are much more likely to fall below the poverty line than intact black families are (see Figure 2.10). Farley (1988) points out that if black family structure had been the same in 1987 as in 1970, poverty rates in 1987 would have been four points lower.

To acknowledge the negative income effect of living in a female-headed household is not to deny the impact of race and racial discrimination on family income.[17] There is obviously a racial gap, too: black female-headed families have only 57 percent of the income of white female-headed families (Cotton, 1989b: 814).

The only good news in this story is that increasing numbers of female-headed families, black and white, have pulled themselves out of poverty in the last three decades. Although slightly more than half of black female-headed families are in poverty, in 1960 70 percent were. However, black female-headed families have not escaped from poverty nearly as fast as other black families, whose poverty rates plummeted from 51 percent in 1960 to 12 percent in 1987. At the other end of the income ladder, one estimate is that 17 percent of intact black families are "affluent," while only three percent of female-headed black families fall into that category (Smith and Welch, 1987).

The increasing concern about black female-headed households does not mean that they are worse off than they were two decades ago; in fact, a much smaller percentage are in poverty now than in the past. Rather, the problem stems from the large increase in female-headed families. Only 40 percent of black women between ages 20 and 54 live with a husband, compared to 61 percent in 1960 and to 60 percent of white women in the same age group (Farley, 1988).[18] This is a particularly disheartening trend, in that the majority of intact black families have achieved at least middle class status (Smith and Welch, 1987).[19] Indeed, among black families with two wage earners, the poverty rate is only eight percent (U.S. Bureau of the Census, 1987: Table 734).

Neither wage levels nor family composition alone explains the wide gap between black and white family incomes. Part of the gap is also attributable to racial differences in unemployment and nonparticipation in the labor force (see also Cotton, 1989a). Black and white wages could be equal, and black families could be similar in composition to white ones, but black incomes would continue to lag far behind because of the high proportion of blacks who are unemployed or are not in the labor force.

We must also recognize the complex interplay among these factors. For example, male unemployment fosters marital instability, and thereby contributes indirectly to poverty (Joe and Yu, 1984). Whereas young black men who are employed are just as likely as employed young white men to marry and to have stable marriages, many unemployed black males do not marry but do father children. Thus, continuing high rates of unemployment among black males ultimately impose a limit on the number of households with income earners capable of supporting a family.

Another aspect of the middle-class status of blacks is heavy reliance on government employment. Whereas in 1960 about the same proportion of blacks (13 percent) as whites (12 percent) worked for government, by 1982 fully 23 percent of blacks did so, compared to 16 percent for whites (Collins, 1983: 373). The discrepancy is even larger among managerial employees. Thirteen percent of all whites working in managerial capacities are employed by government, but twice that many black managers are. This does not necessarily make black middle-class status less secure, because positions in government are probably more secure than jobs in other sectors, but it does indicate that the black middle class has fewer opportunities for the extremely high salaries that are found in some private firms.

In sum, many blacks have moved ahead to middle-class status. Opportunities have opened for blacks with the education and skills to capitalize on them (see Smith and Welch, 1989), although these opportunities do not yet equal those available to whites. Meanwhile, for those who have few skills or little education, there are ever fewer opportunities. For them and their children, both the present and the future are bleak.

Wealth

Income comparisons tell an important story, but what is also crucial, in terms of a group's material well-being and life chances, is wealth (Oliver and Shapiro, 1989). Black-white differences in wealth are of an even larger magnitude than black-white differences in income.

Between 1967 and 1984 the average net worth of black families rose from $3,779 to $19,736 (Cotton, 1989b; Oliver and Shaprio, 1989). However, this seemingly impressive gain was overshadowed by the increasing wealth of whites, whose average net worth increased from $20,153 to $76,297. In other words, in less than two decades the black-white wealth gap grew from approximately $16,000 to almost $57,000. Indeed, by 1984 the average white household with an income in the $7,500–$15,000 range still had a greater net worth than the average black household with an income between $45,000 and $60,000. These trends in wealth represent "progress" of a type that many blacks are understandably reluctant to applaud.[20]

Are blacks moving ahead or falling behind?

Whether blacks are catching up or falling behind is a matter of intense controversy. Many observers assert that blacks have been moving ahead since the 1970s, pointing to such visible signs of progress as the following: college-educated blacks are attaining occupational parity with college-educated whites (Freeman, 1976); in the North, young two-income black families are earning about as much as similar white families (Moynihan, 1972); black families are steadily moving toward middle-income status (Scammon and Wattenberg, 1973; Smith and Welch, 1987); and the earnings of black men are converging with those of white men (Featherman and Hauser, 1978; Smith and Welch, 1989).

Based on these and related trends, Wilson (1978) argued a decade ago that race is becoming less important as a determinant of socioeconomic success than are skills, education, and ability. Conservatives, both black and white, have embraced this argument, celebrating the apparent victory of meritocracy (see, e.g., Gilder, 1981).

At the other extreme, many other observers are much less sanguine. They argue that blacks are actually worse off today than they were fifteen or twenty years ago, pointing to high black unemployment, the declining labor force participation of young black males, the widening real income gap between blacks and whites, declining college attendance, and increasing poverty levels among blacks (Cotton, 1989a; Hill, 1981; Jordan, 1980; Smith and Welch, 1989; Swinton, 1987; see also Lazear, 1979). The economic slump of the early 1980s intensified these concerns, as black unemployment shot up and poverty levels rose (Vaughn-Cooke, 1985). Coincident with this slump, an administration wedded to the "market mentality" deemphasized spending on social programs, leading many analysts to blame the deteriorating conditions of blacks directly on the Reagan administration (see, e.g., Center on Budget and Policy Priorities, 1986) and at least one observer to raise the possibility that we may be witnessing a "prelude to genocide" (Willhelm, 1986). Tellingly, when asked in 1988 whether the Reagan administration had "tended more to help blacks or . . . to keep blacks down," 78 percent of the respondents in a national survey of blacks answered "keep blacks down." By contrast, only 32 percent of whites agreed (Louis Harris and Associates, 1989: Appendix B).

Something of a synthesis of the optimistic and pessimistic views comes from those who see the black population as increasingly polarized (Auletta, 1982; Wilson, 1978, 1987). According to this view, a comfortable black middle class has developed whose members are able to take advantage of the opportunities opened by civil rights legislation and changing white attitudes. On the other hand, a great mass of ghetto blacks remains trapped in poverty, and a generation of children grows up in poverty-stricken female-headed homes, many of them without much prospect of improving their lives (for earlier statements of this view see Brimmer, 1966; see also Farley, 1984, for a summary). The flight of the upwardly mobile black middle class from the ghettos may itself have worsened the plight of those left behind, who no longer can look to middle-class families as a source of community stability and successful role models (Wilson, 1987).

In a careful examination of evidence bearing on this polarization thesis, Farley (1984) shows that, as of 1982, the black population was becoming more homogeneous educationally but more heterogeneous occupationally. In terms of income, there is a significant and growing gap between more and less affluent blacks. Increasing black unemployment and the growing number of single-parent black families are also consistent with the polarization thesis.

For the most part, the evidence viewed in this chapter bears out Farley's contention that one can find both glimmers of hope and reasons for despair in the current status of blacks. In many respects, black progress has been nothing short of spectacular, especially in light of the heritage of slavery and discrimination blacks have faced. But behind this progress lie bleaker realities: Unemployment is a heavy anchor weighing down black economic advancement, and the achievement of racial economic parity promises to stretch over many decades, rather than, as optimists once considered possible, occurring within the foreseeable future. Far more common among blacks than whites, unemployment limits the formation of stable black families, and family instability diminishes family income and prospects for meaningful advancement (see Wilson, 1987). And whereas blacks have registered important gains during the postwar era, if the present rates of black and white mobility in occupation and other aspects of socioeconomic status continue, several more generations will pass before racial equality is achieved (see Oliver and Glick, 1982).

The impact of socioeconomic diversity on racial perceptions, explanations, and policy preferences

We have seen that there is great social and economic diversity among blacks. Because of this diversity, we expect blacks to differ in their perceptions of racial discrimination, their explanations for racial inequality, and their views about the course government should take follow in ameliorating discrimination and inequality. Of course, while we can realistically expect to uncover some factors that more or less consistently shape perceptions, explanations, and solutions, anything approaching a deterministic model lies well beyond our grasp. Ideologies, independent of objective circumstances, shape people's ideas about social advantage and disadvantage (Lane, 1978).

How do we expect blacks' ideas to be patterned? In Chapters 6 and 8 we lay out our interpretation of the ties among perceptions of, explanations for, and preferred solutions to racial inequality. Here we pause to consider the impress of social and economic factors on these perceptions, explanations, and opinions. Our model suggests that age, gender, interracial friendship, and various components of socioeconomic status directly affect each of the three sets of phenomena. We will discuss our expectations about their effects in light of prior research on blacks, and the considerably more abundant literature on whites.

Age

Perceptions. We expect younger blacks to perceive more discrimination even though older blacks are likely to have experienced first-hand the harsh realities of "old-style" white racism and legally imposed segregation. Even though younger blacks have lived in an era marked by the elimination of legally imposed segregation and the expansion of opportunities for blacks, they may be more acutely aware of discrimination that still exists. Several researchers (e.g., Edwards, 1972; Paige, 1970; Schuman and Hatchett, 1974) have documented strong age effects on blacks' racial attitudes, with the young – those who came of age during the disorder- and violence-filled 1960s and 1970s – standing out as most alienated from white society. The ideational basis of their alienation is the belief that a pervasive racism is deeply ingrained in American society. Their basis of judgment about the extent of racism is not the pre-civil rights era that older blacks can still recall, but democratic ideals of equality.

Some research does not support our expectation, however, indicating that older blacks' greater experience with discrimination in effect "cancels out" younger blacks' greater alienation. Kluegel and Smith (1986: 196) report only small, inconsistent age differences in blacks' estimates of the extent of racial discrimination in the United States, and O'Gorman (1979) finds that age is not consistently related to blacks' belief that most whites in the area where they live are segregationists.

We also expect younger whites to perceive greater racial discrimination than older whites do. A long series of studies of white attitudes toward racial integration (e.g., Hyman and Sheatsley, 1956; Greeley and Sheatsley, 1971; Taylor, Sheatsley, and Greeley, 1978) reveals that younger people have long held more liberal racial attitudes than their senior counterparts, suggesting a heightened sensitivity to racial discrimination (see also Schuman et al., 1985: 199–200). Moreover, young people are generally more tolerant than older ones (Stouffer, 1955; Nunn, Crockett, and Williams, 1978), although it is not clear that aging itself brings about lower tolerance (Nunn et al., 1978).

Explanations. We expect age to have little effect on explanations of racial inequality, even though the impact of age on whites' explanations is clear. Whites' likelihood of blaming blacks for racial inequality increases with age, apparently because basic political orientations, including ideas about racial and other inequalities, are acquired early in life. Today's senior citizens first learned about blacks and race relations at a time when most white Americans believed that the inferior status of blacks was divinely ordained, genetically determined, or self-inflicted. Accordingly, more "traditional" explanations of inequality, which seem to place the blame everywhere except on whites, appeal most to older whites (Sniderman with Hagen, 1985; see also Apostle et al., 1983; Kluegel and Smith, 1986; for parallel research on socioeconomic inequality, see Feagin, 1975; Kluegel and Smith, 1986). It is not aging per se that affects whites' causal attributions, but rather that younger whites acquired their basic sociopolitical views in a later, more enlightened time.

This logic is inapplicable to blacks. After all, when they were growing up members of the older generation of blacks were acutely aware of the shackles imposed by racial discrimination. Indeed, Parent (1985), analyzing the 1981 ABC News/*Washington Post* data, detected no significant age effect on blacks' tendency to attribute racial inequality to the shortcomings of blacks themselves (see also Bobo, 1989).

Solutions. We expect that younger blacks, perceiving more discrimination and being more alienated, will also be more supportive of governmental activity as a solution to inequality. The limited existing evidence is mixed, however. Bolce and Gray (1979) note that younger blacks are more likely to support affirmative action programs than are older blacks are, but Jacobson (1983) and Welch and Foster (1987) find no relationship; nor do Welch and Foster find any relationship between age and support for welfare spending.

Among whites, there is a clear tendency of older people to hold more conservative policy views than younger ones (Gilliam and Whitby, 1989; Welch and Foster, 1987). Indeed, the replacement of older generations by younger ones seems to have been a driving force in the liberalization of white attitudes toward policies dealing with racial inequality (Hyman and Sheatsley, 1964; Schuman et al., 1985: 199–200).

Gender

The impact of gender on blacks' racial perceptions, attributions, and policy preferences has been little studied, so our expectations are based largely on indirect evidence.

Perceptions. We expect black women to perceive less discrimination against themselves than black men do despite the fact that black women are victimized on the basis of both race and gender. There are two reasons for this. Because black women have almost attained parity with white women in pay, black women who compare themselves to white women may feel less discriminated against than do black men who compare themselves to white men. Second, among women of all races there is an inclination to deny having been personally discriminated against (see the literature cited by Crosby, 1982). We expect gender to have a negligible effect on perceptions of discrimination against blacks as a group. Women apparently find it more acceptable to claim that their group is discriminated against than to claim discrimination against themselves (Crosby, 1982).

Explanations. We expect little effect of gender on explanations. Although Kluegel and Smith (1986: 89–100) observe that women rely more on "structural" explanations of racial inequality and less on "individual" explanations, others have uncovered few gender-based differences in these attributions (Apostle et al., 1983; Parent, 1985; Sniderman with Hagen, 1985).

Solutions. The male-female opinion differential is both real and widening ("Opinion Roundup," 1982; Shapiro and Mahajan, 1986; see also Smith, 1984; for contrary points of view, see Bolce, 1985; Poole and Zeigler, 1985). It is widest on attitudes relating to violence and the use of force, but it is growing on the so-called compassion issues, such as treatment of the poor, an issue of special concern to us here. But we doubt that the gender gap is as evident among blacks as it is among whites. Indeed, our own previous analysis of blacks' policy opinions and partisanship pinpointed few significant gender differences (Welch and Sigelman, 1989; for similar findings, see Walton, 1985; but see Bolce, 1985; Welch and Foster, 1987).

When such gender-based differences do appear, it should be black women who are more supportive of government programs to ameliorate racial and economic inequality (see, e.g., Shingles, 1986). Almost 45 percent of black families are now headed by women (U.S. Bureau of the Census, 1987). The women who head these families, a large proportion of whom are poor, seem especially likely to support activist policies to reduce poverty and discrimination. Moreover, because black women bear the double burden of racial and gender discrimination, they earn far less than black men (Farley, 1984, 1988; McCrone and Hardy, 1979). This double burden seems likely to predispose them to take a somewhat more favorable view of programs for minorities and the poor.

Interracial friendship

Perceptions. We expect blacks who have at least one white friend to perceive racial discrimination as less widespread. However, we know of no reason why such friendship should be related to either causal attributions or policy views.

Students of race relations have long assumed that close, positive interpersonal contacts between members of different races foster favorable racial perceptions and attitudes (see, e.g., Allport, 1954). Adherents of this "contact theory" consider isolation to be a source of ignorance, which serves as a breeding ground for derogatory and hostile racial stereotypes. Consistent with this view, racial prejudice is less often observed among young whites who maintain closer contacts with blacks (Aberbach and Walker, 1973; Deutsch and Collins, 1951; Meer and Freedman, 1966; Wilner, Walkley, and Cook, 1955). However, the contact theory has not always withstood rigorous testing (Ford, 1973; Robinson and Preston, 1976). Sometimes such contact has little effect one way or the other (Jackman and Crane, 1986), and sometimes it can even increase prejudice. Nonetheless, guided by indications that among blacks, socializing with white neighbors or co-workers is associated with less alienation from and distrust of whites (see, e.g., Schuman and Hatchett, 1974), we expect interracial friendship to reduce blacks' perceptions of discrimination and prejudice.

As for whites, we might expect close personal interaction with blacks to increase sensitivity to the problems blacks face (see, e.g., Deutsch and Collins, 1951; Meer and Freedman, 1966; Wilner et al., 1955), and hence to increase perceptions of racial discrimination. However, some evidence suggests that whites who have black friends may not be aware of the degree of racial prejudice and discrimination on the part of other whites (Ford, 1973; Jackman and Crane, 1986; Robinson and Preston, 1976).

Explanations and Solutions. Interracial friendship should have little or no impact on blacks' causal understandings of racial inequality or policy views. It is true that one study of whites found that, compared to other whites, whites who have black friends are less likely to blame blacks for racial inequality and more likely to blame white discrimination (Apostle et al., 1983), but there is no reason to expect the same for blacks. It is possible that blacks who interact more with whites, perhaps being better integrated into the larger society, may see less need than other blacks for policies designed to reduce racial discrimination and its consequences.

Socioeconomic status

Behavioral and attitudinal differences between blacks of lower and higher socioeconomic status have long been noted (Drake and Cayton, 1945; Franklin, 1967; Frazier, 1939, 1957; Johnson and Roark, 1984; McBride and Little, 1981; Moynihan, 1972; Myrdal, 1944; Pettigrew, 1964; Sites and Mullins, 1985), despite a tendency by some to treat these differences as "politically irrelevant" (Hamilton, 1976).

Perceptions. We expect more affluent blacks to perceive less discrimination than do those lower on the status ladder. More economically comfortable blacks may live in environments in which racial discrimination is less overt or may simply be less discriminated against because they share many of the same values as middle-class whites (Giles and Evans, 1986). Black community studies conducted during the 1940s and 1950s generally concluded that lower income groups were more alienated than their middle- and upper-income counterparts. Better-off blacks tended to want to move closer to whites and to achieve desegregation by proving their worth, while those less well-off wanted to move away from or to challenge whites by engaging in aggressive personal behavior or by joining such collective movements as the Garveyites or later the Muslims (for a summary, see Pettigrew, 1964: ch. 2).

On the other hand, more affluent blacks are less satisfied than those of lower status with the progress that has been made toward racial equality and also tend to identify more with "blacks," while others identify more with "the poor" (Parent and Stekler, 1985; but see Dillingham, 1981).[21]

Although we expect income to be inversely related to perceptions of racial discrimination, we expect increasing education to heighten these perceptions, other things being equal. Education can be viewed as a source of enlightenment, fostering knowledge about members of different races, teaching people to recognize prejudice and to understand its dangers, and providing cognitive skills that enhance the capacity to detect and reject prejudice (Quinley and Glock, 1979: 188). Indeed, Sniderman, Piazza, Finifter, and Tetlock (1989) have shown that for blacks as well as for whites, education is associated with tolerance. Higher levels of formal education should therefore be associated with greater awareness of racial discrimination (but see O'Gorman, 1979); among blacks, those with the most education have traditionally been in the forefront of attempts to bring about greater racial equality (Marx, 1967).

As for whites, we expect those with more education to perceive greater discrimination against blacks. Schwartz (1967: 73), for example, found that white college graduates were much more likely than those with only a grade school or high school education to believe that blacks do not have as good a chance as whites to earn a living or get a job. Drawing on data collected almost two decades later, Kluegel and Smith (1986) show that whites with more education perceive greater discrimination against blacks.

Explanations. We do not expect large effects of socioeconomic status on blacks' causal understandings of racial inequality. Since schooling is not required for blacks to learn about racial discrimination, education seems to hold less potential for shaping blacks' thinking about racial inequality than it does for whites. Nonetheless, we believe that blacks with less education and fewer economic resources will tend to blame blacks themselves for their lower socioeconomic status. To the extent that blaming blacks for racial inequality reflects what social psychologists call "learned helplessness" (see Chapter 5), then it should be less successful blacks who manifest this tendency (Parent, 1985). The scanty empirical evidence does not, however, indicate a large effect (Bobo, 1989; Parent, 1985).

We also expect that less economically successful whites will be more likely than others to blame blacks (Parent, 1985; Sniderman with Hagen, 1985). However, we expect to find minimal effects of education among whites. Better educated whites may have more knowledge of the difficulty blacks face in making their way in white-dominated society, and should thus be less likely to blame blacks themselves for their problems. On the other hand, this difference is probably canceled out by education's role as a marker of social class. In this guise education may increase the blame aimed at blacks for not improving their lot.

Solutions. Generally, we expect blacks who are better off economically to be less supportive of welfare programs than lower-income blacks are,[22] but we expect education to have little impact on opinions about these policies. These expectations are based on several different analyses. Welch and Combs (1985) conclude that poorer blacks are significantly more supportive of welfare spending, but find no relationship between level of education and blacks' support for welfare spending. However, while education is positively associated with approval of greater spending on other social programs, such as health and education, income is not (see also Parent and Stekler, 1985; Seltzer and Smith, 1985; Welch and Foster, 1987). Thus, among blacks the higher one's socioeconomic status, especially as measured by income, the more conservative one's attitudes toward welfare, but not toward other kinds of social welfare issues. These differences are reasonably consistent, though not particularly large. Many members of the black middle class feel an ambivalence about being black and relatively well off, and this propels them to be sensitive to the plight of those less well off than themselves (Hochschild, 1990). As we have seen, middle-class blacks are likely to be employed by government. It therefore comes as no great surprise that they are supportive of government programs in ways that the white middle class often is not.

We expect to find no relationship between socioeconomic status and blacks' attitudes toward policies aimed specifically at blacks, such as special financial help, civil rights programs, and affirmative action. This expectation is based on several studies that have uncovered no strong or consistent socioeconomic differences between elements of socioeconomic status and views on affirmative action (Jacobson, 1983; Welch and Foster, 1987) or school busing and spending to improve the condition of blacks (Seltzer and Smith, 1985; Welch and Combs, 1985; see also Gurin et al., 1988). There is some contradictory evidence: Bolce and Gray (1979: 68) observe that in New York City blacks with lower incomes and less education are more supportive of quotas, and Parent and Stekler (1985) document a negative relationship between income and blacks' support for the idea that "blacks should get additional help from the government above that given to whites in similar economic circumstances." To some extent, these divergent findings reflect variations in question wording and the use of small samples, different sampling frames, and disparate years. We hesitate to attribute the contradictory findings wholly to methodological differences, however, and can only conclude that for blacks a consistent link between socioeconomic status and views of affirmative action, busing, and government aid for minorities remains unproven.

Among whites, we expect a straightforward link between socioeconomic status and support for government aid to the poor, with those of higher status being less likely to support such aid. We expect the impact of socio-economic status on support for aid to blacks and other minorities to be weaker. Even so, studies such as those of Schuman et al. (1985: 199) and Hyman and Sheatsley and their colleagues (Hyman and Sheatsley, 1956, 1964; Greeley and Sheatsley, 1971; Taylor et al., 1978; Smith and Sheatsley, 1984) have shown that education is associated with greater support for racial integration and policies promoting racial equality.

Conclusion

In some cases, prior studies provide strong reasons to anticipate linkages between socioeconomic status, on the one hand, and racial perceptions, explanations, and solutions, on the other. In other cases, there are no immediately relevant studies, or prior research conveys mixed messages. Bearing in mind the injunction with which we began this discussion – that even under the best of circumstances we should not expect too much by way of predictive power on the part of socioeconomic characteristics – we are now prepared to launch our own investigation of these issues.

Notes

1. Farley's analysis extends through 1982, whereas Farley and Allen present some analyses with data as recent as 1985. However, much of their analysis is based on 1980 data. Although *A Common Destiny* was published in 1989, most of the analyses reported therein draw on data from 1985 or earlier.
2. This conclusion was based on an analysis of a national survey done in 1975. Among blacks, education, income, and occupational status explained only three percent of the variance in subjective class identification. The same variables explained 28 percent of whites' subjective class identifications (Jackman and Jackman, 1983:83).
3. Gurin et al. (1988) also employ separate components of black socioeconomic status in their recent analysis of blacks' participation and attitudes during the 1984 election campaign. A recent analysis of blacks' class status is presented by Boston (1988).
4. Between 1790 and 1910, the proportion of blacks living in the South varied only between 89 percent and 92 percent.
5. An even earlier organization, the Niagara Movement, founded in 1905 by William Monroe Trotter and W. E. B. DuBois, was composed solely of blacks. Most of its leaders later became part of the NAACP leadership.
6. During the 1890s, about 100 lynchings took place annually, declining to about 80 in the

1900s and betweeen 55 and 60 in the 1910s. After averaging somewhat over 40 per year in the first half of the 1920s, the number fell to 14 per year after 1923, continued at about that level in the 1930s, and in the 1940s dropped to three annually; these figures are cited by McAdam, 1982:89.

7. As early as 1915, in *Guinn v. United States,* the U.S. Supreme Court struck down grandfather clauses in many southern states' laws. These were provisions that exempted people from having to pass a literacy test for voting if their grandfathers had been eligible to vote – in effect, if they were white.

8. Of course, the anti-German propaganda coexisted not only with continuing racism against black Americans, but also with virulent American racism against the Japanese, including Japanese Americans (Dower, 1986).

9. Two other civil rights organizations in addition to the NAACP and SCLC formed the heart of the protest movement: the Congress of Racial Equality, organized in 1942 and revitalized in the 1950s, and the Student Nonviolent Coordinating Committee, organized in 1960.

10. The black poor in some urban ghettos do, however, have mortality rates similar to those in poor Third World countries.

11. A special methodological problem in comparing blacks over time is that until the 1970s blacks were lumped with other nonwhites in most census classifications. This problem is not too serious, however, because as late as 1950, 96 of every 100 nonwhite Americans were black. However, that proportion has been steadily decreasing, and in 1980 only 85 percent of the nonwhite population was black (Farley, 1984: 37).

12. Economic status is a primary determinant of whether one goes to college: nearly 70 percent of all students whose families are in the highest income quartile attend college, but only 29 percent of those whose families are in the lowest income quartile do so (Vobejda, 1989). The declining college attendance rate of blacks, and lower-income students generally, probably is due in part to declining federal student aid. In constant 1982 dollars, the proportion of aid given in grants shrank from 43 percent in 1976 to 27 percent in 1988. In real dollars, the value of both grants and loans has fallen since the late 1970s (Moulton, 1988; U.S. Bureau of the Census, 1989: Table 268). Blacks, having on average much lower incomes than whites, are much more reliant on student aid. Moulton's (1988) analyses of aggregate enrollment and financial aid data show a strong positive relationship between real dollar aid and minority enrollment in colleges and universities. The drop in college attendance has been more dramatic for black men than for black women.

13. See also Lichter (1988). Willhelm (1986) disputes this, but the evidence in Figure 2.4 indicates a strong negative relationship between more education and unemployment.

14. Indeed, it has been argued that the unemployment rate is itself not an especially useful indicator. The unemployment rate is the proportion of the labor force actively looking for work, including answering help-wanted ads, registering at an employment service, or just "checking around." People are counted as employed even if they have only part-time work. Some critics argue that this measure overstates unemployment; others argue exactly the opposite. On the one hand, it overestimates unemployment by counting as unemployed those who look for work only sporadically, or who would accept only an ideal job. More commonly, critics charge that the official unemployment rate is an underestimate because it ignores unemployed people who are too discouraged even to try to find work; thus it is argued that the "real" black unemployment rate is really at least half again the official rate (Hill, 1981).

15. Smith and Welch (1987) show that about 8 percent fewer 24 year-old black males were employed or in school in 1980 than in 1960, and 3 percent fewer thirty-five to thirty-six year-olds.

16. Blacks with high school degrees or less are less likely than similarly educated whites to hold managerial and professional jobs, but the differences are small, as only a small number of either achieve such positions.

The changing occupational distribution among black men has a negative side, too. The black-white income ratio of the blue-collar jobs blacks are leaving is higher than the income ratio of some of the white-collar jobs blacks are gaining (Cotton, 1989: 808). Moreover, the closing of blue-collar jobs to black (and white) workers with limited educations is undoubtedly partially responsible for the increased unemployment and decreased labor force participation of young black males (Bluestone and Harrison, 1988; Cotton, 1989).

17. Willhelm (1986), for example, argues that discussions of the "feminization of poverty" inappropriately downplay the impact of racial discrimination on poverty. We consider the two explanations mutually reinforcing rather than mutually exclusive. Within each type of family, blacks are more likely to be poor. But intact black families are less likely to be poor than white female-headed ones. Thus both race and family composition are crucial.

18. Sixty percent of all black children are now born to unmarried women, and half of all black families with children are female-headed.

19. However, as Collins (1983) argues, the black middle class relies somewhat more on the public sector for employment opportunities than does the white middle class. Within the public sector, blacks are more likely to hold positions in public administration, teaching, or personnel administration than in finance or less "helping"-oriented occupations.

20. Comparing median rather than mean estimates of net worth controls for the impact of a relatively few extremely wealthy individuals who might skew the means. However, huge differences in wealth between the races remain even in this comparison. In 1984, white households had a median net worth of nearly $40,000 more than twelve times as large as the $3,400 median net worth of black households (U.S. Bureau of the Census, 1989: Table 746).

21. Studies conducted during the civil rights movement show that blacks with more education and in higher status occupations were more militant about equal rights (Marx, 1967; Orbell, 1967). Schuman and Hatchett (1974: 69), drawing on surveys conducted in 1968 and 1971, reported a relatively weak inverse relationship between income and alienation.

22. A somewhat discordant note is sounded in a recent study by Gilliam and Whitby (1989), who detect no relationship between either income or occupation and blacks' support for spending on social programs. Upon reflection, this seemingly anomalous finding makes considerable sense. Gilliam and Whitby measure support for social spending via a composite scale of support for spending on education, welfare, aid to the cities, antidrug programs, blacks, health care, and anticrime programs. We have already noted that blacks split along income and education lines on some of these programs, but not on others. Indeed, the direction of the relationship between income and support for government spending varies from one type of program to another. So, it is hardly surprising to find no relationship between income or occupation and blacks' support for government spending on social programs in general, because Gilliam and Whitby's composite measure lumps together programs whose primary appeal is to different parts of the black community.

3

Blacks' perceptions of racial inequality

As we have just seen, during the last three decades blacks have moved toward equality with whites in several areas of life, but at the same time many blacks have fallen farther and farther behind, especially in employment and income. In this light, it becomes particularly important to examine blacks' attitudes concerning their progress toward overcoming the bitter legacy of white supremacy and black enslavement.

Do most blacks now regard out-and-out white racism as largely a thing of the past, or is it still seen as widespread? What about the concrete manifestations of such racism – inadequate education, unemployment, and poverty? Are these conditions seen as improving or worsening? How do blacks explain persisting racial inequalities? How do they explain any recent progress toward closing these gaps? And what solutions do they endorse for the problems they continue to face? Because blacks' understandings of the causes and solutions of racial inequality are based, in part, on their perceptions of the current situation, our task in this chapter is to describe these perceptions.

Perceptions of black-white inequality

In analyzing blacks' perceptions of racial inequality, we distinguish between views of racial prejudice and views of racial discrimination (see, e.g., Dovidio and Gaertner, 1986). Racial prejudice is attitudinal, so when we describe someone as being prejudiced against blacks, we mean that he or she judges blacks unfavorably because of their race. Racial discrimination, on the other hand, is behavioral, so when we characterize someone as discriminating against blacks, we mean that he or she treats blacks unfavorably because of their race. It is relatively easy to imagine a person who holds prejudiced attitudes about blacks but does not act on the basis of these attitudes, that is, does not discriminate. It is not quite as easy, but it is again possible, to imagine a person who engages in discrimination against blacks without being prejudiced, as could be the case for a well-intentioned person. In practice, of course, one would expect prejudice and discrimination to be traveling companions, so it is often difficult to tell the two apart. As both social psychologists and constitutional lawyers can attest, the distinction between attitudes and behavior, or between belief and action, is too simplistic for many purposes, but the distinction does provide a useful starting point for the discussion that follows. We shall begin by considering blacks' perceptions of white prejudice, and then turn to perceptions of white discrimination.

The prevalence of prejudice against blacks

Asked directly about their feelings toward blacks, white Americans have become much less likely than they were only a few decades ago to espouse racial segregation or to express a belief in white supremacy. For example, according to a series of NORC surveys conducted over the last three decades, white support for racial integration has increased markedly (Greeley and Sheatsley, 1971; Hyman and Sheatsley, 1956, 1964; Sheatsley, 1966; Smith and Sheatsley, 1984; Taylor, Sheatsley, and Greeley, 1978; see also Condran, 1979; Jaynes and Williams, 1989). Indeed, Taylor et al. (1978: 43) note that several of the questions NORC once asked to tap whites' racial attitudes now evoke such broad agreement that they are no longer useful for research purposes.[1]

Figure 3.1 brings this point home by portraying trends in white racial prejudice from the 1940s to the early 1970s (Schuman et al., 1985). In general, by the end of this period, whites rarely expressed the overt hostility toward blacks that had still prevailed during the 1940s. In 1942, for example, two out of every three whites reacted negatively to the prospect of having a black of their own income and educational level move onto their block, but by 1972 85 percent of whites denied that it would bother them to have a black neighbor of this description. Nor by 1972 did more than a trace of disagreement remain among whites that blacks "should have as good a chance as white people to get any kind of job" – a dramatic change from the prevailing sentiment of thirty years earlier, when most whites still endorsed the idea that "white people should have the first chance at any kind of job."

This is not to say that white prejudice against blacks has disappeared or that most whites would now welcome blacks with open arms into their neighborhoods, homes, or families. Many whites now tend to eschew overt expressions of racist sentiment, but at the same time want to keep blacks at arm's length. Instructive in this regard are answers to a pair of

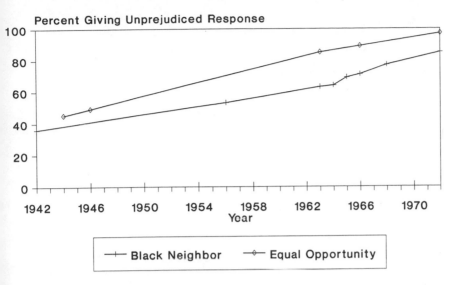

Figure 3.1. Signs of decreasing prejudice, whites, 1942–1972
Source: NORC surveys summarized by Schuman et al. (1985: 106–7 and 74–5). Question wording: "If a Negro with the same income and education as you have moved into your block, would it make any difference to you?" "Do you think Negroes should have as good a chance as white people to get any kind of job, or do you think white people should have the first chance at any kind of job?"

questions that were asked in Harris surveys over a fifteen-year period. In 1963, almost half the whites surveyed said they would relocate if a black family moved in next door, but by 1978 this proportion had fallen to roughly one in six. On the other hand, in 1978 almost half the whites surveyed said they would move if blacks came to live "in great numbers" in their neighborhood, implying something less than a wholehearted personal commitment to the goal of racial integration (see also Jaynes and Williams, 1989).

The same impression comes through in responses to a question asked in several American National Election Studies: "Are you in favor of desegregation, strict segregation, or something in between?" From the mid-1960s to the late 1970s, the percentage of whites who classified themselves as segregationist declined almost to the vanishing point, but expressions of support for desegregation rose by only eight percentage points (see Figure 3.2). Even in 1978, the great majority of whites described themselves as taking an "in between" stance on segregation versus desegregation. In fact, the "in between" category was also embraced by almost 40 percent of blacks, the rest of whom favored integration (Schuman et al., 1985: 144–

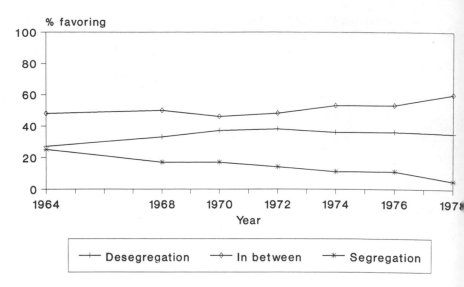

Figure 3.2. Attitudes toward segregation, whites, 1964–1978
Source: American National Election Studies, summarized by Schuman et al. (1985: 74–5). Question wording: "Are you in favor of desegregation, strict segregation, or something in between?"

5). However, we must be careful about drawing any conclusions based on fluctuating responses to this particular survey item, because, as Schuman and Bobo (1988: 62–7) have shown, changes in the question that served as a lead-in to this item could account for the observed trend.

Historically, racist sentiment was rooted in the belief that blacks were morally and intellectually inferior (Jordan, 1968, 1974; Morgan, 1890; Newby, 1968; Phillips, 1966; Rhodes, 1966). At the turn of this century, scientists were actively engaged in "proving" that blacks are less intelligent than whites (Bean, 1906), while historians busied themselves with demonstrating that blacks are less civilized than whites (Bancroft, 1912; for reviews see Cartwright and Burtis, 1969; Newby, 1968). As the decades have passed, such sentiments have become less respectable. In the 1978 Louis Harris nationwide survey of whites, the statement "Blacks are inferior to white people" was endorsed by "only" one white in seven, although substantial minorities of whites did ascribe to blacks such stigmatized traits as low intelligence, laziness, and a propensity toward violence (see Figure 3.3). And more whites accepted than rejected the idea that blacks are less ambitious than whites are (see also Jackman and Senter, 1980, 1983). Happily, when a few of the same questions were repeated ten years later in the

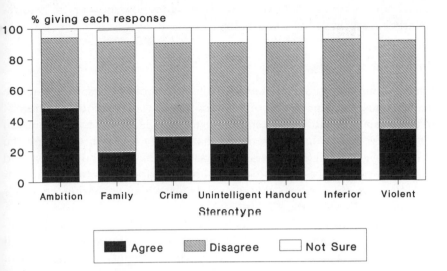

Figure 3.3. Stereotypes of blacks, whites, 1978
Source: 1978 nationwide survey of whites by Louis Harris and Associates, machine-readable data file. Question wording: "Now let me ask you some questions about blacks as people, leaving aside the whole question of civil rights and laws. I'd like to know how you feel as an individual. On this card are some statements people sometimes make about black people. As I read the number next to each statement, please tell me whether you personally tend to agree or disagree with that statement." "Blacks tend to have less ambition than whites." "Blacks care less for the family than whites." "Blacks breed crime." "Blacks have less native intelligence than whites." "Blacks want to live off the handout." "Blacks are inferior to white people." "Blacks are more violent than whites."

white portion of Harris's 1988 national survey, negative stereotyping of blacks had faded somewhat. For example, 60 percent of whites now disagree with the statement that blacks are less ambitious than whites (Louis Harris and Associates, 1989: Appendix B).

During the postwar era, the accumulated evidence from national opinion surveys indicates a substantial liberalization of whites' attitudes toward blacks in other ways, too. This liberalization seems to have taken the form of genuine attitudinal change, accompanied by the replacement of cohorts of older, more prejudiced whites by younger, less prejudiced ones (Firebaugh and Davis, 1988; Schuman et al., 1985; but see Dowden and Robinson, 1990). Social scientists are still debating whether old-style white racial prejudice is actually as rare as data from recent surveys suggest, and, if it is, whether it has been supplanted by more egalitarian racial attitudes or by subtle new forms of prejudice, often labeled "symbolic" racism.[2] We make no attempt to solve these thorny issues here, because our focus is on what and how *blacks* think about black-white inequality. For our purposes the crucial point is simply that overtly racist attitudes now show up fairly infrequently in surveys of the white public.

Perceptions of racial prejudice

Whatever most white Americans really believe about blacks, they perceive that the most virulent strains of white racism are confined to an extremist fringe. Responding to the September–October 1989 ABC News/*Washington Post* survey, three whites in ten said that "only a few" whites "share the attitudes of groups like the Ku Klux Klan toward blacks," and another third pegged the prevalence of Klan-type sentiments at approximately 10 percent. Only four percent of whites characterized most whites as sharing the Klan's extreme racial views.[3] (See Table 3.1.)

By contrast, most blacks still perceive overt white hostility as fairly widespread. In fact, almost one black in four claims that *more than half* of all white Americans accept the Klan's racial views – significantly higher than the corresponding percentage for whites – and just one black in ten perceives overt racism among "only a few" whites – significantly lower than the corresponding percentage for whites.[4] These estimates are consistent with responses to a question asked in the 1986 ABC News/*Washington Post* survey. Virtually no black respondents (only two percent) perceived "almost no" antiblack prejudice among whites, and only 12 percent perceived "not much." Almost half detected a "fair amount" of prejudice, and, most strikingly, a third beheld "a great deal" of white prejudice against blacks.

So no matter what national opinion surveys say about whites' attitudes toward blacks, and no matter what whites assume to be the racial attitudes of other whites, most blacks see racism living on in a sizable part of the white public. That so many blacks still consider old-style white racism, let alone some more "genteel" form of antiblack sentiment, alive and well in white America bespeaks a vast perceptual gulf between blacks and whites. The existence of this perceptual gulf helps define the context within which members of the two races consider the causes and solutions of racial inequality.

Perceptions of racial discrimination

In this psychological climate, how do blacks appraise their material well-being? Do they tend to believe that the most important barriers to black social, economic, and political advancement have largely been overcome, or are they convinced that some of the most important battles in the struggle for racial equality have yet to be won?

One answer can be found in the 1978 Louis Harris survey, in which a

Table 3.1. *Perceptions of white prejudice against blacks, 1981 and 1986* (in %)

Just your best guess – how many white Americans would you say personally share the attitudes of groups like the Ku Klux Klan toward blacks? Would you say only a few Americans share that attitude, about ten percent, less than a quarter, less than half, or over half of white Americans share that attitude?

	Blacks			Whites	
	1981	1986	1989	1981	1989
Only a few	13	10	11	29	30
About ten percent	23	24	25	31	34
Less than a quarter	18	15	11	16	17
Less than half	19	21	25	11	12
Over half	18	23	26	7	4
Don't know/No opinion	9	8	3	7	2

Now I want to ask you about prejudice against blacks. Please tell me whether you think that in the following groups there's a great deal of prejudice against blacks, a fair amount, not much, or almost no prejudice.

	Blacks
	1986
Whites in general	
Great deal	34
Fair amount	48
Not much	12
Almost no	2
Don't know/no opinion	4
No answer/refused	0

Sources: February–March 1981 ABC News/*Washington Post* nationwide survey, January 1986 ABC News/*Washington Post* nationwide survey of blacks, machine-readable data files, and September–October 1989 ABC News/*Washington Post* nationwide survey, unpublished summary provided by Richard Morin.

plurality of blacks denied experiencing or anticipating discrimination in housing or on the job, and most asserted that their children were receiving an education equal or superior to that received by white children (see Table 3.2). Wage discrimination was seen as a more common problem, a finding that resurfaced in the 1986 ABC News/*Washington Post* survey (see Figure 3.4). According to the 1986 survey, one black in four recalls encountering discrimination in getting "a quality education," and one in four also recalls being discriminated against in getting "decent housing." In contrast, about four in ten say they have experienced discrimination in getting a job, and about four in ten also see themselves as victims of wage discrimination.[5] This perception of greater discrimination in employment than in education

Table 3.2. *Blacks' perceptions of discrimination against themselves, 1963 and 1978* (in %)

Do you feel that if you do the same work as a white you will be paid the same as the white will get for that work, or will you probably get paid less?

	Blacks	
	1963	1978
Same pay	33	44
Less pay	56	46
Not sure	11	9

Have you or has anyone in your family been discriminated against in trying to get ahead on the job or in trying to get a job, or not?

	Blacks
	1978
Discriminated against	39
Not discriminated against	50
Not sure	11

In general, if you were to get a house or apartment, the same as a white person, do you feel you would pay the same rent or more than the white person would pay?

	Blacks	
	1963	1978
Same	30	39
More	53	45
Not sure	17	15

All in all, do you feel children in your family are receiving a better education than white children around here, as good an education as white children get around here, or are they getting not as good an education?

	Blacks	
	1963	1978
A better education	0	9
As good as whites	35	50
Not as good an education	48	25
Not sure	17	14
No answer/Refused	0	2

Sources: Louis Harris 1963 survey of blacks reported in Brink and Harris (1964: 55, 57, 59), and Louis Harris and Associates 1978 nationwide survey of blacks, machine-readable data file.

comports fairly closely with the situation described in Chapter 2. Blacks are moving ahead in education, but their unemployment situation has worsened relative to that of whites. Even though those blacks who are employed are gaining on whites in salary and occupational status, in the real

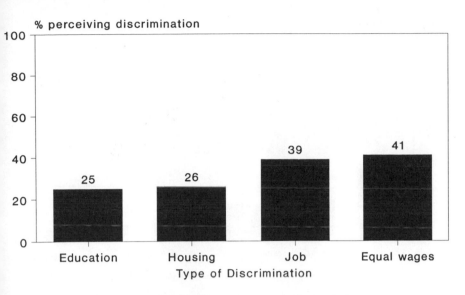

Figure 3.4. Type of perceived discrimination against oneself, blacks, 1986
Source: January 1986 ABC News/*Washington Post* nationwide survey of blacks, machine-readable data file. Question wording: "Have you yourself ever been discriminated against or not in:" ". . . getting a quality education . . ." ". . . getting decent housing . . ." ". . . getting a job . . ." ". . . getting equal wages for a job . . ."

world that blacks are perceiving, black males pay at least a 12 percent salary penalty for being black (Farley, 1984).

So it is hardly surprising that many blacks feel personally victimized by discrimination. In fact, even though there is currently no single type of discrimination from which more than 40 percent of blacks claim to have suffered, approximately 60 percent of those responding to all four questions say they themselves have been affected by at least one of these types of discrimination (see Figure 3.5).[6] Nor is it at all unusual for blacks to claim that they have been discriminated against in more than one way, for example, in getting decent housing *and* getting equal wages for a job. Indeed, one black in three recalls discrimination against himself or herself in more than a single realm, and one in ten alleges that he or she has suffered discrimination in getting an education *and* housing *and* a job *and* equal wages.

Blacks are consistently more likely to perceive widespread discrimination against blacks as a group than against themselves in particular (compare Figure 3.4 and Table 3.3). The perceptual gap in 1986 ranged from 10 percentage points in getting a quality education to 22 points in getting

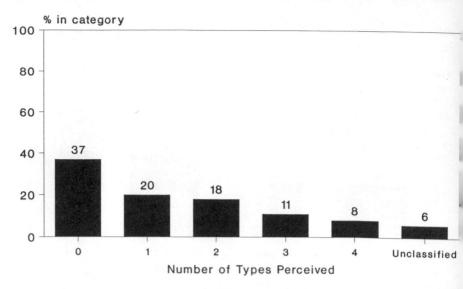

Figure 3.5. Extent of perceived discrimination against oneself, blacks, 1986
Source: See Figure 3.4. "Unclassified" means that the respondent did not answer one or more of these items, making it impossible to calculate a meaningful summary score.

decent housing.[7] As for whites, in 1989 as in 1978, approximately nine out of every ten perceive no discrimination against blacks in education, while almost four blacks in ten do perceive discrimination. So although "only" a minority of blacks perceives the schools as a site of discriminatory treatment, this is almost four times the proportion of whites who share that perception. Here again, then, a wide perceptual gulf between blacks and whites is evident.

The same gap recurs throughout Table 3.3, where, depending on the specific question, two, three, four, or even more times as many blacks as whites perceive white discrimination against blacks as a group. Although about four blacks in ten say that blacks generally are discriminated against in getting a quality education, blacks' estimates of discrimination in housing and on the job go well beyond that. Approximately five blacks in ten perceive discrimination in housing and in the market for unskilled labor; roughly six in ten point to wage discrimination; and at least that many say that discrimination still keeps many blacks out of skilled and managerial positions. Whites' estimates of the prevalence of racial discrimination pale by comparison; in every case they are far lower than blacks' estimates in the same survey.

Thus blacks perceive discrimination against blacks as a group as being

Table 3.3. *Perceptions of discrimination against blacks, 1978, 1981, 1986, and 1989 (in %)*

Louis Harris and Associates [1978]: "Let me ask you about some specific areas of life around here. Tell me for each if you feel blacks are discriminated against or not in that area around here."
ABC News/Washington Post [1981, 1986]: "In your area, would you say blacks generally are discriminated against or not in:"

	Blacks				Whites		
	1978	1981	1986	1989	1978	1981	1989
Getting a quality education							
Discriminated	42	27	35	37	9	6	11
Not discriminated	49	68	59	61	88	90	87
Don't know/No opinion	7	4	6	2	3	4	2
No answer/Refused	1	0	0	0	0	0	0
Getting decent housing							
Discriminated	58	42	48	52	25	16	20
Not discriminated	36	53	48	47	68	78	76
Don't know/No opinion	5	4	4	1	6	6	4
No answer/Refused	1	0	0	0	1	0	0
Getting unskilled labor jobs							
Discriminated	36	41	49		8	10	
Not discriminated	55	50	44		86	83	
Don't know/No opinion	7	8	7		5	7	
No answer/Refused	1	0	0		1	0	
Getting skilled labor jobs							
Discriminated	67	56	66	53	23	19	15
Not discriminated	26	36	26	44	68	72	79
Don't know/No opinion	6	7	7	3	8	9	6
No answer/Refused	2	0	0	0	1	0	0
Getting [Harris: promoted into]							
managerial jobs							
Discriminated	72	57	68	61	30	22	23
Not discriminated	18	31	24	36	55	64	71
Don't know/No opinion	8	12	7	3	14	14	7
No answer/Refused	2	0	0	0	1	1	0
The wages they are paid [ABC News/							
Washington Post: in most jobs]							
Discriminated	60	50	61	57	18	12	14
Not discriminated	27	37	32	40	72	80	81
Don't know/No opinion	12	13	7	3	8	8	6
No answer/Refused	1	0	1	0	1	0	0

Sources: Louis Harris and Associates 1978 national surveys of blacks and whites, machine-readable data files; February–March 1981 ABC News/*Washington Post* nationwide survey; January 1986 ABC News/*Washington Post* nationwide survey of blacks; and September–October 1989 ABC News/*Washington Post* nationwide survey.

Table 3.4. *Number of types of discriminatory treatment against blacks mentioned, 1978, 1981, and 1986* (in %)

Number mentioned	Blacks			Whites	
	1978	1981	1986	1978	1981
0	7	12	7	43	48
1	5	10	6	10	10
2	8	8	9	7	6
3	10	11	13	6	4
4	11	10	15	6	3
5	17	9	14	3	3
6	15	14	15	3	1
Unclassified	26	26	22	23	25
Mean	3.7	3.1	3.6	1.2	0.9
Median	4.1	3.1	3.8	0.4	0.3
Standard deviation	1.9	2.1	1.9	1.7	1.5

Note: As in Figure 3.5, "unclassified" means that the respondent did not answer one or more of these items, making it impossible to calculate a meaningful summary score.
Sources: Louis Harris and Associates 1978 national surveys of blacks and whites, machine-readable data files; February–March 1981 ABC News/*Washington Post* nationwide survey, machine-readable data file; and January 1986 ABC News/*Washington Post* nationwide survey of blacks, machine-readable data file.

most problematic in getting good jobs and getting appropriate pay for their jobs, the very same areas in which they are most likely to report having personally experienced discrimination. By the same token, they do not consider getting a quality education to have been one of the main obstacles they have personally had to face, and neither do they rank it among the most common problems for blacks as a group.

Using the 1978, 1981, and 1986 surveys, we counted the number of areas in which each respondent perceived discrimination against blacks, in order to obtain a summary measure of the perceived scope of discrimination. Scores on the scale run from 0, for those who perceived discrimination in none of the six areas, to 6, for those who perceived discrimination in all six. The results, which are shown in Table 3.4, document the gross black-white perceptual difference. Blacks on average have perceived racial discrimination in three or four of the six areas, but whites, responding to the same questions, have perceived discrimination in an average of only one area. For the 1978 and 1981 surveys, in which direct black-white comparisons can be made, these differences are highly significant and very substantial.[8]

The ability of many whites to persuade themselves that blacks are treated well in American society is nothing new. Whites, particularly those who are not especially sympathetic to blacks, have historically taken comfort in the ideas that the situation of blacks is not all that bad and that blacks do not mind their status in American society. Bancroft (1909), for example, portrayed the black slave as "the happiest of mortals," content with good food and "undisturbed by thoughts of having to go into the boiling pot for somebody's breakfast in the morning." According to this view, it was emancipation, not slavery, that brought troubles to blacks. Thirty years later, Senator Allen Ellender of Louisiana, reflecting the views of other white segregationists, argued that "the Negro of the South loves the white people of the South; he always has" (quoted by Newby, 1968: 128–33). By 1960, after several years of intense civil rights activity, only 22 percent of white southerners knew that most blacks were in favor of integration; as Donald Matthews and James Prothro, considering this fact, concluded: "Inaccurate information about the views of the subordinate group may be considered one of the prices the superordinate group must pay for a repressive social system" (1966: 351–2).

Whereas whites tend to downplay the extent of discrimination against blacks, blacks tend to downplay the extent of discrimination against themselves as compared to discrimination against blacks in general (see Figures 3.4 and 3.5 and Table 3.3). Thus, many blacks say that they themselves have not been directly affected by racial discrimination, but they do perceive discrimination as a problem besetting blacks in general. Part of the difficulty in assessing exactly what this means is the looseness of the term "generally" in the question, "Would you say blacks generally are discriminated against or not?" Agreement could mean that most blacks are discriminated against, or that there is a general condition in which some blacks are sometimes discriminated against. But whatever the question is supposed to mean, it is clear that blacks see racial discrimination as an everyday occurrence, not an historical curiosity.

The extent of discrimination might appear even more widespread if our measures of discrimination were more refined. The questions national surveys use to tap perceptions of discrimination are fairly crude; they deal with broad dimensions of the quality of life (such as housing and education) and ignore possible discrimination in the daily routines of life (shopping, enrolling children in a sports or art program, getting medical care, dealing with coworkers, and so on). Perhaps because social scientists are so new at examining blacks' attitudes and perceptions about race and inequality, we may still only be scratching the surface of the depths of discrimination. We hasten to add that even a score of zero on our scales of perceived discrimination against oneself or against blacks as a group would not necessarily indicate an absence of perceived discrimination; rather, it would indicate an absence of perceived discrimination in the areas about which survey respondents have been asked. Discrimination in other, subtler forms could coexist with an absence of discrimination in the areas included in our discrimination scales.

Nonetheless, the questions asked in these surveys do provide at least a rough profile of perceived discrimination in important and varied aspects of life. Although they may lead us to underestimate the overall prevalence of discrimination, the picture they paint of perceived discrimination, especially in the workplace, is bleak enough to give pause.

Perceptions of trends in prejudice and discrimination

Even though blacks see racial prejudice and discrimination as still widespread, do they believe that, generally speaking, things are getting better? And how optimistic are they that the situation will improve in the future?

The data summarized in Table 3.5 reveal a lack of consensus among both blacks and whites about whether prejudice against blacks is on the rise. Most whites think white attitudes are in flux, but there is little agreement among them about whether antiblack feelings are ebbing or flowing. The same holds true for blacks. Most blacks characterize whites' attitudes as undergoing change, but there is no consensus concerning the direction of this change. A third of the blacks surveyed in 1981 sensed less white prejudice than had prevailed five years earlier, a third detected more, and a quarter noted no change. A similar pattern was evident in 1986, but in 1989 a substantially larger percentage of blacks perceived an increase in antiblack feelings among whites, and a substantially smaller percentage of blacks perceived a decrease in antiblack feelings among whites. Several racial incidents that attracted national attention, including the Howard Beach and Bensonhurst cases, undoubtedly contributed to these perceptions of rising white prejudice.

The geographic referent in the item we have just been examining must also be taken into account. Respondents in the 1981 ABC News/*Washington Post* survey, after answering several questions about conditions "in your area," were asked about an increase or decrease in antiblack feeling "on a national basis." The importance of this distinction becomes clear when we see, in Table 3.5, that both blacks and whites were more likely to perceive an increase in antiblack feeling nationwide than in their own area. Surveys of opinion on nuclear power plants, hazardous waste dumps, and other potentially dangerous facilities have often documented a "not in my backyard" or "NIMBY" phenomenon, that is, a tendency to favor such facilities as long as they are far away from one's own abode (e.g., Mitchell, 1984). To this we can

Table 3.5. *Perceived trends in racial prejudice and discrimination, 1981, 1986, and 1989 (in %)*

On a national basis, do you think today there is more, less, or about the same amount of antiblack feeling among whites as compared to four or five years ago?

	Blacks			Whites	
	1981	1986	1989	1981	1989
More	34	27	44	26	23
About the same	25	34	33	27	39
Less	34	35	21	42	36
Don't know/No opinion	7	4	1	5	3
No answer/Refused	0	1	0	0	0

What about in the area where you live? Do you think today there is more, less, or about the same amount of antiblack feeling among whites as compared to four or five years ago?

	Blacks			Whites	
	1981	1986	1989	1981	1989
More	21	17	25	13	10
About the same	33	39	44	42	48
Less	37	37	29	36	36
Don't know/no opinion	10	7	2	9	5

Looking back over the last ten years, do you think the quality of life for blacks in the United States has:

	Blacks		Whites	
	1986	1989	1981	1989
Gotten better	60	47	77	69
Stayed about the same	21	30	15	24
Gotten worse	18	22	7	6
Don't know/no opinion	2	1	1	1

Would you say that over the past year the economic position of blacks has gotten?

	Blacks
	1984
Better	27
Same	33
Worse	35
Don't know/no opinion	4

In terms of income and living conditions for most blacks, would you say things are getting better, getting worse, or staying about the same?

	Blacks
	1986
Better	13
About the same	37
Worse	48
Don't know/no opinion	2
No answer/refused	0

Table 3.5. *(cont.)*

How about you personally? Would you say your income and living conditions are getting better, getting worse, or staying about the same?

	Blacks
	1986
Better	29
About the same	48
Worse	23
Don't know/No opinion	1
No answer/Refused	0

Sources: February–March 1981 and 1986 ABC News/*Washington Post* nationwide surveys, machine-readable data files; September–October 1989 ABC News/*Washington Post* survey, unpublished summary provided by Richard Morin; 1984 National Black Election Study, machine-readable data files.

add a different sort of "NIMBY" phenomenon – a tendency (also observed by Cataldo et al. [1970] in a survey of Buffalo blacks) to believe that racial discrimination is not as serious in one's own area as it is elsewhere. This gap suggests to us that to a marked extent blacks, lacking first-hand information about national trends, often use notorious cases reported in the media as a basis for their impressions concerning how whites in general feel about blacks. On the other hand, most whites, though confronted with the same media reports, continue to perceive white prejudice as holding constant or lessening, resisting the inference that large numbers of blacks have drawn.

The next two items in Table 3.5 indicate that blacks perceive a slowing of racial progress during the early 1980s. By more than a three-to-one ratio, blacks in 1981 assessed "the quality of life for blacks in the United States" as getting better rather than worse. But in their 1984 responses, and even more so in 1986 and 1989, blacks began to sound much more bearish. In fact, almost half described "income and living conditions for most blacks" as "getting worse," and only one in eight contended that conditions are improving. This is a realistic assessment of the trends affecting blacks in the early 1980s, as we saw in Chapter 2. Black income dropped, unemployment and poverty grew, and college enrollment leveled off. Progress slowed and in some cases halted. Obviously, then, the "objective" upturn in black economic fortunes that began in late 1983 was not yet reflected in black attitudes in 1986 or 1989 – hardly surprising in light of the continuing deficit of real black income below its 1978 level and of the Reagan administration's efforts to sidetrack civil rights and affirmative action programs.

Blacks are far less negative about their personal situation than about the situation for blacks in general. Approximately 30 percent describe their own income and living conditions as "getting better," and almost half describe their economic situation as steady.[9]

Whites, as we have seen several times in this chapter, are more impressed than blacks are by the gains blacks have registered: Seven whites in ten see the quality of life as having improved for blacks during the last decade, ten times the proportion who say that things have gotten worse for blacks. This perception of the improvement of blacks' lives during the 1980s flies in the face not only of blacks' perceptions but also of the "objective" reality of declining black income and fragmenting black family structure that occurred during this decade.

Conclusion

In sum, blacks' views of how things have been shaping up for themselves and for blacks in general are full of crosscurrents – perceptions of gain and loss, of personal well-being and collective deprivation, of long-term gain and short-term reversals. Blacks concede that in the long run their situations have improved, but they are not satisfied with the pace or the scope of that improvement. Their pessimism has a basis in reality. It reflects the rising rates of black unemployment and falling black income of the early 1980s, as well as a political climate not positively attuned to enhancing the well-being of the poor and minorities.

Where blacks perceive limited, halting gains, whites tend to see great and rapid improvement. Whatever the cognitive or motivational mechanism may be, such as ignorance, suppressed guilt, projection, or indifference, the present generation of whites, like its predecessors, prefers to believe that blacks are doing well.[10]

In looking toward the future, most blacks are optimistic (see Figure 3.6). Responses of "better" outrun "worse" by a four-to-one margin when blacks compare "life for blacks in this country" in the future to life in the present. And even though three blacks in ten take the pessimistic view that "There will always be many blacks living in extremely bad conditions no matter how much effort is made to change that," many more (two out of every three) express confidence that "With enough effort, those extremely bad conditions can be almost entirely eliminated." The 1984 NBES indicated that slightly less than half (46 percent) of a large black sample thought blacks would ever achieve full social and economic equality, 35 percent were dubious, and the rest were undecided.

Optimism has been a perennial feature of the attitudes of black Ameri-

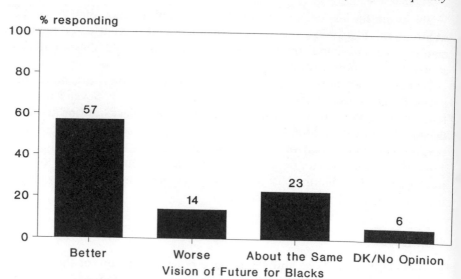

Figure 3.6. Optimism about the future for blacks, blacks, 1986
Source: January 1986 ABC News/*Washington Post* nationwide surveys, machine-readable data file. Question wording: "Thinking of the future, all in all would you say that life for blacks in this country will be better, about the same, or worse than it is now?"

cans, through good times and bad. Long before surveys became available to quantify such measurements, the idea of progress infused black thought and opinion (Meier, 1968), and surveys conducted over the last thirty years have documented the continuing hold this idea exercises over blacks (McCready with Greeley, 1976). In the 1950s, more blacks than whites believed life would be better in the future (Pettigrew, 1964). In the early 1960s, at the height of the sometimes violent civil rights struggle in the South and before the passage of the Civil Rights Act, Southern blacks were extremely optimistic about the future of race relations (Matthews and Prothro, 1966). Indeed, in 1964 blacks across the nation were more optimistic than they had been a decade earlier (Brink and Harris, 1964: 238). At the height of the 1960s riots, blacks in Detroit felt optimistic about their own lives and the future of race relations (Aberbach and Walker, 1973: 46–7). And researchers in Buffalo reported that blacks were even more optimistic than whites (Cataldo et al., 1970).

Amid all these crosscurrents of positivity and negativity about the past and optimism and pessimism about the future, what stands out most clearly about perceptions of white prejudice and discrimination is the massive perceptual gap that divides blacks from whites. It is hardly an overstatement to say that blacks and whites inhabit two different perceptual worlds. Whites simply do not acknowledge the persisting prejudice and discrimination that are so obvious to blacks. Besides the black-white perceptual gap, it is important to recognize that blacks, for their part, vary widely in their perceptions of how widespread prejudice and discrimination are and whether these conditions are improving or worsening. Even so, there is something approaching consensus among blacks that prospects for the future are brighter than the record of the past and present.

Notes

1. For example, questions concerning access to public accommodations were once quite controversial but now are not even asked, and it is impossible even to imagine today's pollsters asking the following question, which appeared in a 1949 survey: "Scientists are reported to be working on a drug that turns colored skins white. If such a drug were perfected, people with colored skins who wanted to do so could turn their skins white. Do you think that would be a good thing or a bad thing to have happen?" (Roper Center, 1982).

2. See, e.g., McConahay and Hough (1976). For an exchange that touches on most of the relevant issues in this debate, see Sniderman and Tetlock (1986a,b) and Kinder (1986). For a biting critique of both the Sniderman and Kinder positions, see Roth (1990). A somewhat different interpretation of the apparent decline in "old-style" white racism would be that whites have simply learned to avoid publicly expressing overt hostility to blacks. That is, as norms of social desirability have changed, whites may have become more adept at camouflaging their prejudices, which they have not abandoned. From this perspective, survey-based estimates of racial prejudice are inherently suspect. For some evidence consistent with this interpretation, see Crosby, Bromley, and Saxe (1980).

3. Here and throughout this chapter, it must be borne in mind that we are dealing in perceptions of prejudice or discrimination, not in prejudice or discrimination per se. The accuracy or inaccuracy of these perceptions is beside the point for our purposes, since we are taking an explicitly subjectivist approach. That is, our interest lies not in the "facts" of prejudice and discrimination, but rather in blacks' and whites' perceptions of prejudice and discrimination.

   Still, it bears mentioning that such perceptions can be reasonably accurate, even when they are based on minimal information. Brady and Sniderman (1985), for example, have shown that members of the mass public can accurately describe the policy positions of Democrats and Republicans, liberals and conservatives, and blacks and whites. The explanation, they argue, is that even though most people may not really "know" where these groups stand, they can use what little they do know to infer where the groups are likely to stand, and such inferences are, by and large, correct. Thus, at least under some conditions blacks' perceptions of where whites stand closely match whites' actual stands, and vice versa. This argument contradicts, at least in part, O'Gorman's (1975, 1979; O'Gorman with Garry, 1976–7; see also O'Gorman, 1988) contention that whites' and blacks' conceptions of one another's racial values tend to be grossly distorted.

4. In this chapter and in Chapters 5 and 7, all references to statistically significant differences are based on tests for differences of proportions or differences of means, as appropriate in a particular case. Only black-white differences within a survey were so tested; given differences in sampling frames, question order, question wording, and a host of other sources of variability, no tests were conducted for intersurvey differences.

5. Perhaps surprisingly, except in the area of education, a larger proportion of blacks in this 1986 survey reported discrimination against themselves than did a sample of Detroit blacks in 1971 (Aberbach and Walker, 1973). This could, however, reflect the existence of more pervasive discrimination in the South than in northern cities.

6. Only the 1986 ABC News/*Washington Post* data from Figure 3.4, and not the 1978 Louis Harris data from Table 3.2, are used in Figure 3.5. The ABC News/*Washington Post* questions focused on the respondent's personal experience of discrimination. So did two of the four Louis Harris questions, but the other two posed hypothetical situations rather than asking for a recall of actual experiences. As a consequence, it would be misleading to sum the Harris respondents into a scale of respondents' perceptions of how much discrimination they had actually suffered.

7. Here and throughout Table 3.3, we tend to discount year-to-year differences in perceived discrimination against blacks due to (1) question wording differences between the Louis Harris and ABC News/*Washington Post* items and (2) the relatively small size of the 1981 and 1989 ABC News/*Washington Post* samples of blacks. Some of these yearly differences might indicate real opinion trends, but question wording and sampling differences make it impossible to separate fact from artifact.

8. On the reliability of this scale and the scale of perceived discrimination against oneself, see note 4 in the next chapter. In Table 3.4 we do not show mean scores for blacks or whites on the scale of perceived discrimination against blacks for the 1989 ABC News/*Washington Post* data because one of the items on which the scale is based for the other years was not used in the 1989 survey. Accordingly, the 1989 mean, based on five items rather than six, is not strictly comparable to the 1978, 1981, and 1986 means. Because the black-white differential in 1989 is of interest, though, we will report here that on the 0–54 scale for 1989, the mean for blacks is 2.7 and the mean for whites is 0.9 – an extremely sizable difference, just as in prior years.

9. The same phenomenon is evident in the results of the 1984 NBES, which showed that more blacks believed that the condition of blacks had worsened than believed that their own condition had deteriorated.

10. Some findings from Kluegel and Smith's (1986: 190) nationwide survey in 1980 are instructive in this regard. Asked for their assessments of whether "the chances for blacks to get ahead" have improved during the last ten to twenty years, 61 percent of whites but only 31 percent of blacks answered "improved greatly."

4

The sources of blacks' perceptions of racial inequality

We have examined perceptions of racial inequality but have not yet determined whether these perceptions fit together in any interpretable fashion. Do blacks who perceive greater prejudice and discrimination against themselves also tend to see blacks in general as more victimized by whites, or are perceptions of prejudice and discrimination against oneself largely divorced from broader perceptions of prejudice and discrimination against blacks? Is the idea that discrimination is widespread tied to the idea that prejudice is on the rise? Do blacks tend to differentiate among different aspects of discrimination – educational, residential, occupational – or do they perceive discrimination as more of a unified whole, or *gestalt?* And how do the interrelationships among these perceptions compare between blacks and whites? Not until we know more about the structure of perceptions of inequality will we be prepared to address the central questions of this chapter.

Answering these questions necessarily involves us in some fairly sophisticated statistical operations. In order to keep our presentation as accessible as possible, we shall provide a brief, nontechnical overview of the statistical results and invite technically minded readers to peruse these results more closely in the Appendix, at the end of this book.

The dimensionality of blacks' perceptions of racial inequality

To probe the interrelationships among the various aspects of blacks' perceptions of racial inequality, we undertook an exploratory factor analysis of responses to the sixteen perceptual items in the 1986 ABC News/*Washington Post* survey (see Chapter 3). These items include six concerning discrimination against blacks, four concerning discrimination against oneself, two concerning the trend in antiblack feelings, two concerning the trend in living conditions, and one each concerning the prevalence of Klanlike attitudes and white prejudice. In essence, exploratory factor analysis amounts to a search for order beneath the surface of a large number of variables. In the present case, the question is whether one or more "dimensions" or "factors" underlie the various perceptual items. If these items converge on some factor or factors, then we will have empirical warrant to speak of the underlying dimensions rather than having to deal with the idiosyncracies of sixteen different items.

Analysis of these sixteen items uncovered five underlying factors, dominated by the first (see Table A.1 in the Appendix).[1] The five factors are easy to identify, because they correspond perfectly to the five sets of items mentioned in the last paragraph. Only the six items pertaining to discrimination against blacks are highly correlated with the first, and strongest, factor; this, then, is obviously a "perceived discrimination against blacks" dimension. The second factor, though considerably weaker, is no less identifiable, since it involves only the two items relating to the trend in antiblack feelings, making it a "perceived trend in antiblack feelings" factor. The only items correlated with the third factor are all four of the items on discrimination against oneself; so this is a "perceived discrimination against oneself" factor. The fourth and fifth factors, weaker still, respectively involve only the items pertaining to the perceived trend in black living conditions and the two items about the prevalence of white prejudice. Based on these results, we conclude that blacks' perceptions are mentally organized according to a simple, readily interpretable structure. That is, the sixteen individual perceptual items cluster into the five basic factors just identified.[2]

To find out whether whites' perceptions are structured in the same way, we conducted a parallel exploratory factor analysis for whites, based on the 1981 ABC News/*Washington Post* survey. Because six of the sixteen items were not used in the 1981 survey (the five questions about discrimination against oneself and the question about the prevalence of racial prejudice among whites)[3], the factor analysis for whites was restricted to ten items.

The results for whites are quite similar to those for blacks, though for whites only two significant factors emerge. Just as for blacks, the dominant first factor for whites links the six items concerning perceived discrimination against blacks. The second factor for whites also matches the second factor for blacks, in that both are composed of the two items on perceptions of the trend in antiblack feelings. Because all the items on perceptions of discrimination against oneself are obviously missing for whites, there is no such factor in the white analysis, nor is it surprising, in light of the absence of two of the remaining four items, that neither of the other two factors from the factor analysis for blacks shows up for whites.

Because these results suggest a perceptual structure common to both blacks and whites, it seems reasonable to search for the social and economic sources of various perceptual dimensions rather than undertaking item-by-item analyses of sixteen different items. We therefore created three separate composite perceptual measures by summing the scores (0 or 1, or, in the case of the trend variables, 0, 1, or 2) on each item that correlates highly with a given factor. For blacks, there are three such scales. The first is the index of perceived discrimination against blacks, which ranges from 0 (for those who perceive no discrimination at all) through 6 (for those who perceive all six forms of discrimination). The second is the index of perceived discrimination against oneself, which ranges from 0 through 4. And the third is the index of the perceived trend in anti-black feelings, which ranges from 0, for those who see antiblack feelings abating both locally and nationally, to 4, for those who see antiblack feelings growing both locally and nationally. (The first two of these scales were already introduced in Chapter 3.) For whites, only the first and third scales come into play.[4]

Testing the model

Our model of blacks' perceptions of racial inequality focuses on the relationships between the three scales we have just described, on the one hand, and a series of predictor variables, on the other, the intent being to determine whether blacks' perceptions of inequality vary as a function of differences among them in various personal characteristics. The predictors are described in Table 4.1. They include seven socioeconomic variables[5] along with indicators of the other personal attributes mentioned above. In comparing the sources of blacks' perceptions with those of whites, we draw on the 1981 ABC News/*Washington Post* survey, the most recent source of comparable data. Every independent variable from the 1981 survey is identical to its 1986 counterpart, but, as noted in Table 4.1, two items from the 1986 survey were not included in the 1981 survey.

In the analyses reported here and in Chapters 6 and 8, we use probit analysis to test our model. Probit analysis is a statistical technique quite similar to the much more familiar technique of ordinary least-squares regression analysis. But whereas regression analysis assumes that the dependent variable is measured on a precise interval scale (like age in years), probit analysis assumes only that the dependent variable is measured in terms of ordered categories (like "strongly agree," "agree," "disagree," and "strongly disagree"). Since the dependent variables of interest to us here all have relatively few ordered categories, probit analysis is clearly the appropriate statistical technique.

In discussing the probit results for a particular dependent variable, we

Table 4.1. *Description of predictors in the analyses of perceptions of discrimination, whites, 1981 and blacks, 1986*

Predictor	Description
Demographic characteristics	
Gender	0 = male, 1 = female
Age, in years	Number of years since year of birth.
Interracial friend-ship	"Do you yourself know any white person whom you consider a fairly close personal friend?" 0 = no, 1 = yes. (If white) "Do you yourself know any black person whom you consider a fairly close personal friend?" 0 = no, 1 = yes.
Socioeconomic status	
Family income, in thousands	"If you added together the yearly incomes, before taxes, of all the members of your household for last year, would the total be . . . ?" Responses recoded as midpoints of response categories.
Homeowner	"And are you or your family the owners, or are you renting?" 0 = renting, 1 = owners.
Subjective middle-class member	"When asked, most people say that they belong to either the middle class or to the working class. If you had to make a choice, would you call yourself middle class or working class?" 0 = working, 1 = middle.
Unemployed	"At present, are you yourself employed part-time or full-time, unemployed, laid off, retired, or something else?" 0 = employed, retired, or something else, 1 = unemployed or laid off.
Government aid recipient[a]	"Do you or anyone in your household receive food stamps or aid for dependent children or some other government welfare assistance, other than Social Security benefits?" 0 = no, 1 = yes.
Perceived economic pressure[a]	"How difficult is it for you to meet your monthly household expenses: would you say it is [1] not difficult at all, [2] somewhat difficult, [3] very difficult, or [4] are there some months when you cannot meet your monthly household expenses?"
Years of education	"What was the last year of school you completed?" Responses recoded as midpoints of response categories.

[a]This item did not appear in the 1981 ABC News/*Washington Post* survey.

highlight the independent variables that exert a statistically significant influence; that is, we focus on the predictors that are too closely connected to the dependent variable for the relationship to be ascribed to chance. However, because statistical significance is a product not only of the strength of the relationship but also of the number of cases being analyzed, it is not an especially telling criterion for samples the size of the ones analyzed here. Therefore, whenever we uncover a statistically significant effect, we go on to examine its magnitude, in order to see whether statistical significance translates into substantive importance. In this regard the coefficients from the probit analysis are of no immediate help, since they are not directly interpretable in the same way as the coefficients from an ordinary least-squares regression would be, that is, as the number of units of change in the dependent variable associated with a one-unit change in an independent variable, holding constant the effects of every other independent variable. However, based on the probit coefficients we can perform some simple calculations, described below, that convey these impacts quite effectively. Accordingly, in order to keep our statistical presentations as simple as possible, we relegate the probit results to the Appendix, at the end of this book, and focus our discussion on the calculations derived from the probit results.[6]

Sources of blacks' perceptions pf discrimination against themselves

Our initial probit analysis reveals that blacks' perceptions of discrimination against themselves are significantly affected by gender, age, and four aspects of socioeconomic status. Bearing out our earlier prediction, black women are significantly less likely than black men to see themselves as victims of discrimination. Older blacks more frequently claim to have been targets of discriminatory treatment.

Several indicators of socioeconomic status have contradictory effects. When all the other variables in the model are held constant, education exerts a significant positive effect on perceived discrimination; this means that, *ceteris paribus,* more highly educated blacks perceive greater discrimination against themselves than less educated blacks do. This could indicate greater awareness of the totality of racial discrimination, or it could mean that more educated blacks perceive themselves as further removed from their white peer group than less educated blacks do.

On the other hand, as predicted, perceived discrimination against oneself is also more common among those who consider themselves members of the working class, receive government assistance, and admit to having trouble paying their bills. With the exception of education, then, the factors contributing to higher socioeconomic status decrease the sense that one is a victim of racial discrimination.

Just how much do gender, age, and the various aspects of socioeconomic status, affect blacks' perceptions of discrimination against themselves? For example, controlling for the other predictors in the model, how much more discrimination against themselves do black men perceive than black women do? To answer questions of this nature, we need to translate the maximum likelihood estimates (the probit equivalents of unstandardized regression coefficients) from the probit analysis into the much more readily interpretable probability that those with certain characteristics – by which we mean people with a specified score on each predictor – perceive themselves as victims of discrimination; such individuals can then serve as a "baseline" for purposes of gauging the effects of other characteristics, such as gender, one at a time or collectively.

We could assign the hypothetical baseline person any attributes we wish, but it makes sense to define someone who is as "normal" or "typical" as possible. Accordingly, we stipulate that on every predictor in the model the baseline black is modal or falls close to the mean for all respondents in the 1986 ABC News/*Washington Post* survey. By these criteria, the baseline black is an employed forty-year-old woman with twelve years of education who has a close white friend, owns her own home, has a family income of $25,000, receives no government assistance, finds it "somewhat difficult" to meet her family's monthly expenses, and considers herself a member of the working class. As indicated above, we use information from the probit analysis to calculate the probability that such a person has a particular score on the 0–4 scale of perceived discrimination against oneself. Then, to see how much of an effect, say, gender has on perceptions of discrimination, we hold each of the baseline individual's remaining characteristics constant at its designated level, transform her into a man by changing her score on the female dummy variable from 1 to 0, recalculate the probability of perceiving a given amount of discrimination, and treat the difference between the estimate for the baseline person and that for the otherwise identical man as an expression of the impact of gender for a "typical" black. Similar calculations permit us to gauge the effects of other personal attributes.

In our analyses in this chapter and in Chapters 6 and 8, we also compare a hypothetical "poverty-stricken" black with a hypothetical black in "economically comfortable" circumstances. To create a composite poverty-stricken black, we alter the baseline person by stipulating that she completed only ten years of schooling instead of twelve, that she is unemployed rather than employed, that her family income is $10,000 rather than $25,000, that she is not a home owner, that she does receive government aid, and that some months her family cannot pay its bills. To create a composite black living in comfortable economic circumstances, we modify the baseline profile by having her identify with the middle class, by making her a college graduate, by raising her family income to $50,000, and by specifying that it is "not difficult at all" for her to meet monthly expenses.[7] The difference in projected scores on the 0–4 scale between the "poverty-stricken" and the "economically comfortable" person summarizes the overall effect of socioeconomic factors on perceptions of discrimination.

The projections shown in Table 4.2 sound a note of caution against

Table 4.2. *Projected scores on the scales of perceptions of discrimination against oneself and against blacks, blacks, 1986*

Personal characteristics	Discrimination against self	Discrimination against blacks
Baseline	1.2	3.3
Male	1.4	
25 years old	1.1	
65 years old	1.4	
Subjective middle-class member	1.0	
Not a homeowner		3.7
Government assistance recipient	1.5	
Economic pressure = 0	0.9	3.0
Economic pressure = 4	1.7	3.9
10 years of education	1.1	
16 years of education	1.3	
In poverty	2.0	3.9
Comfortable	1.0	3.2

Notes: N = 750 and 636, respectively. The projections are calculated from the coefficients of Table A.2 and the *mu* values for the probit solution, using a cumulative normal distribution. An example follows. The calculated probability that the "baseline" respondent would have a scale score of 0 is .42; the probability that the same respondent would have a score of 1 is .23; the probability of a score of 2 is .184; the probability of a score of 3 is .09; and the probability of a score of 4 is .08. Multiplying each scale score by its associated probability and summing yields a projected scale score of 1.2 for the "baseline" respondent.
Source: January 1986 ABC News/*Washington Post* nationwide survey of blacks.

overstating the magnitude of the male-female differential, which for a typical black amounts to only two-tenths of a point on the 0–4 scale. On the other hand, no matter how narrow this gap is, the fact remains that black women are slightly less likely than black men to view themselves as victims of discrimination. Assuming, as seems highly possible, that as a consequence of their susceptibility to discrimination on the grounds of both race and gender black women actually experience greater discrimination than black men do, this finding bears out indications from prior research that women either are more likely than men to discount the discrimination they face or compare themselves against a different reference group. The latter interpretation is buttressed by our observation (based on analyses not shown here) that the male-female difference is more apparent on the items pertaining to getting a job and receiving equal wages than it is on items concerning education and housing. Black women may feel less discriminated against than black men in job-related concerns if they use white women as a reference group while black men use white men, since black and white women are much more similar in employment characteristics than black and white men are (see Chapter 2).[8]

So gender has a modest, but provocative, effect on blacks' perceptions of discrimination against themselves. The effect of age on these perceptions, though statistically significant, is also modest. Between a 25- and a 65-year-old black who share every other baseline characteristic, we project a difference of only three-tenths of a point on the perceived discrimination scale.

The remaining statistically significant effects on perceived discrimination against oneself all relate to socioeconomic status. We noted earlier that, controlling for all the other variables in the model, blacks who consider themselves members of the working class perceive significantly greater discrimination against themselves than do their middle class counterparts. But according to Table 4.2 a working-class black is projected to score only two-tenths of a point higher on the 0–4 scale. Virtually the same small gap (.3) separates recipients of government assistance from others. However, the gap based on economic pressures is more appreciable: between those who say they have no difficulty paying their bills each month and those who sometimes cannot pay their bills, the projected score on the perceived discrimination scale varies by eight-tenths of a point.

So there are several indications that the better off one is, the less discrimination one perceives against oneself. Level of education, alone among the badges of socioeconomic status, pulls significantly in the opposite direction. But even though more highly educated blacks perceive greater discrimination against themselves than do less educated blacks who are otherwise identical, the effect of education is not very strong. The difference between an otherwise typical black who dropped out of school after tenth grade and one who graduated from college translates into a gap of only two-tenths of a point in the perceived discrimination scale.

Even with education pulling in the opposite direction, the cumulative effects of all the socioeconomic factors on blacks' perceptions of discrimination against themselves is fairly substantial. We project a perceived discrimination score for a poverty-level black of 2.0, as compared to the projected score for the composite economically comfortable black of only 1.0. This difference of a full point (which is approximately one standard deviation) on the 0–4 scale means, first, that the effect of education is more than counterbalanced by the effects of other socioeconomic status variables, and, second, that there is a wide socioeconomic gap in the extent to which blacks see themselves as victims of discrimination. Those who live in poverty tend to perceive that the deck is stacked against them, but this perception is much less likely to be shared by blacks at medium or higher levels of socioeconomic attainment.

Sources of blacks' perceptions of discrimination against blacks

Blacks' perceptions of discrimination against blacks as a group are less sharply differentiated by the predictors in the model. For example, neither gender nor age significantly affects blacks' perceptions of discrimination against blacks.

The only statistically significant effects on blacks' perceptions of discrimination against blacks are registered by two socioeconomic variables, home ownership and perceived economic pressure, both of which pull in the same direction. Those who rent their living quarters and who have trouble paying their bills perceive significantly greater discrimination against blacks than do home owners and those who are not under great financial pressure. Whereas the baseline black, a home owner, has a projected discrimination scale score of 3.3, the projected score for a renter who is identical in every other respect is 3.7. This finding seems consistent with the idea that owning a home is a conservatizing force (Castells, 1975; but see Kingston, Thompson, and Eichar, 1984; Schuman and Hatchett, 1974: 73), perhaps because it accentuates one's concern for property values (Jelen, 1990). Similarly, there is a difference of almost a full point (.9) on the perceived discrimination scale between those who do not find it difficult to pay their bills and those who sometimes cannot meet their monthly expenses.

Of the remaining socioeconomic predictors, income, subjective class membership, employment status, and government assistance all display virtually no trace of any independent impact on perceptions of discrimination against blacks. As for education, again we observe a positive effect, but this time it falls well short of statistical significance.

In general, then, perceptions of discrimination against blacks are less clearly patterned than are perceptions of discrimination against oneself. Even so, there is an observable perceptual gap between blacks who are socially and economically far removed from one another. According to Table 4.2, between the composite economically comfortable black and her poverty-stricken counterpart the disparity amounts to seven-tenths of a point on the 0–6 scale. We said in Chapter 3 that in many respects blacks and whites inhabit two separate perceptual worlds. We cannot say the same about poverty-stricken blacks and those living in relatively comfortable circumstances, because the .7 gap between them is only about one-third as large as the 2.2 gap between blacks and whites (see Chapter 3). Still, it is no exaggeration to conclude that the significant economic divisions documented in Chapter 2 do affect the way blacks perceive their own situation and that of blacks in general.

Table 4.3. *Projected scores on the scale of perceptions of the trend in antiblack feelings, blacks, 1986*

Personal characteristics	Projected score
Baseline	1.7
In poverty	1.9
Comfortable	1.6

Notes: N = 758. These projections are based on Table A.3.
Source: January 1986 ABC News/*Washington Post* nationwide survey of blacks.

Sources of blacks' perceptions of the trend in antiblack feelings

Finally, what factors distinguish between blacks who perceive an intensification of antiblack feelings and those who see such feelings as abating? We have already observed that there is no real consensus among blacks about trends in racial prejudice (see Table 3.5 and Figure 3.6) and that prior studies say little about cleavages among blacks in optimism concerning the future of race relations. It therefore comes as no great surprise to see that optimism and pessimism about the future of race relations do not follow any well-defined social and economic lines (see Table 4.3).

More specifically, not a single one of the ten predictors in the model significantly affects blacks' perceptions of the trend in antiblack feelings. Nor can we detect much by way of an overall socioeconomic effect. The difference in projected scores between the composite poverty-level black (1.9) and the composite comfortable black (1.6) is slight, bespeaking a lack of perceptual differentiation along socioeconomic lines.

A black-white comparison of the sources of perceptions of racial inequality

For blacks, we have seen some fairly clearcut differences in perceptions of discrimination based on socioeconomic status: the lower one stands on the socioeconomic ladder, the more discrimination one perceives against oneself and against blacks as a group. Is there any similarity between blacks and whites in the sources of their perceptions of racial discrimination?[9] The first of the expectations outlined earlier, that younger whites will be more aware of racial discrimination, proved to be valid. Although there is no significant tendency for age to affect blacks' perceptions of discrimination against blacks, Table 4.4 reveals that younger whites do perceive signifi-

Table 4.4. *Projected scores on the scales of perceptions of discrimination against blacks and the trend in antiblack feelings, whites, 1981*

Personal characteristics	Discrimination against blacks	Trend in antiblack feelings
Baseline	0.7	1.5
25 years old	0.8	
65 years old	0.6	
No black friends		1.6
Not a homeowner	1.1	
10 years of education	0.8	1.6
16 years of education	0.6	1.2
In poverty	1.1	1.7
Comfortable	0.8	1.4

Notes: N = 933 and 1,071, respectively. These projections are based on Table A.4.
Source: February–March 1981 ABC News/*Washington Post* nationwide survey.

cantly more racial discrimination than older whites do (cf. Kluegel and Smith, 1986: 186–96). As a consequence, we project a 65-year-old white as perceiving a bit less discrimination than an otherwise identical 25-year-old.[10]

Among whites, the relationship between socioeconomic status and perceived discrimination against blacks is rather ambiguous. Neither family income nor self-perceived class status significantly affects whites' perceptions of racial discrimination, paralleling our findings for blacks. Nor does being unemployed have any bearing on perceptions of discrimination. On the other hand, white homeowners, like their black counterparts, perceive significantly less discrimination against blacks, though for neither whites nor blacks is this difference appreciable. Whereas education does not significantly influence blacks' perceptions of discrimination against blacks, it does have a significant effect on whites' perceptions. Contrary to expectations, it is the least educated whites who consider discrimination most widespread, though here again statistical significance must not be confused with substantive importance; as the projections in Table 4.4 show, the education-based differential in whites' perceptions of discrimination against blacks is not very wide.

Among blacks the impact of education can be explained to some extent by an enlightenment interpretation, because more informed blacks perceive somewhat greater discrimination against blacks than less informed blacks do. However, this difference is small and statistically nonsignificant. Moreover, the enlightenment interpretation fails utterly for whites, among whom, other things being equal, the "more informed" are significantly less likely to acknowledge discrimination against blacks than other whites are.

How can we explain the differing relationships between education and perceptions held by both blacks and whites? Though we know of no single interpretation that can provide a full account, one outlined by Jackman and Muha (1984; see also Smith and Seelbach, 1987) holds out considerable promise. According to Jackman and Muha, educational attainment does not reduce intergroup negativism, but is essentially a measure of advocacy of one's group interest. "An advanced formal education," they argue (1984: 752), "equips its recipients to . . . become the state-of-the-art apologists for their group's social position." Thus, for whites an advanced education might enhance the sense of *class* identification and solidify individualistic, middle-class values, while for blacks an advanced education might, to some extent at least, foster a greater sense of *racial* identification and intensify the sense of collective injustice. Indeed, blacks of higher social status are more likely to identify as blacks than are lower-status blacks (Jackman and Jackman, 1983).

Another consideration is that highly educated whites may not witness overt racial discrimination as often as less educated whites do. In the college classroom or the corporate boardroom, racial discrimination is usually much more subtle than it is on the assembly line or in a working-class bar. Still, the findings for whites in Table 4.4 are so inconsistent with other findings about the relationship between education and inequality-related attitudes that we shall reserve final judgment for subsequent chapters, in which we examine educational differences in whites' explanations for, and solutions to, problems of racial inequality. If being well educated really turns whites into apologists for the status quo, then we might expect more highly educated whites to pin the blame for racial inequality on blacks themselves rather than faulting "the system"; similarly, we might expect them to oppose policies like affirmative action, which, to some extent at least, alter the rules by which social and economic mobility can be attained.

Overall, for whites the socioeconomic differential in perceived antiblack discrimination is minuscule. That is, between poverty-stricken and economically comfortable whites there is little difference in projected scores on the 0–6 scale – a stark contrast to the pattern for blacks, whose perceptions are sharply differentiated on the basis of socioeconomic status. One reason for the small net status-based difference for whites is that the leading predictor of blacks' perceptions of discrimination against blacks, economic pressure, could not be used in our analysis of whites' perceptions, since that question was not asked in the 1981 survey. The variables that we could use do not differentiate nearly as well as the omitted variable, so it is little wonder that the net contrasts are fuzzier.

Then, too, for whites the overall socioeconomic effect is considerably less than the sum of its parts. That is, the socioeconomic variables that do affect these perceptions cancel one another out. It would be misleading to conclude from Table 4.4 that socioeconomic factors do not affect whites' perceptions of discrimination against blacks, but we must take care to specify the particular components of socioeconomic status in which we are interested. Notwithstanding the lack of a net status-based perceptual gap among whites, some individual status components – namely, home owner ship and education – are associated with significant perceptual differences.

Finally, the projections in Tables 4.2 and 4.4 illuminate the black-white difference in perceptions of racial discrimination that we spotlighted in Chapter 3. This black-white difference interacts with socioeconomic status differences between blacks and whites. Between the hypothetical poverty-level black and her exact white counterpart there is a gap of 2.8 on the 0–6 scale of perceived discrimination against blacks, while between the hypo-thetical economically comfortable black and her exact white counterpart the gap is somewhat smaller: 2.4. Thus, if blacks stood higher on the socioeconomic scale, their perceptions of the extent of racial discrimination would probably be more similar to those of whites. On the other hand, the crucial point is that even when socioeconomic differences are taken into account, an enormous perceptual gap remains between blacks and whites. Whites simply do not perceive nearly as much discrimination against blacks as blacks do, and this perceptual difference holds up even when social and economic differences are taken into account.

Perceptions of the trend in antiblack feelings

Earlier we noted that blacks' perceptions of the trend in antiblack feelings cannot be predicted by the factors in our model. According to Table 4.4, the same is true for whites. However, in contrast to the results for blacks, for whom nothing in the model is related to perceptions of the trend in antiblack feelings, two predictors do affect whites' perceptions. Neither has a truly major impact, but both impacts are statistically significant.

The first of these is interracial friendship. Whites who have one or more black friends are less likely to see race relations as worsening than are whites who have no black friends. This difference is by no means major, as the comparison between the composite white with and without black friends in Table 4.4 makes clear, but it is still worth noting that among both blacks and whites, having a friend of the other race is associated with the view that antiblack sentiments are abating.

Education is the other significant predictor for whites. Earlier we noted a weak tendency for more educated blacks to perceive increasing antiblack feelings, but here we observe a significant tendency in the opposite direction for whites. That is, more educated whites are more likely to see antiblack sentiments as decreasing. Perhaps more educated whites come into more frequent contact with the black middle class, whose size and status have grown, while less educated whites are more familiar with working-class and poor blacks, whose status and economic well-being have declined during the 1980s. Again, though, this effect is not major: in Table 4.4 we project a difference of only .4 on the 0–4 scale for otherwise identical whites, one of whom dropped out after her sophomore year in high school, while the other completed college.

Overall, the impact of socioeconomic differences is slight, as indicated by the small difference in projected scores for a poverty-level white (1.7) and her economically comfortable counterpart (1.4). Of greater interest is the lack of any major black-white difference in these perceptions. According to Table 4.3, the projected score for the baseline black is 1.7, while according to Table 4.4, the projected score for her exact white counterpart is an almost identical 1.5. Once again, then, there is a wide gulf between blacks' and whites' perceptions of discrimination against blacks, but their perceptions of the trend in antiblack feelings are quite similar.

Conclusion

How have our expectations stood up in light of our empirical findings?

We expected older blacks to be more likely than younger blacks to view themselves as victims of discrimination, and this expectation has been borne out, even though the age gap in blacks' perceptions of discrimination against themselves is not extremely wide. With regard to the impact of age on blacks' perception of discrimination against blacks in general, our expectations were that younger blacks would perceive more, given their greater sense of alienation. In fact, there proves to be no significant age differential one way or the other in blacks' perceptions of discrimination against blacks and of the trend in antiblack sentiments.

Our companion analyses of whites' perceptions of discrimination against blacks revealed that the older a white person, the less likely he or she is to view discrimination as widespread. As expected, then, the effect of age on perceptions of discrimination operates differently for blacks than it does for whites.

We expected black women to perceive less discrimination than black men do because women are less likely to acknowledge discrimination and because black women might have a different reference group than black men do. We actually observed an inconsistent gender effect. Black men are more prone to report discrimination against themselves than black women are, but this difference is not large. With regard to perceived discrimination against blacks in general and perceptions of the trend in antiblack feelings, there is no significant gender difference among blacks. Nor is there any indication that among whites gender plays any significant role in shaping perceptions of racial discrimination or of the trend in antiblack feelings.

With regard to interracial friendship, we expected blacks with at least one fairly close white friend to perceive less discrimination than do blacks with no white friends. Our analyses uncovered some signs of such an effect, but these signs are too faint for us to advance interracial friendship as an important influence on blacks' perceptions. This is not to say that interracial friendship plays no part at all, since having a white friend may significantly affect aspects of blacks' perceptions that we have not considered here. Because perceptions of prejudice and discrimination come in many subtle forms and shadings, factors that affect one specific type of perception may have little or no bearing on another. But for now the most we can say is that for both blacks and whites, interracial friendship appears to have only a minimal perceptual impact.

The remaining predictors in our model all pertain, in one way or another, to socioeconomic status. We expected blacks of lower status to perceive more discrimination, and this is largely true. One socioeconomic indicator stands out above all the rest – and, indeed, above all the other elements in the model – in terms of its impact on blacks' perceptions of discrimination. There is a wide perceptual gap between blacks who have difficulty meeting their monthly household expenses and those who do not. Those who say it is "very difficult" to pay their bills perceive markedly greater discrimination against themselves and against blacks in general than do those who find it "not difficult at all," and blacks who sometimes cannot pay their bills perceive even greater discrimination than those for whom it is "very difficult." These effects are sufficiently strong that perceived economic pressure can legitimately be said to dominate our model of blacks' perceptions of discrimination.

The effects of most of the other socioeconomic status indicators are nonsignificant. One exception is owning one's home, which among both blacks and whites is associated with the perception that discrimination against blacks is less common. Perhaps, as we speculated earlier, owning a home is indeed a conservatizing force.

Our expectation was borne out that more highly educated blacks would perceive significantly more discrimination against themselves. They are not, however, more likely to perceive greater discrimination against other blacks or to sense a more rapid growth of antiblack feelings. For blacks, then, the effect of education is restricted to perceptions of discrimination against oneself, with the more educated perceiving more widespread discrimination by whites. However, among whites education has the opposite effect. More educated whites perceive significantly less discrimination against blacks and are also less likely to perceive antiblack feelings as worsening. The impact of education on whites' perceptions is consistent with Jackman and Muha's (1984) argument that education tends to make members of the in-group apologists for the socioeconomic status quo, but it is inconsistent with most previous analyses of the impact of education on whites' perceptions of racial discrimination.

We argued earlier that although many of the factors that shape perceptions of discrimination are complex and idiosyncratic, these perceptions might still be patterned in ways that enable us to offer some reasonably reliable generalizations about their sources. This argument has, we believe, been sustained by our data analysis. Now, having described perceptions of racial discrimination and having explored the sources of some of these perceptions, we proceed to the next link in the chain – explanations of racial inequality. Discrimination, of course, is one way of explaining inequality, but there are several others. We examine these in Chapter 5.

Notes

1. The factor analyses, like those reported in the next chapter, were based on matrices of *tetrachoric* or *polychoric* correlation coefficients (O'Brien and Homer, 1987; Olsson, 1979), depending upon the number of categories in the variables. Because every item under consideration was measured at the ordinal level, product-moment correlations would be inappropriate. Each ordinal measure can, however, be regarded as an indicator of an underlying continuous variable, in which case tetrachoric and polychoric correlation coefficients estimate the correlation between a pair of underlying continuous variables for which only ordinal measures are available. These factor analysis results and those reported in the next chapter are products of a principal component analysis with oblique rotation. Oblique rotation was employed because it seemed unreasonable to assume that the underlying factors would be uncorrelated with one another. The between-factor correlations are shown in Appendix Table A.1.
2. An alternative hypothesis is that an instrumentation effect could be at work, since the similar wording within each group of items may have caused respondents to answer in a patterned way. We cannot definitively rule out such an interpretation, though we obviously prefer a much more straightforward substantive interpretation.
3. The 1981 and 1986 versions of one question also differed. In 1981, respondents were asked, "Looking back over the last ten years, do you think the quality of life for blacks in the United States has gotten better, stayed about the same, or gotten worse?" In 1986, the referent changed from "the quality of life" to "income and living conditions," and the ten-year time frame was dropped: "In terms of income and living conditions for most

blacks, would you say that things are getting better, getting worse, or staying about the same?"
4. The scale means and standard deviations are as follows:

	Blacks		Whites	
	mean	s.d.	mean	s.d.
Discrimination against oneself	1.3	1.3		
Discrimination against blacks	3.6	1.9	0.9	1.5
Trend in antiblack feelings	1.7	1.4	1.6	1.3

We experimented with composite scales for the fourth and fifth factors for blacks, but because these two-item scales fell short of conventional levels of reliability and because we could not create parallel scales for whites because of missing items from the 1981 survey, we discarded these factors. The reliability of all perceptual three scales, as measured by coefficient *alpha* calculated from matrices of tetrachoric and polychoric correlations, is quite acceptable. For blacks, *alpha* = .87, .82, and .80 for the scales of perceived discrimination against blacks, perceived discrimination against oneself, and the perceived trend in antiblack feelings, respectively. Scale reliability is acceptable for whites: *alpha* = .94 and .76 for the scales of perceived discrimination against blacks and the perceived trend in antiblack feelings, respectively.

5. The presence of several different measures of socioeconomic status in the model makes multicollinearity a matter of obvious concern. However, our investigations revealed that the interrelationships between pairs and among combinations of socioeconomic variables are never appreciable enough to make multicollinearity a credible threat to our conclusions. For example, among black respondents in the 1986 ABC News/*Washington Post* survey, the correlation (*tau-b*) between income and education is .370; the corresponding relationships for whites are similarly modest.

6. Although techniques for structural equation modeling of ordinal variables are now available (see Muthen, 1987), the exploratory character of much of our analysis means that specifying a precise causal model of attitudes toward inequality would have outstripped our understanding of the phenomena being investigated. The general model given earlier in Chapter 1 guides our analysis, but it would be woefully insufficient in the structural equation context. A related point is that when we discuss the impact of a given variable on a particular dependent variable, we are referring to its direct effect, controlling for the effects of the other predictors in the model. This reflects our inability, within the data-analytic framework we employ, to decompose total effects into direct effects, indirect effects, and spurious effects. In discussing the statistical results, however, we do note some instances in which the total effect of a variable appears to be considerably greater than its direct effect, although we do not provide a precise numerical estimate of such indirect effects.

7. We have already indicated that the definition of socioeconomic status is a complicated matter, which we necessarily greatly oversimplify in our stipulations of the composite "in poverty" and "comfortable" blacks. On this point, see Vanneman and Cannon (1987: ch. 10).

8. We thought that the scale of perceived discrimination against oneself might be biased toward uncovering more discrimination against men than against women, since two of the four items focus on job-related discrimination and since a higher proportion of men than women are employed outside the home. However, analyses not detailed here reveal that using each of the four component items in turn as the dependent variable instead of the 0–4 scale produces exactly the opposite pattern, as discussed in the text.

9. As noted in Table 4.1, the items concerning government assistance and perceived economic pressure were not used in the 1981 survey. This is unfortunate, since perceived economic pressure was the leading predictor in the analyses reported earlier in this chapter. The omission of these variables from the analyses for whites does not, however, invalidate the black-white comparisons. At least, this is the inference we would draw after rerunning the probit analyses for blacks without these two predictors; few of the parameter estimates for the other predictors were perceptibly different from those reported above.

10. By definition, the "baseline," "in poverty," and "comfortable" whites are identical, except for race, to their black counterparts. Because blacks as a group are measurably different on some of these dimensions from whites as a group (for example, average number of school years completed), the baseline white is therefore not as typical of whites as the baseline black is of blacks. The baseline white, then, is not a typical white; rather, she is a white with the characteristics of a typical black. Had we defined the white baseline to be typical of whites, then the black and white baselines would have differed from one another, confounding direct black-white comparisons. The black-white comparisons summarized in the text are much more straightforward, since the blacks and whites being compared have identical personal characteristics. However, it must be borne in mind that the baseline white does not bear the same relation to whites in general that the baseline black does to blacks in general.

5

Blacks' explanations of racial inequality

In order to repair a problem, in this case, the uneven socioeconomic advancement of blacks and whites, we need to understand what is causing the problem. Too often it has been exclusively the white community's understanding of the nature and sources of racial inequality that has shaped public policy, with blacks relegated to the role of policy "targets." How do blacks account for racial inequality? Do they attribute it largely to the discrimination they perceive as so pervasive? Instead, or in addition, do they blame the black community itself? And how do they explain the opening of opportunities during the postwar era?

Success and failure in the American political culture

Blacks' causal understandings of racial inequality reflect the broad impress of the American political culture as well as distinctive cultural heritage of blacks and their individual life experiences. The American political culture is not highly "ideological," in the strong sense of the term. That is, it is not dominated by an all-encompassing *Weltanschauung* that provides a ready explanation for the diverse array of social, economic, and political phenomena that people encounter every day. Nor do the mass media, from which we derive so many of our impressions of the community, the nation, and the world, provide much by way of an explanatory framework (see, e.g., Barkin and Gurevitch, 1987). Accordingly, when Americans pause to reflect on important developments in the news, including events that may directly affect them, they have no official or quasi-official "line" to fall back on. They do, however, have some characteristic American ways of thinking about such issues. Among the somewhat contradictory cardinal elements of the American political culture are the belief that people should get ahead on their own merit through hard work, support for the free enterprise system, and commitment to equality (Feldman, 1983, 1988; Hochschild, 1981; McClosky and Zaller, 1984; Merriman and Parent, 1983; Sniderman and Brody, 1977). The "lesson" of the Horatio Alger story – that anyone willing to work hard can get ahead – is deeply rooted in American values.

A comprehensive investigation of the American political culture would deflect us from our main task of analyzing blacks' understandings of racial inequality. But before we turn to the question of what blacks see as the sources of their disadvantaged status, let us briefly consider the broader constellation of attitudes and values that help define the American political culture.

Table 5.1 presents some survey-based evidence about how Americans account for the existence of poverty in their affluent soci   These responses, like responses to all survey questions, are subject t both short-term fluctuations and long-term change. However, because attitudes concerning the locus of responsibility for economic success or failure are among the deeply ingrained components of the American political culture, they presumably remain fairly stable over time. Indicative of such stability are some results from Caplow and Bahr's fifty-year follow-up to the classic sociological study of "Middletown" (Muncie, Indiana). In 1924, 47 percent of the high school students surveyed in Muncie agreed that "It is entirely the fault of the man himself if he cannot succeed" (Lynd and Lynd, 1929). When the same question was posed again half a century later, the identical percentage of Muncie's high school students expressed the very same opinion (Caplow and Bahr, 1979).

Table 5.1, drawing upon national surveys of the adult population (of which blacks comprise approximately 12 percent) during the 1970s and 1980s, bears testimony to the prevailing American faith that in economic affairs "God helps those who help themselves." The main premise of the average American, as Howard Schuman (1975: 375) puts it, "is that people are free to do as they will." This strong strain of individualism is evident in the widespread tendency to blame the poor for their poverty. Most Americans consider insufficient effort, lack of ability, weak motivation, and immoderation to be among the most important reasons for poverty in this country, and a sizable minority would include "loose morals and drunkenness" as well. Explanations of poverty that place the blame on the "top dogs" rather than the "underdogs," or which point toward shortcomings of the American system, are less popular. (A conspicuous exception is the concession that inadequate access to good schools is a prime cause of poverty; Americans do believe in education.) Americans tend to agree that poverty results from failures of the individual rather than of the system, even though empirical evidence strongly indicates, contrary to the Horatio Alger myth, that educational, occupational, and economic success are largely inherited traits (Alwin and Thornton, 1984; Duncan, Featherman,

Table 5.1. *Americans' explanations of poverty, 1972 and 1980*

The importance of various "reasons some people give to explain why there are poor people in this country."

Reason	Percentage saying "very important"
Lack of thrift and proper money-management skills	64
Lack of effort by the poor themselves	53
Lack of ability and talent	53
Their background gives them attitudes that keep them from improving their condition.	46
Failure of society to provide good schools for many Americans	46
Loose morals and drunkenness	44
Sickness and physical handicaps	43
Low wages in some businesses and industries	40
Failure of private industry to provide enough jobs	35
Prejudice and discrimination against blacks	31
Being taken advantage of by rich people	20
Just bad luck	12

As you know, even though America is a wealthy nation, there are still many people living here who are poor. I will read you some reasons people have offered to explain why this is so, including some things that other people don't agree with at all. For each, I'd like you to tell me whether you agree a great deal, agree somewhat, disagree somewhat, or disagree a great deal.

Reason	Percentage agreeing
Poor people didn't have a chance to get a good education – schools in poor neighborhoods are much worse than other schools.	67
Most poor people don't have the ability to get ahead.	57
Many poor people simply don't want to work hard.	57
Maybe it is not their fault but most poor people were brought up without drive or ambition.	56
People are poor because there just aren't enough good jobs for everybody.	56
Good skilled jobs are controlled by unions and most poor people can't get into the skilled unions.	47
The poor are poor because the wealthy and powerful keep them poor.	39
The seniority system in most companies works against poor people – they're the last to be hired and the first to be fired.	39
The poor are poor because the American way of life doesn't give all people an equal chance.	38

Sources: The first set of items is from a 1980 national survey by Kluegel and Smith (1986: 79). These were patterned after items used by Feagin (1975) in a 1969 national survey; since the 1969–80 differences are minimal, only the 1980 responses are shown. These items were also adapted by Smith (1985a,b) for his surveys in a Texas metropolitan area, and by Feather (1974) and Furnham (1982) for their surveys in Australia and Britain, respectively. The second set of items is from the 1972 American National Election Study (Miller, Miller, Brody, Dennis, Kovenock, and Shanks, 1975); the percentage is the sum of those who answered "agree a great deal" or "agree somewhat" divided by the number of respondents who answered, including those replying "don't know." For earlier analyses focused on these data, see Nilson (1980) and Feldman (1983).

and Duncan, 1972; Lipset and Bendix, 1959; Sewell and Hauser, 1975; Thomas, 1979). And, as we noted earlier, the heritability of these traits is greater for whites than it is for blacks.

These beliefs about economic success and failure provide a cultural context within which Americans think about equality and inequality. We expect the high value that is placed on individual responsibility for economic success or failure to be reflected in whites' evaluations of racial inequality. But to what extent do black Americans, in trying to assess where the responsibility for racial inequality lies, articulate this mainstream mentality?

Explanations of the persistence of racial inequality

In many respects the core sociopolitical values of black and white Americans are similar to one another, but for reasons that are not all that difficult to fathom blacks tend to be more concerned about the issue of inequality than whites are (see, e.g., Fine, 1990). Thus Feldman (1988) finds no significant black-white difference in acceptance of economic individualism or support for free enterprise, two of what he considers the three cardinal elements of the American political culture, but does uncover a sizable black-white gap in support for the third element, belief in equality of opportunity.[1] Similarly, consistent with the principle that those who benefit least from a stratification system are most likely to consider it unjust, Robinson and Bell (1978) find that in both England and the United States blacks are much more proegalitarian than whites are.

Rokeach's (1973, 1979) research on basic values bears out this conclusion. When asked in a 1968 national survey to rank the importance of eighteen different "terminal values" (e.g., "a world of peace," "freedom," "pleasure," "wisdom," and "a comfortable life") as guiding principles in their lives, blacks and whites responded in virtually the same way. But there was one outstanding exception: the priority given to "equality (brotherhood, equal opportunity for all)," which blacks ranked second (just behind "a world at peace") but whites only eleventh (Rokeach, 1973: 67). However, the timing of the survey, which was administered just a few weeks after the assassination of Martin Luther King, probably polarized the priorities. Thus, when the values items were presented in another national survey three years later, the racial gap in the ranking of "equality" shrank considerably, although it was still statistically significant. This time "equality" ranked fourth (behind "a world at peace," "freedom," and "family security") among blacks and sixth among whites (Rokeach, 1979: 138–9). Subsequent research (e.g., Christenson and Dunlap, 1984) reveals that this black-white differential in the value placed on equality has persisted.

In short, equality and inequality seem to occupy a rather different place in the value systems of black and white Americans. Beyond this, however, little can be said about how blacks think about inequality in general and racial inequality in particular, since most prior research has focused on whites, not blacks (see, e.g., Apostle et al., 1983; Kluegel, 1990; Kluegel and Smith, 1986; Sniderman with Hagen, 1985; for rare exceptions, see Parent, 1985; Bobo, 1989). How, then, do blacks account for black-white socioeconomic differences? It has been established that black political leaders are more likely than their white counterparts to blame "the system" rather than the poor or blacks themselves for the existence of poverty (Verba and Orren, 1985: 74). However, these differences are not especially large, especially between black leaders and the predominantly white leaders of other liberal-oriented groups, such as feminists, college youth, labor unions, and the Democratic Party. What is unclear at this point is how the black rank and file, rather than black leaders, account for racial inequality, and how their accounts compare to those advanced by whites.

To address these questions, we draw on responses to a series of questions in the 1981, 1986, and 1989 ABC News/*Washington Post* surveys and the 1985 and 1986 General Social Surveys.[2] After being told that "Most people agree that, on the average, blacks have worse jobs, income, and housing than whites," respondents in the ABC News/*Washington Post* surveys were asked to accept or reject each in a series of four potential explanations for these differences. These explanations placed the blame on white discrimination, low black learning ability, inadequate black access to education, and blacks' lack of motivation or willpower.[3] Later in the ABC News/*Washington Post* interviews, respondents were asked to react to the statements that blacks have not achieved equality because "many whites don't want them to get ahead," and that "many of the problems which blacks in this country have today are brought on by blacks themselves." These two items have never appeared in the GSS.

Virtually everyone, irrespective of race, accepts at least one of these explanations. Looking first at the six ABC News/*Washington Post* items (see Table 5.2), we see that only one person in a hundred, black or white, rejects all six explanations, and the average person accepts three. Overall, blacks accept more of these explanations than whites do, and for both blacks and whites acceptance of these explanations appears to be becoming somewhat less widespread than it was in the past. However, we consider these differences too narrow to warrant serious attention. A similar pattern holds in the GSS data, with blacks being slightly more likely than whites to embrace the four explanations.

According to approximately two out of every three blacks, blacks' infe-

Table 5.2. *Number of inequality attributions, blacks and whites, 1981, 1986, and 1989* (in %)

Number of attributions made	ABC News/*Washington Post* Blacks			Whites		GSS Blacks	Whites
	1981	1986	1989	1981	1989	1985–6	1985–6
0	0	1		1		4	6
1	4	7		7		24	34
2	16	16		25		48	42
3	31	33		32		16	15
4	24	25		24		9	3
5	16	14		8		NA	NA
6	9	5		4		NA	NA
Mean	3.6	3.3	3.4	3.1	2.8	2.0	1.8
Median	3.5	3.3		3.0		2.0	2.0
Standard Deviation	1.3	1.3		1.2		1.0	.9

Notes: See the text for a description of the attribution items. The 1989 scale means are calculated from the item frequencies given in Table 5.3, which were provided by Richard Morin of the *Washington Post;* because the 1989 data set was not yet available when this book was completed, we were unable to calculate scale medians and standard deviations or to show the distribution of scores on the scales.

Sources: February–March 1981 ABC News/*Washington Post* nationwide survey; January 1986 ABC News/*Washington Post* nationwide survey of blacks; September–October 1989 ABC News/*Washington Post* nationwide survey; and 1985 and 1986 GSS.

rior jobs, income, and housing are "mainly due to discrimination" (see Table 5.3). Although it would be unwise to jump from responses on this single item to the conclusion that most blacks see discrimination as the primary source of the black-white socioeconomic differential, Table 5.3 also shows three blacks in four agreeing that "black people are not achieving equality as fast as they could because most whites don't want them to get ahead." Thus, the great majority of blacks view discrimination as a major cause of the persisting black-white gap. By contrast, most whites do not attribute blacks' lagging fortunes to discrimination by whites, although the willingness of whites to blame discrimination by whites grew during the 1980s. On the related question of whether blacks "are not achieving equality as fast as they could because many whites don't want them to get ahead," whites are again split and are again becoming more open to the idea that whites themselves may be a cause of blacks' problems.

Noting these differences between the dominant black and white opinions, we must also recognize that many whites – almost half – concede that discrimination is at least partially responsible for racial inequality.[4] Still,

Table 5.3. *Attributions for persisting racial gaps, blacks and whites, 1981, 1986, and 1989* (in %)

Most people agree that, on the average, blacks have worse jobs, income, and housing than whites. Do you think the differences are:

	ABC News/*Washington Post*					General Social Survey	
	Blacks 1981	Blacks 1986	Blacks 1989	Whites 1981	Whites 1989	Blacks 1985–6	Whites 1985–6
Mainly due to discrimination?							
Yes	67	64	69	38	46	70	40
No	27	31	29	58	52	22	57
DK/no opinion	6	5	1	4	2	7	3
No answer/refused	0	1	0	0	0	1	0
Because most blacks have less in-born ability to learn?							
Yes	25	19	24	23	14	18	20
No	69	77	76	74	84	79	76
DK/no opinion	6	3	0	3	2	2	4
No answer/refused	0	0	0	1	0	1	0
Because most blacks don't have the chance for the education it takes to rise out of poverty?							
Yes	72	67	67	53	63	66	51
No	25	29	31	44	36	30	47
DK/no opinion	2	4	2	2	1	3	2
No answer/refused	0	0	0	0	0	2	0
Because most blacks don't have the motivation or willpower to pull themselves out of poverty?							
Yes	47	42	44	58	43	34	60
No	47	51	54	36	54	58	36
DK/no opinion	6	5	2	5	3	6	4
No answer/refused	0	3	0	1	0	2	0
Black people are not achieving equality as fast as they could because many whites don't want them to get ahead							
Agree	74	76	75	46	43		
Disagree	20	18	20	47	52		
DK/no opinion	6	5	5	7	5		
No answer/refused	0	1	0	1	0		
Discrimination has unfairly held down blacks, but many of the problems which blacks in this country have today are brought on by blacks themselves							
Agree	50	47	52	73	56		
Disagree	40	44	42	19	35		
DK/no opinion	10	8	6	8	8		
No answer/refused	0	1	0	1	0		

Sources: February–March 1981 ABC News/*Washington Post* nationwide survey; January 1986 ABC News/*Washington Post* nationwide survey of blacks; September–October 1989 ABC News/*Washington Post* nationwide survey; and 1985 and 1986 GSS.

most whites do not share the majority black viewpoint, indicating an attributional difference substantial enough to warrant attention. In Chapter 3 we noted a recurrent gap between blacks and whites in *perceptions* of racial inequality, and here we first encounter a complementary black-white gap in *explanations* of racial inequality.

Having said this, we should immediately note that whites express no greater agreement than blacks do with the idea that blacks fare worse than whites because of any black deficit in "in-born ability to learn." Indeed, whites have, if anything, become even less likely than blacks to say that racial inequality is a product of black learning disabilities, the explanation most evocative of old-style racism.[5] What we consider most surprising about these figures is that one black in four or five accepts a view that assumes their innate intellectual inferiority, paralleling, to some degree, the antisemitism that has sometimes been observed among Jews and, more generally, the tendency of oppressed peoples to take on the perspective of their oppressors (see, e.g., Sarnoff, 1951).

Although relatively few blacks or whites see racial inequality as a product of any innate black learning deficiency, many do regard blacks' poor access to education as part of the problem. Approximately two blacks in three, and a similar proportion of whites, count poor educational access among the reasons why blacks have not made greater progress. This explanation gained significant ground among whites during the 1980s.[6]

How can we reconcile the fact, noted in Chapter 3, that neither blacks nor whites perceive discrimination against blacks in the educational arena to be especially widespread, with the fact that both blacks and whites see inadequate black access to education as a major source of black-white inequality? To some extent, this seeming contradiction probably reflects the pervasive American faith in the powers of education, a sense that if everyone could be appropriately educated any number of social ills would vanish. Hence, when asked why a particular problem such as racial inequality continues to exist, many Americans reflexively cite educational deficits as a cause. Moreover, poor educational access poses an inviting explanation because it can be invoked without giving offense – it is, after all, far less insulting to say that blacks have had poor access to education than to claim that they are intellectually inferior – and also because it points to a fairly straightforward solution. It may also be that what initially seems to be a contradiction between the widespread perception that racial discrimination is not a great problem in education and the widespread reliance on poor black access to education as an explanation of racial inequality is not really a contradiction at all. The survey questions about perceived discrimination in education have been framed in the present tense; that is, respondents have been asked how widespread discrimination in education *is*, not how widespread it has been within the lifetime of today's black adults. In light of the highly visible progress that has been made in desegregating the nation's schools, that is by no means a minor, semantic difference. On the other hand, the pertinent attributional question points to the inability of today's blacks to rise out of poverty due to poor access to education. It hardly seems illogical to perceive this as a cause of poverty among blacks who are now in their forties or older, or those who are even in their twenties or thirties, while denying that racial discrimination in education is currently a great problem. When considering the plight of blacks who are living in poverty, one is likely to think first of unemployment and under-employment, problems for which poor educational backgrounds are a major source.

Black opinion is split almost evenly on the two remaining explanations, that blacks lag behind whites because "most blacks don't have the motivation or willpower to pull themselves out of poverty" and because many of the problems blacks face "are brought on by blacks themselves." Even though many blacks reject these ideas, many do accept the notion that blacks are at least partially responsible for their inferior socioeconomic status in American society. Among whites, agreement with these explanations was common in 1981, when six whites in ten blamed blacks for lacking the determination to climb out of poverty[7] and seven in ten faulted blacks for bringing many problems upon themselves. Since then, however, considerably larger numbers of whites have rejected these explanations, with the percentages of whites in agreement falling by 15 percentage points or more for each.

Overall, three of the six explanations stand out as blacks' favorites. These are the ideas, each acceded to by at least two blacks in three, that blacks tend to have poorer jobs, income, and housing than whites because of discrimination, white opposition, and inadequate access to education. Only one of these three explanations, inadequate access to education, is accepted by a majority of whites. It now ranks first among whites, having moved ahead of blacks' ostensible tendency to create problems for themselves.

So, even though there is some consensus that black-white socioeconomic differences are not due to racial differences in in-born ability and are due to blacks' inadequate chances for education and even though whites' explanations have been growing more similar to blacks' in recent years, there remain some noteworthy differences between the way blacks and whites explain racial inequality. What is there about these explanations that might make some of them more attractive to blacks and others to whites?[8]

"Dispositional" and "situational" explanations of racial inequality

Perhaps the most obvious contrast among the six explanations lies in where they place the locus of responsibility for racial inequality. Some point to a purported shortcoming of blacks themselves. According to these explanations, blacks lag socioeconomically because they have inadequate learning ability, because they lack motivation or willpower, or because they bring many problems upon themselves. By contrast, other explanations put the blame on shortcomings of American society in general or of the white population in particular. Such explanations show up in references to white discrimination, roadblocks erected by whites, and inadequate black access to education.

Many different terms have been used to distinguish between these two types of explanations, including "endogenous" versus "exogenous," "internal" versus "external," and "individualistic" versus "social" – or, in the racial context, "distribution" versus "discrimination" (Herrnstein, 1990). We prefer the terminology of Fritz Heider (1958), a founder of attribution theory, who distinguished between "dispositional" and "situational" sources of behavior. To oversimplify somewhat, dispositional attributions concentrate on the person whose actions are being explained, while situational attributions emphasize the circumstances surrounding the person's actions. Thus, a standard dispositional explanation for why someone succeeds or fails at a task might refer to the degree of effort the person has expended or to the person's level of ability. On the other hand, situational sources of success or failure, such as, say, the difficulty of the task or sheer luck, are external to, and beyond the control of, the person. Two aspects of this distinction, its dimensionality and its biases, are of particular interest here.

The dimensionality issue. For Heider and for many others who have followed in his footsteps, dispositional and situational attributions "are yoked together inversely such that an increment in one necessarily accompanies a decrement in the other" (Miller, Smith, and Uleman, 1981: 81). In a representative treatment, Zeitz and Lincoln (1981: 284) conceive of "individualistic" and "social" explanations as opposite poles of a single continuum. At one pole, people are considered to be free to make decisions as they choose, while at the other pole they are seen as restricted by the social structures in which they operate.

This interpretation has been the target of considerable criticism (see, e.g., Gurin, Gurin, Lao, and Beattie, 1968; Miller et al., 1981), the most pertinent of which is empirical in nature. There is, it is argued, little evidence that dispositional and situational explanations are actually "yoked together" in the manner Heider and his successors anticipated. In their review of research on dispositional and situational attributions, Miller et al. (1981: 81) indicate that "when the two types of attributions are measured independently, the predicted negative relationship has often not been found."

To derive summary measures of these two attributional concepts, we need to determine whether there is a measurable tendency among blacks or whites to array themselves along a continuum ranging from reliance on dispositional (black-centered) explanations of racial inequality, on the one hand, to reliance on situational (society- or white-centered) explanations, on the other. Or do dispositional and situational attributions constitute two separate, uncorrelated dimensions rather than opposite poles on a single dimension?[9] Or, indeed, do they encompass more than two dimensions, as has also been suggested (Apostle et al., 1983; Sniderman with Hagen, 1985)?

To answer these questions, we undertook a factor analysis of the six explanations of black-white economic inequality introduced in Table 5.3.[10] The analysis, summarized in Table A.5 in the Appendix, at the end of this book, indicates that dispositional explanations of racial inequality constitute a dimension entirely separate from, and essentially uncorrelated with, situational explanations. The six explanations are not components of a single, bipolar attributional dimension.[11] Nor do they correspond to the more complex categorization schemes employed elsewhere (Apostle et al., 1983; Sniderman with Hagen, 1985; Kluegel and Bobo, 1990).[12]

The three explanations that place the blame on factors beyond the effective control of blacks (discrimination, insufficient access to education, and opposition from whites) form one attributional dimension, while the three that point the finger at alleged shortcomings of blacks (lack of learning ability, lack of motivation or willpower, and a tendency to bring problems on themselves) form a separate dimension. This two-dimensional structure is even more evident in the explanations accepted by whites than it is in those accepted by blacks.

Having observed that acceptance of dispositional explanations of racial inequality is unrelated to acceptance of situational explanations, we cannot assume that a person who agrees with dispositional explanations rejects situational explanations, or vice versa. A person may well accept both types of explanations, only one, or neither.

Biases in attribution. Can the distinction between dispositional and situational attributions help us understand the differences we glimpsed earlier between blacks' and whites' explanations of racial inequality? That is, as blacks and whites try to account for black-white socioeconomic differences, do they tend to invoke explanations of different types?

Before examining the data, we need to consider certain attributional biases that can color the way people account for specific actions or outcomes. In explaining what happens in their lives, people have a need not only for objective understanding, but also for ways of presenting and justifying their actions to themselves and others (Tetlock, 1985). These social and psychological functions of attribution introduce various types of "bias" or "error" into people's answers to "why" questions (see especially Ross and Anderson, 1982). Perhaps the best known of these biases is the so-called "fundamental attribution error," the tendency to focus unduly upon the actor as the cause of whatever happens to him or her (Ross, 1977). This common tendency is reinforced, in the American case, by the prevalence of the individualistic creed that people succeed or fail largely as a result of their own efforts – that they can be whatever they want to be, if only they work unstintingly in pursuit of their goals. Moreover, there seems to be a natural tendency for people to accept their lot if they see it as the consequence of their own actions (Shepelak, 1987); therefore, the need to believe that the world is just (Lerner, 1975) reinforces, and is reinforced by, the need to attribute one's outcomes to one's own actions.

Neglected in such highly individualized accounts of why things turn out the way they do is the often appreciable extent to which outcomes can be affected by factors beyond the control of the individual. As we have already discussed, the probabilities are high that a child born to poor parents will grow up to be a poor adult and that a child born to wealthy parents will become a wealthy adult. These outcomes suggest an entirely different type of attributional bias: the tendency to see whatever happens as beyond the actor's control, which goes by such names as "fatalism," "inefficacy," "passivity," or "helplessness." Chronic failure or victimization often activates this bias. Of course, people sometimes react to consistent failure or victimization by working to change the circumstances that led to these unsatisfactory outcomes, but the lesson people frequently learn is that since they are not masters of their own fate it is futile to try to change the world. This is what social psychologists call "learned helplessness" (Seligman, 1975; Peterson and Seligman, 1983).

These two biases would yield wholly different responses to the six explanations of black-white socioeconomic inequality. The actor-centered bias associated with the fundamental attribution error meshes far more naturally with dispositional than with situational explanations of racial inequality, while the opposite is true for the helplessness bias.

We also need to consider a third type of attributional bias: the "self-serving bias" and, by extension, the "group-serving bias." When they can plausibly do so, people try to explain their actions in ways that cast themselves in a favorable light (Heider, 1958: 172). Thus the self-serving bias is simply that "We attribute success to our own dispositions and failure to external forces" (Schneider, Hastorf, and Ellsworth, 1979).[13]

We can extend this idea from individuals explaining their own successes or failures to group members explaining the successes or failures of their group. Among blacks, a group-serving bias would be consistent with blaming whites or society in general for blacks' problems while crediting blacks for the progress they have made in recent years. Among whites, a group-serving bias would be consistent with blaming blacks for their problems while crediting whites or society in general for the progress blacks have made in recent years. With regard to explanations of black-white economic inequality, the group-serving bias would, then, be expected to yield fatalistic response patterns for blacks but to produce, for whites, the response patterns associated with the fundamental attribution error. Our extension of the "self-serving bias" from the individual to the group level is by no means novel (see, e.g., Hewstone and Jaspers, 1982; Zaccaro, Peterson, and Walker, 1987; for relevant examples of materially-based group models, see, e.g., Bobo, 1983; Brady and Sniderman, 1985). Indeed, Pettigrew (1979) coined the term "ultimate attribution error" to refer to just such an attributional tendency among members of a particular group.

The evidence. Let us now return to the data on explanations of the black-white economic gap, bearing in mind, first, the distinction between dispositional and situational attributions and, second, the potential operation of various types of attributional bias. In so doing, we rely on summary scales of each person's proclivity toward dispositional and situational explanations of racial inequality, created from the ABC News/*Washington Post* survey data. The first scale indicates how many of the three dispositional explanations a person agrees with, while the second indicates how many of the situational attributions the person accepts. Each scale ranges from 0, for those who reject every explanation of a particular type, to 3, for those who accept all three explanations of that type.[14]

In Table 5.4 we see considerable variability among blacks in acceptance of dispositional explanations. On average, blacks agree with 1.2 of the dispositional explanations, virtually the same as their 1981 mean of 1.3. However, they are much more likely to agree with the situational explanations: in 1986 almost half accepted all three situational explanations, and another 30 percent accepted two of the three situational explanations. Whereas nearly 30 percent of blacks in 1986 rejected all three dispositional explanations, only six or seven percent rejected all three situational explanations. Consequently, the mean number of situational attributions accepted by blacks, which held steady during the 1980s, is high – 2.3 in 1981, and 2.2 in 1986 and 1988.

Table 5.4. *Dispositional and situational inequality attributions, blacks and whites, 1981, 1986, and 1989* (in %)

Number of attributions	Relative frequency for:				
	Blacks 1981	Blacks 1986	Blacks 1989	Whites 1981	Whites 1989
	A. Dispositional attributions				
0	30	28		14	
1	28	37		25	
2	25	26		42	
3	17	9		19	
Mean	1.3	1.2	1.2	1.7	1.2
Median	1.2	1.1		1.8	
Standard Deviation	1.1	0.9		0.9	
	B. Situational attributions				
0	6	6		26	
1	14	16		27	
2	26	30		25	
3	54	48		23	
Mean	2.3	2.2	2.2	1.4	1.6
Median	2.6	2.4		1.4	
Standard Deviation	0.9	0.9		1.1	

Notes: See the text and Table 5.3 for a description of the dispositional and situational inequality attribution items. The 1989 scale means are calculated from the frequencies for each scale item given in Table 5.3, which were provided by Richard Morin of the *Washington Post;* since the 1989 data set was not yet available when this book was completed, we were unable to calculate scale medians and standard deviations or to show the distribution of scores on the scales.
Sources: February–March 1981 ABC News/*Washington Post* nationwide survey; January 1986 ABC News/*Washington Post* nationwide survey of blacks; and September–October 1989 ABC News/*Washington Post* nationwide survey.

Overall, then, it seems fair to characterize the majority of blacks as likely to blame the persistence of racial inequality on factors beyond the effective control of blacks, and less likely to blame the black-white gap on blacks themselves.[15] Parent (1985), also examining the 1981 ABC News/ *Washington Post* survey data, perceived a tendency among blacks toward the "market mentality," an individualistic mode of thinking in which people attribute their failures to their own shortcomings rather than to situational deficiencies. Although we can see traces of that mentality, in our view the overriding consideration is that most blacks reject the majority of the dispositional explanations while only a tiny majority reject all three situational explanations. At the same time, few blacks accept all three dispositional explanations, but almost half accept all three situational explanations. Thus, although most blacks accept at least one dispositional explanation, they accept almost twice as many situational ones. There is, as Parent says, some tendency toward self-blame, but there is a greater tendency to blame external forces.

Table 5.4 also reveals some appreciable differences between blacks and whites in the explanations they offer for black-white inequality, and a notable trend for whites during the 1980s. First and most importantly, far fewer whites than blacks accept the proposition that racial inequality is a product of situational constraints on blacks. The mean 1989 white score of 1.6 on the situational attribution scale is well below the mean of 2.2 registered by blacks, so it is clear that the black-white difference from the early 1980s had by no means disappeared as the nation entered the 1990s. In 1981 the black-white gap in situational attributions was matched by another black-white gap in acceptance of dispositional accounts of racial inequality; in fact, six whites in ten – roughly double the proportion of blacks – agreed with at least two of the dispositional explanations in the 1981 survey. However, this black-white differential faded during the decade, to the point that by 1989 the mean dispositional attribution score for whites was identical to that for blacks. This might simply be a sign of the continuation during the 1980s of the long-term trend toward moderation in whites' racial attitudes (Schuman et al., 1985), but we suspect that it also reflects a widening sense, spawned by eight years of exposure to criticism of a conservative Reagan administration, that it is inadequate to blame blacks for the problems they face.

On the other hand, even though the 1989 black and white means on the dispositional attribution scale are identical, whites are relatively more likely than blacks to accept the dispositional explanations. That is, blacks agree with an average of 3.4 of the six attributions, and 1.2 of these 3.4 are situational in nature; whites also agree with 1.2 situational explanations on average, but this constitutes a larger portion of the attributions accepted (2.8) than is true for blacks. So what one makes of the "identical" mean situational attribution score for blacks and whites depends, to some extent at least, upon whether one views those scores from an absolute or a relative perspective.

Conclusion. Most blacks place the primary responsibility for racial inequality on whites or on shortcomings of American society, giving lesser credence to explanations that blame blacks themselves. By contrast, whites give shorter shrift to explanations that place the primary blame on whites or on American society in general. These findings parallel Kluegel and

Smith's (1986: 89–100) conclusion that nonwhites rely much more on "structural" and somewhat less on "individual" explanations of poverty and wealth than whites do (see also Feagin, 1975).

How can we account for these black-white differences in explanations of racial inequality? Two of the three attributional biases discussed earlier appear to be consistent with at least part of the pattern observed so far. The fundamental attribution error seemed to hold for whites' explanations in 1981, but based on the changes we have observed during the 1980s it can no longer be argued that whites are still more likely than blacks to blame blacks for their own problems. So the applicability of the fundamental attribution error to these explanations seems to have diminished. The helplessness bias could be why blacks are so inclined toward situational explanations of the black-white economic gap rather than dispositional explanations. Finally, the idea of a group-serving bias is consistent with the differences between blacks' and whites' attributions: blacks rely heavily upon explanations of racial inequality that point the finger at whites or at American society in general, while whites are much more likely to deny that the responsibility lies with them or with society at large. At this juncture, then, we can say that both the helplessness and group-serving biases are consistent with the attributional patterns we have observed. As yet we have no firm basis for choosing between them, though that task should be easier after we examine explanations of recent black progress.

Explanations of recent black progress

Although we are primarily concerned with blacks' explanations of racial inequality, we are also interested in how they explain progress in the opportunities available to them. As we saw in Chapter 2, various observers have reached remarkably divergent conclusions about whether blacks are catching up to whites economically or falling farther behind. Even so, no one seriously doubts that blacks now have opportunities for social and economic advancement that were not generally available a few decades ago. Recognition of these emerging possibilities is manifest in the belief that the quality of life for blacks has been improving, a proposition with which three times as many blacks agree as disagree. It is also reflected in blacks' basic optimism about the future, observable in the four-to-one ratio of those answering "better" rather than "worse" when asked how life will be for blacks in the future (see Figure 3.6).

How do blacks account for the opening up of opportunities that were denied to them until relatively recently? The 1986 ABC News/*Washington Post* survey posed six potential explanations of why "things have changed

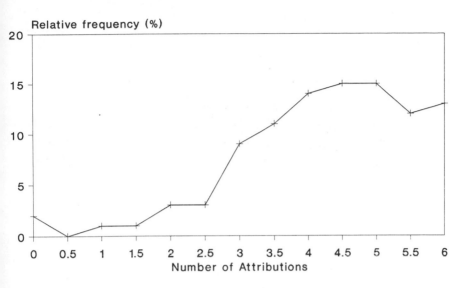

Figure 5.1. Number of progress attributions, blacks, 1986
Source: January 1986 ABC News/*Washington Post* nationwide survey of blacks. Mean = 4.3, median = 4.4, standard deviation = 1.4.

so that many blacks these days have jobs or positions that were open to only a few blacks years ago." These explanations focused on declining white prejudice against blacks, federal laws and court decisions banning racial segregation, assertiveness on the part of younger blacks, government financial assistance to blacks, increasing educational attainment by blacks, and blacks' hard work and determination. After hearing a given explanation, each respondent was asked to characterize it as "a major reason," "a minor reason," or "not a reason at all" for the changes that have occurred. Unfortunately, no comparable data are available for whites, because these questions were asked in neither the 1981 nor the 1989 ABC News/ *Washington Post* polls, nor in the GSS or any other national survey with which we are familiar.

Figure 5.1 summarizes the responses. We award full credit for any reason a respondent considered "major" and half credit for any reason deemed "minor." Of course, this distribution is not strictly comparable to those for inequality attributions (Table 5.2), because it is based on different questions and different response categories. Thus, even though in both instances the fewest explanations a respondent could agree with is 0 and the most is 6, a given score on the one scale is not necessarily equivalent to the same score on the other.

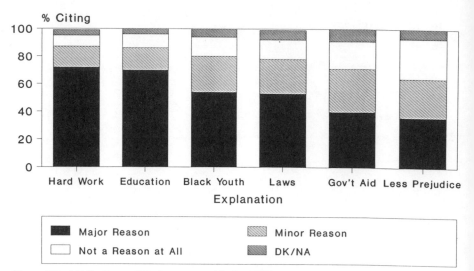

Figure 5.2. Attributions of black progress, blacks, 1986
Source: January 1986 ABC News/*Washington Post* nationwide survey of blacks. Question wording: "Things have changed so that many blacks these days have jobs or positions that were open to only a few blacks years ago. Do you feel that _____ is a major reason, a minor reason, or not a reason at all for the change?" ". . . a decrease in whites being prejudiced against blacks . . ." ". . . federal government laws and court decisions ending formal racial segregation . . ." ". . . younger blacks asserting their rights . . ." ". . . government financial assistance to blacks . . ." ". . . an increase in education for many blacks . . ." ". . . hard work and determination by blacks . . ."

Just as is true for explanations of the persistence of racial inequality, virtually every black accepts at least one of the six explanations for black progress, and most accept several. The mean of 4.3 attributions indicates that on average, blacks find most of the explanations reasonable. Indeed, about one in eight considers all six to be "major" reasons for black progress. On the other hand, one black in five is leery of at least half the explanations. As a consequence, there is substantial diversity among blacks in the number of explanations accepted for whatever progress blacks may have made in recent years.

Of the six explanations, two – "an increase in education for many blacks" and "hard work and determination by blacks" – stand out in terms of the frequency with which they are seen as having led to black progress on the job front (see Figure 5.2). Only one black in ten gives no credit at all to either of these reasons, while seven times that many consider increasing educational attainments and hard work and determination to have been major ingredients in improving blacks' access to good jobs.

Just over half hail the judicial decisions highlighted by *Brown v. Board* in

1954 and the federal legislation highlighted by the Civil Rights Act of 1964 and the Voting Rights Act of 1965 as major factors in blacks' on-the-job progress. This is approximately the same proportion as regards the assertiveness of younger blacks as a major source of progress. Although, as noted above, we have no comparable data for whites, we strongly suspect that whites are much less likely than blacks to give credit to greater black assertiveness as a source of economic advancement; indicative in this regard is the existence of a gross black-white difference in evaluations of the black political movement (Bobo, 1988). In any event, while neither greater black assertiveness nor new federal laws and court decisions is flatly rejected by many blacks as a cause of progress, neither is regarded as having been as crucial as increasing education and black initiative.[16]

Only about one black in three views declining white prejudice as a major reason for blacks' occupational advancement. In light of the substantial percentage of blacks who perceive white racial prejudice as still rampant and as not abating, the unpopularity of this explanation is hardly surprising. On the other hand, only about 30 percent wholly reject this explanation, while two-thirds are willing to concede that "a decrease in whites being prejudiced against blacks" has played at least a minor role in blacks' recent occupational gains.

Finally, though seven blacks in ten give some share of the credit to federal spending programs and only two in ten completely demur, "government financial assistance to blacks" does not rank among the main sources that blacks credit for recent black progress. Only 40 percent call federal spending programs a major factor in black advancement, placing this explanation alongside "a decrease in whites being prejudiced against blacks" as the least popular of the six explanations.

Now let us examine these six explanations in light of the same distinction between dispositional and situational explanations that proved so useful for explanations of the black-white gap. Dispositional explanations of black advancement focus on characteristics of blacks themselves. In this category we include the assertiveness of younger blacks, blacks' hard work and determination, and blacks' increasing educational attainments.[17] On the other hand, situational explanations trace black progress to developments outside the black community. Federal legislation and court decisions, government financial assistance programs, and the putative decline in prejudice among whites are all situational sources of black progress.

Before we follow these distinctions any further, we must refer back to the factor analysis results. These factor analyses were undertaken in order to address the competing expectations that (1) dispositional and situational attributions occupy opposite poles of a single dimension, and (2) dispositional and situational attributes constitute two or more separate dimensions. The results for explanations of racial inequality are consistent with the two-dimensional interpretation. However, the results for progress attributions suggest an entirely different factorial structure. There is no hint of bidimensionality in explanations of black economic progress. Rather, what emerges from the factor analysis is a clear-cut single dimension. But this dimension does not fit the bipolar pattern, either, because the six items fail to group into two sets of dispositional and situational items, one positively and the other negatively correlated to the dimension. Instead, all six items display positive correlations.

The simple fact, then, is that blacks' progress attributions do not conform to any of the expectations with which we began. Because all six items exhibit high positive correlations with the single dimension, the tendency to accept any particular explanation of black progress turns out to be positively related to the tendency to accept any other explanation, whether dispositional or situational.[18] Thus, in these explanations the distinction between dispositional and situational explanations is nowhere to be found. The dimensional solution is consistent with a 0–6 scale summarizing the total number of progress attributions with which each respondent agreed (see Figure 5.1). It provides no empirical basis for differentiating between the tendencies to offer dispositional or situational explanations of black progress.

We created separate 0–3 scales of dispositional and situational progress attributions nonetheless, so that we could further explore attributional biases. While for explanations of black-white inequality the correlation between the number of dispositional and situational explanations a respondent accepted is modest for both blacks and whites, this is decidedly not the case for blacks' progress attributions. Rather, agreement with a relatively large number of dispositional explanations of black progress suggests agreement with a relatively large number of situational explanations as well.[19]

The response distributions in Figure 5.3 are strikingly different from what we encountered in blacks' explanations of black-white inequality. Whereas blacks tend to reject dispositional explanations of racial inequality and to accept situational explanations, they are much more likely to accept dispositional than situational explanations for black progress. Only about 18 percent of blacks have scores of 1.5 or less on the 0–3 dispositional attribution scale, while more than twice as many have scores of 1.5 or less on the situational attribution scale. At the top of the scales, approximately two out of every three blacks have scores of 2.5 or 3 on the dispositional attribution scale, almost twice the proportion as on the situational attribution scale.

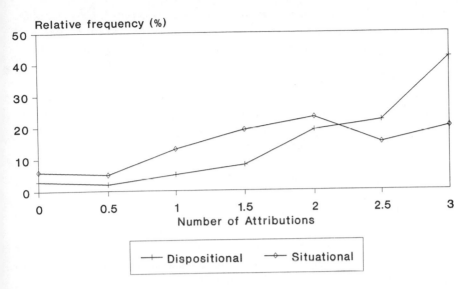

Figure 5.3. Number of progress attributions by type, blacks, 1985
Source: January 1986 ABC News/*Washington Post* nationwide survey of blacks. See the text and Figure 5.2 for a description of the dispositional and situational attribution items. For the dispositional scale, N = 915, mean = 2.4, median = 2.6, standard deviation = 0.7. For the situational scale, N = 852, mean = 1.9, median = 1.9, standard deviation = 0.9.

In sum, a conspicuous reversal in blacks' attributional tendencies accompanies the substantive shift from accounting for blacks' relatively low socioeconomic standing to accounting for the progress they have made in recent years. The blame for the former is largely directed at white-dominated American society and at whites in particular. The credit for the latter is largely directed at blacks themselves.

How can we account for this reversal? Dispositional explanations of racial inequality involve agreement with some negative stereotypes about blacks: that they lack in-born ability, ambition, and motivation. In this light, it is perhaps more surprising that many blacks agree with some of these explanations than that they reject most of them. On the other hand, dispositional explanations for black progress permit the expression of positive images of blacks, such as persistence, educational achievement, and hard work. If we compare the response distribution of blacks' explanations of socioeconomic inequality and recent progress, we see that blacks are twice as likely to accept dispositional explanations that involve positive images of blacks (2.4) as negative ones (1.2).

Similarly, blacks' agreement with situational explanations of black-white inequality involves negative portrayals of whites, whereas their acceptance of situational explanations of black progress involves positive images of whites and the federal government. In this connection, blacks are somewhat more likely to agree with the negative (2.2) than the positive (1.9) features of whites, though the difference is not large.

This brings us back to the issue of biases in attribution. Earlier, we were unable to determine which of two biases, helplessness or group-serving, better accounted for the patterns we had observed in blacks' explanations of black-white socioeconomic inequality. This was because both of these biases would be expected to produce the same heavy reliance on situational explanations accompanied by avoidance of dispositional explanations. Blacks' explanations of their recent progress add a vital new piece to this puzzle. If blacks' causal understandings of their current situation are shaped largely by a sense of their own helplessness, how could blacks simultaneously be so likely to view their recent gains as products of their own efforts? Blacks' reliance on dispositional explanations of their progress on the job front is not at all what would be expected if blacks were truly weighed down by a sense of helplessness. However, reliance on dispositional explanations of the group's successes, accompanied by rejection of dispositional explanations of the group's failures, is exactly what would be expected on the basis of a group-serving bias. Because this is precisely the pattern we have observed, it seems fair to conclude that blacks' accounts of the sources of their relative deprivation and their recent progress show signs of being influenced by a group-serving bias.

To say that attitudes are affected by a group-serving bias is not to say that they are false, or that blacks are any more likely to be group-serving than whites are. Indeed, though we lack measures of whites' explanations of black progress, their explanations of black inequality are also entirely consistent with a white group-serving bias. Whites are much less likely than blacks to blame whites for black-white socioeconomic inequality. We cannot say with certainty whether whites' relative distaste for situational attributions would carry over into whites' explanations for recent black gains, but we strongly suspect that it would not. While it is possible that whites would assign blacks the credit for their progress, it seems more likely that for whites as well as blacks, the resort to dispositional or situational explanations has less to do with a general predilection toward one or the other than with a selective mode that can be turned on or off to serve one's particular purposes. That is, we suspect that whites' attributions, like blacks', would show strong evidence of a group-serving bias. If this were so, then whites would tightly embrace situational explanations of black progress while rejecting dispositional explanations, unlike the way they account for black-white economic inequality. Our data are consistent with this latter speculation, but unfortunately these data do not extend far enough to pose a definitive test of it.

Conclusion

In Chapter 3 we encountered a vast gap between blacks and whites in their perceptions of the extent to which blacks are victims of prejudice and discrimination. In Chapter 5, we have encountered another black-white difference, this one attributional rather than perceptual. In trying to account for why blacks, on average, have poorer jobs, lower incomes, and worse housing than whites, blacks tend to see themselves largely as victims of white-dominated society, but whites are likely to downplay their own responsibility for blacks' problems. In direct contrast to their situational explanations of black-white economic inequality, blacks are more likely to invoke black-centered explanations of why blacks have made progress on the occupational front in recent years. These responses are exactly what would be expected if a group-serving bias were at work, as it often is when people try to account for success or failure in situations with which they are associated.

Despite the group-serving tendencies of both blacks and whites, it is important to note that most blacks do not forswear all black responsibility for black-white inequality, nor do whites forswear all white responsibility. Most whites accept at least one of the three situational explanations for racial inequality, and most blacks accept at least one of the three dispositional explanations. And almost all blacks are willing to give at least some of the credit to the federal government and to whites for helping improve the status of blacks in recent years. Thus both groups do balance group and external forces in their causal thinking about racial inequality. It is in the relative weights accorded to these forces that blacks differ from whites, and, indeed, that both blacks and whites differ among themselves. Our task in Chapter 6 is to try to account for these differences by exploring the extent to which blacks' and whites' explanations of black-white inequality reflect differences in personal backgrounds, socioeconomic standing, and perceptions of racial discrimination.

Notes

1. Another treatment of fundamental American sociopolitical values also reveals that across the broad range of values black-white differences tend to be relatively modest. A 1987 nationwide Gallup survey for the Times Mirror Company (reported by Colasanto, 1988) identifies six value dimensions: tolerance (support for civil liberties, free speech,

and personal lifestyle choice); social justice (beliefs about welfare and the role of government in providing for the needy); militant anticommunism (perceptions of threat, support for the use of international force, and ethnocentrism); statism (beliefs about the size and effectiveness of government); American exceptionalism (love of country and conviction that America's future is unlimited); and free enterprise (beliefs about the power and influence of big business). On all six value dimensions, there are statistically significant differences between blacks and whites, but most of these are differences of only a few percentage points. The primary exception, in keeping with Feldman's (1988) findings, is on the social justice scale, on which 58 percent of blacks but only 17 percent of whites fall into the top quartile.

2. In addition, the 1984 NBES and the 1988 Harris survey asked one forced-choice question apiece about why blacks trail whites economically. According to 33 percent of the NBES respondents, "In the U.S. if black people don't do well in life it is because they don't work hard to get ahead"; 58 percent demurred, stating that blacks "are kept back because of their race"; and 9 percent declined to choose between these two alternatives. In the Harris survey, 58 percent of blacks and 42 percent of whites said that blacks lag behind whites in getting equal pay and equal jobs because blacks are given inferior training; 19 percent of blacks and 12 percent of whites said that tests favor whites; and 14 percent of blacks and 26 percent of whites said that blacks lack a work ethic (Louis Harris and Associates, 1989: Appendix B). The validity of the forced-choice approach to measuring explanations of inequality is discussed in Note 18 of this chapter.

3. These four items were patterned after items from the 1977, 1985, and 1986 GSS, except that the GSS items omitted the introductory phrase "Most people agree that."

4. As early as 1944, survey data indicated that approximately 40 percent of whites recognized that blacks did not have as good a chance as whites to earn a living, and 70 percent realized that blacks had a poorer chance to get a job (reported by Schwartz, 1967).

5. Even as late as 1963, 66 percent of whites believed that blacks have less ambition than whites, 55 percent that they have looser morals, 41 percent that they want to live off the handout, 39 percent that they are less intelligent, and 31 percent that they are inferior (Brink and Harris, 1964: 140–1). Comparison with the somewhat differently worded items in Figure 3.3 shows that whites are now considerably less likely to consider blacks genetically inferior in intelligence and somewhat less likely to ascribe a lack of motivation or ambition to blacks.

6. For the four explanations discussed so far, rates of acceptance and rejection among whites were virtually identical in the 1977 and 1981 GSS.

7. Similarly, 57 percent of the white respondents in the 1988 ANES agreed, and only 28 percent disagreed, with the statement that "It's really a matter of some people not trying hard enough; if blacks would only try harder they could be just as well off as whites." This information was taken from the machine-readable 1988 ANES data set supplied by the Inter-University Consortium for Political and Social Research.

8. In the remaining analyses of explanations of black-white inequality attributions in this chapter and the next, we focus exclusively on the six items from the ABC News/ *Washington Post* survey. This focus is based on the more complete set of attribution items in that survey (six, as opposed to four in the GSS) and on the much larger size of the black sample.

9. This would be analogous to the finding that liberalism and conservatism are two separate dimensions, not opposite ends of the same underlying continuum (Conover and Feldman, 1981; but see Green, 1988, for a contradictory view).

10. As in Chapter 4, these factor analyses were based on matrices of *polychoric* correlation coefficients. Again, too, we undertook principal component analyses with oblique rotation.

11. By contrast, Bobo (1989) used the attribution items from the 1981 ABC News/ *Washington Post* survey to create a single scale of "racial structuralism." Our factor analysis results are inconsistent with that procedure.

12. However, we do not have any measures of one of Sniderman and Hagen's dimensions, the "fundamentalist," nor of Apostle et al.'s "supernatural."

13. As clear-cut as this formulation seems to be, there is disagreement about exactly what evidence meets the criterion of characterizing success as dispositional and failure as situational (Miller and Ross, 1975; Bradley, 1978), though this controversy is not of central concern to us here.

14. Scale reliability, indicated by coefficient alpha as calculated from the *tetrachoric* correlation matrix, is marginal (.66) for the situational attribution scale and is below conventional levels (.54) for the dispositional attribution scale. The latter coefficient would be somewhat higher if one of the three scale items (the idea that blacks bring problems upon themselves) were omitted, but because dropping this item would depress the reliability of the scale for whites and would lower the number of items in the scale to only two, we decided to retain it. Having done so, we must bear in mind that the reliability of the dispositional attribution scale for blacks is suspect. For whites, scale reliability is acceptable for both situational (.72) and dispositional (.74) attributions.

15. Kluegel and Smith (1986: 90) report parallel findings. Blacks, they find, are significantly more likely than whites to emphasize "structural" explanations of wealth and significantly less likely to emphasize "individual" explanations of wealth. Blacks are also significantly more likely to emphasize structural explanations of poverty, but Kluegel and Smith find no black-white difference in individual explanations of poverty.

    Like Feagin (1975), Kluegel and Smith use "structural" and "individual" rather than "situational" and "dispositional," the terms we prefer. It is worth noting that their application of these terms is somewhat anomalous. For example, when people refer to either "hard work and initiative" or "dishonesty and willingness to take what they can get" as reasons for success or failure, they are obviously citing individual rather than structural causes. However, while the former term loads on Kluegel and Smith's "individual" factor, the latter is actually the highest-loading item on their "structural" factor. Why initiative should be considered an individual explanation but dishonesty a structural one simply escapes us. Our scan of the items with the highest loadings on Kluegel and Smith's second dimension suggests that it could more accurately be labeled "unrespectable" or "unfair" rather than "structural."

16. It could be, of course, that embedded in the agreement that educational attainment has been instrumental in black progress is a recognition that federal court action helped bring about advances in black education. But in the absence of evidence one way or the other, it seems prudent to treat the two explanations separately.

17. We interpret poor black access to education as a situational explanation of black-white inequality, but classify increasing black educational attainment as a dispositional explanation of black advancement. This seems consistent with the basic distinction between dispositional and situational attributions.

18. This finding suggests a danger inherent in forced-choice attribution items, which have been extensively used in prior survey research on issues related to race and poverty. The forced-choice approach is based on the sometimes dicey assumption that acceptance of any particular explanation logically implies rejection of another explanation. Respondents may find themselves being forced to choose one of two or more unpalatable alternatives, or to reject an alternative toward which they feel quite positively. Examples of such forced-choice attribution items can be found in an April 1985 survey by the *Los Angeles Times*, which included several items calling for explanations of poverty (see Lewis and Schneider, 1985: 6–7); in the 1978 and 1988 Harris surveys, which probed explanations of black-white inequality (see Note 2 in this chapter); in a battery of attribution items in the 1972 and 1976 American National Election Study; in the lone 1984 NBES question on explanations of racial inequality (see Note 2 in this chapter); and in poverty attribution items in the 1975–87 "Opinions and Values of Americans" survey (McClosky and Zaller, 1984: 125).

19. The correlation between the two scales is .439, $p < .001$.

6

The sources of blacks' explanations of racial inequality

Most blacks place the primary blame for black-white socioeconomic disparities on discrimination by whites, but some do cite the failings of blacks as the
greater source of the problem. In this chapter we search for demographic,
socioeconomic, and perceptual sources of differentiation among blacks in
the explanations they offer for racial inequality. By undertaking parallel
analyses of the sources of whites' attributions, we also seek to determine
whether these patterns operate in like fashion for blacks and whites.

Expanding the model

In addition to the impact of demographic characteristics, socioeconomic
factors, and interracial friendship, we suspect that blacks' attributions for
racial inequality may be affected by their perceptions of the extent of racial
discrimination. Our primary expectation is that those who perceive widespread discrimination against blacks should be more likely to attribute
black-white inequality to situational factors than those who perceive little
such discrimination (see, e.g., Bobo, 1989). Those who perceive little discrimination against blacks cannot logically attribute black-white inequality
to widespread racial discrimination. It does not follow that those who do
consider racial discrimination widespread must view such discrimination as a
primary cause of racial inequality, but it is at least logically consistent for
them to do so. In this sense, perceptions of discrimination against blacks
constitute a necessary but not sufficient condition for situational attributions
of racial inequality, and empirically the two should be tied strongly together.

With regard to the impact of perceptions of discrimination against oneself, one possibility is that blacks build inductive theories of racial inequality based on their own personal experiences. That is, they might engage in a
process of generalization, moving from specific perceptions of the role
discrimination has played in their own lives to general understandings of
the role of discrimination in retarding the social and economic progress of

110

blacks. However, an alternative possibility is suggested by the concept of "sociotropic" decision-making (Kinder and Kiewiet, 1979), which holds that when people are called upon to make broad social, economic, and political judgments, they typically respond not on the basis of their own personal circumstances, but rather on the basis of how they think things are going in the more inclusive collectivity with which they identify – perhaps the nation as a whole, or perhaps an especially salient group (see Conover, 1985). Because blacks tend to identify strongly as blacks, it follows from the sociotropic perspective that in shaping causal understandings of racial inequality, blacks' perceptions of discrimination against blacks should play a more important role than their perceptions of discrimination against themselves.

Testing the model

In the model of racial inequality attributions, the indicators of demographic characteristics, socioeconomic status, and interracial friendship are identical to those employed in Chapter 4, but perceptions of discrimination against oneself (for blacks only) and against blacks as a group (for both blacks and whites), which served as dependent variables in Chapter 4, are now included as independent variables.[1] The dependent variables here are the dispositional and situational attribution scales that we introduced in Chapter 4.[2]

Findings

The sources of blacks' attributions

Dispositional attributions. The probit analysis indicates relatively little patterned differentiation among blacks in the tendency to view black-white inequality as a function of the shortcomings of blacks. The weak performance of the model of dispositional attribution probably reflects, among other things, the marginal reliability of this scale among blacks, which we noted above.

Within the framework of this generally weak performance, two of the socioeconomic status predictors register statistically significant effects: Those who are less educated and those who receive some type of government aid are significantly more likely than other blacks to view racial inequality as a consequence of the inadequacies of blacks. In both instances, then, it is those who rank lower in socioeconomic status who are more likely to see blacks as the source of racial inequality.

Table 6.1. *Projected number of dispositional and situational attributions, blacks, 1986*

Personal characteristics	Dispositional attributions	Situational attributions
Baseline	1.1	2.4
Government assistance recipient	1.3	
10 years of education	1.2	
16 years of education	0.9	
Black discrimination = 0		1.6
Black discrimination = 6		2.7
In poverty	1.4	2.5
Comfortable	0.9	2.2

Notes: N = 532 and 561, respectively. These projections are based on Table A.6.
Source: January 1986 ABC News/*Washington Post* nationwide survey of blacks.

This finding bears out Parent's (1985) observation that among blacks dispositional attributions are significantly linked to level of education.[3] However, neither the effect of education nor that of government aid is truly substantial: As we see in Table 6.1, when the other predictors in the model are held constant, recipients of government aid score only two-tenths of a point higher than other blacks on the 0-3 dispositional attribution scale, and those who completed only ten years of schooling score only three-tenths of a point higher than college graduates. In combination, these socioeconomic effects add up to a half-point gap between the composite poverty-level black and her more economically comfortable counterpart – not a huge difference, but one that is every bit as large as the one between blacks and whites in the early 1980s (see Table 5.4). The direction of this difference is consistent with the "learned helplessness" interpretation, which holds that people who have consistently failed in their efforts to advance socially and economically should rely most heavily upon dispositional attributions, blaming themselves rather than the external barriers they encounter.

Situational attributions. The socioeconomic configuration of situational attributions is less definitive, as evidenced by the nonsignificant effects of all seven status indicators. Even when all the socioeconomic effects are considered jointly, they matter little, accounting for an overall difference of only .3 between the composite poverty-level black and her comfortable counterpart. To the limited extent that we can speak of socioeconomic differences in these attributions, it is lower-status blacks who are more likely to accept situational explanations of racial inequality, but we should not make too much of this slight difference.

The primary factor bearing on situational attributions is perceived discrimination against blacks. The baseline black, who scores 4 on the 0-6 perceived discrimination against blacks scale, has a projected score of 2.4 on the situational attribution scale. But an otherwise identical black who perceived discrimination in all six of the areas about which she was asked would be expected to score 2.7, whereas if the same person perceived no discrimination her projected score would be only 1.6. This difference is considerably wider than the .6 that now separates the average black from the average white (see Table 5.4). Of course, it is unusual for a black to perceive no discrimination whatsoever against blacks,[4] so we should not gauge the overall impact of perceived discrimination simply by comparing those at the top and the bottom of the 0-6 scale. Nonetheless, these projections do convey the strong linkage that exists between perceived discrimination against blacks and causal understandings of racial inequality. Moreover, since many whites perceive no discrimination against blacks,[5] the projected situational attribution score for a black who scores 0 on the perceived discrimination scale is useful for purposes of interracial comparison, as we shall see shortly.

The sources of whites' attributions

Dispositional attributions. How do the sources of blacks' attributions compare to those that can be observed among whites? In order to address this question, we undertook probit analyses paralleling, as closely as possible, those for blacks.

Differences among whites in endorsement of dispositional explanations of racial inequality are somewhat more predictable than differences among blacks. One reason for this is that age, which has no bearing on the tendency of blacks to subscribe to dispositional explanations of racial inequality, does affect whites' acceptance of such explanations. As we have seen, several prior studies (Apostle et al., 1983; Feagin, 1975; Kluegel and Smith, 1986; Sniderman with Hagen, 1985) have characterized older whites as being more likely to embrace "traditional" explanations of poverty and racial inequality, such as those that place the blame on genetic racial differences or on lack of motivation among blacks and the poor. The same tendency shows up here. The projected differential in scores on the dispositional attribution scale for two otherwise identical whites, one twenty-five years old and the other sixty-five, is roughly .4 (see Table 6.2). This is by no means a night-and-day difference, but it is consistent enough to rank as the most powerful effect in the model.[6]

The remaining effects and noneffects are congruent, for the most part, with those for blacks. For one thing, better educated whites, like better

Table 6.2. *Projected number of dispositional and situational attributions, whites, 1981*

Personal characteristics	Dispositional attributions	Situational attributions
Baseline	1.6	2.3
25 years old	1.5	
65 years old	1.9	
Subjective middle class member	1.5	
Unemployed		1.9
10 years of education	1.7	
16 years of education	1.5	
Black discrimination = 0		1.1
Black discrimination = 6		2.7
In poverty	1.7	2.0
Comfortable	1.3	2.4

Notes: N = 841 and 857, respectively. These projections are based on Table A.7.
Source: February–March 1981 ABC News/*Washington Post* nationwide survey.

educated blacks, are significantly less likely to embrace dispositional explanations of racial inequality, and by approximately the same narrow margin as for blacks. For another, the projected gap on the dispositional attribution scale between a poverty-level and a comfortable white is about on par with the projected differential for poverty-level and comfortable blacks, and once again it is those of lower standing who are more favorably inclined toward dispositional explanations.

Among whites this differential comes about because those who consider themselves members of the middle class are significantly less prepared to accept dispositional explanations than are self-identified working- or lower-class whites (see also Sniderman with Hagen, 1985). However, this difference is offset by others (for home ownership and unemployment) that run in the opposite direction, so that the overall socioeconomic differential in acceptance of dispositional attributions is essentially the same among whites (.4) as it is among blacks (.5). Even so, it seems fair to say that status-based differences in attributional tendencies are virtually as important as race-based differences.

Situational attributions. As for whites' endorsement of situational explanations, the results again parallel those for blacks, with a single noteworthy exception. The exception relates to unemployment. Among blacks, the unemployed are slightly (albeit not significantly) more likely to espouse situational explanations of racial inequality, but among whites the direction of this difference is reversed: unemployed whites are significantly less likely to accept situational explanations of inequality. It may be, as Parent (1985) has speculated, that reversals of this type bespeak the competitive situation that prevails between blacks and whites of a certain social stratum, but if this is so then it is difficult to understand why this reversal is restricted to a single indicator of socioeconomic status. The relatively minor projected difference in situational attributions between two whites who match the profiles of the composite poverty-level and comfortable blacks, respectively, reflects the significant effect of unemployment among whites, without which there would be no socioeconomic differential whatsoever. Because being unemployed significantly decreases whites' acceptance of situational explanations, the overall tendency is for more affluent whites to look somewhat more favorably than less affluent whites do upon situational explanations – a reversal, though not an especially resounding one, of the pattern for blacks.

Just as is true for blacks, perceptions of discrimination against blacks are the most important determinant of whites' situational attributions. Whites who recognize widespread discrimination against blacks are much more likely to attribute racial inequality to situational factors than are whites who fail to perceive much discrimination. Thus, as we see in Table 6.2, there is a projected difference of 1.6 on the three-point situational attributions scale between two "baseline" whites, one of whom scores 0 on the perceived discrimination scale while the other scores 6. This is a huge difference, and it means that for whites, too, perceiving, or failing to perceive, widespread discrimination against blacks is intimately bound to causal attributions.

Conclusion

Until now, little has been known about the sources of variability among blacks in causal understandings of racial inequality. Thus, the major contribution of this chapter is to portray the cleavages – and, in many cases, the lack of cleavages – within the black community in causal interpretations of black-white socioeconomic inequality. Like Parent (1985), we have observed that better educated blacks are less likely to point to blacks as primarily responsible for racial inequality. In Parent's analysis, education emerged as the lone significant predictor of these attributions. Here, however, we have also seen that blacks who receive government aid are more likely to blame blacks for their lesser socioeconomic status. Both of these findings are consistent with the idea that many less successful blacks engage in "learned helplessness" reasoning, turning inward to find reasons why they stand at the bottom of the status ladder.

The learned helplessness interpretation should not be overemphasized, since none of the other indicators of socioeconomic status predicts a tendency toward dispositional attributions. Still, the magnitude of the attributional gap between prototypical poverty-stricken and comfortable blacks equals the gap that separated the average black and the average white a decade ago, indicating that socioeconomic as well as racial cleavages can foster different causal understandings of racial inequality.

Interestingly, the amount of discrimination blacks perceive against themselves and against blacks in general does not affect their acceptance of dispositional explanations of racial inequality. Many blacks, while acknowledging the reality of white discrimination, still place some of the blame on blacks themselves for their problems.

On the other hand, the extent to which blacks perceive discrimination against blacks is a highly significant – indeed, the only significant – predictor of the tendency to accept situational explanations of racial inequality. Blacks who perceive discrimination as more widespread are much more likely to consider discrimination an important reason for racial inequality.

As for whites' explanations of black-white inequality, we have seen that many of the same factors that lead to acceptance or rejection of situational explanations among blacks do so among whites as well. As is the case among blacks, lower status whites are more likely to blame blacks for their own problems, and for whites, like blacks, increased education leads to less reliance on "blame the victim" explanations. One distinctive pattern for whites is the significant effect of age; older whites are much more likely to accept dispositional attributions than are younger whites, a difference that has no counterpart among blacks.

For whites, like blacks, by far the strongest predictor of acceptance of situational explanations is perceived discrimination against blacks. Whites who see discrimination as widespread are likely to attribute racial inequality to such discrimination, a logical but not inevitable linkage. It follows from the perception-attribution link that one key to remedying the effects of discrimination may be to make more whites aware that racial discrimination exists.

Among whites, the higher the socioeconomic status, the greater the acceptance of the idea that societal barriers are an important source of black-white socioeconomic differences. Thus status differences do affect whites' attributional tendencies, and to a greater extent than prevails among blacks. Even so, these socioeconomic differences are small and largely reflect the impact of unemployment.

In Chapter 5, we noted a wide gap between blacks and whites in the way

Table 6.3. *Projected black–white differences in attributions, by socioeconomic status*

	Dispositional		Situational	
	Blacks	Whites	Blacks	Whites
In poverty	1.4	1.7	2.5	2.0
Comfortable	.9	1.3	2.2	2.4

Source: Summarized from Tables 6.1 and 6.2.

they explain racial inequality. Although the former black-white gap in acceptance of dispositional explanations seems to have been bridged, blacks are still much more likely to agree with situational explanations than whites are. The analyses reported in this chapter enable us to determine how much of this attributional difference reflects the socioeconomic disparity between blacks and whites. Comparing the projected scores for our hypothetical comfortable and poverty-stricken blacks and whites holds constant the effects of all the other factors in our model and thus isolates the "pure" race effect, that is, the black-white difference not attributable to any of the predictors in the model.

Table 6.3 displays these scores.[7] The overall .5 black-white gap in dispositional attributions from earlier in the decade does not narrow appreciably when socioeconomic and other factors are held constant, since even then whites are considerably more likely than blacks to accept dispositional attributions. More precisely, the projected dispositional attribution score for a composite poverty-stricken black is 1.4, and the projected score for an otherwise-identical white is 1.7; similarly, the projected scores for the composite more economically secure black and her exact white counterpart are .9 and 1.3, respectively. So most of the original .5 difference remains when blacks and whites with identical socioeconomic characteristics are compared. However, as we have already seen, within-race differences are just as important as between-race differences.

As for situational explanations, the gap between blacks and whites is partially closed when we hold the other factors in the model constant. In fact, although poverty-stricken blacks are considerably more likely than identical whites to accept racial discrimination as an important source of racial inequality, among comfortable blacks and identical whites there is little difference in the willingness to accept situational explanations. Indeed, these blacks are, if anything, slightly less likely than identical whites to accept situational explanations of racial inequality. In sum, the earlier black-white differences in the tendency to blame blacks for their lesser socioeconomic status seem to have been largely independent of the socio economic and perceptual differences between blacks and whites, but acceptance of white discrimination as a barrier to black advancement is a product of socioeconomic and perceptual differences between blacks and whites as well as of race per se.

In the past, researchers have devoted considerable attention to people's explanations of racial inequality, but the people whose explanations have been studied have almost always been white. In this chapter, we have seen that conclusions about the sources of whites' attributions do not always hold for blacks. Nor is there any reason to expect that they should invariably do so.

The primary question to be addressed in the remaining chapters is whether the perceptions blacks hold of racial discrimination and the explanations they provide for racial inequality shape their assessments of various proposed remedies for problems stemming from racial discrimination and inequality. First, though, we must carefully examine these assessments, to gain a firmer grasp on the extent of support for these remedies within the black community.

Notes

1. In the projections, the "baseline" values of these two variables are set at 1 and 4, respectively.
2. We make no attempt in this chapter to pinpoint the sources of blacks' explanations of recent black gains, since (as noted in Chapter 5) these attributions do not factor in any interpretable fashion.
3. Bobo (1989) reports a significant bivariate relationship that vanishes in the multivariate phase of his analysis. In his multivariate analysis, he controlled not only for demographical characteristics such as income, sex, age, and urbanicity, but also several attitudinal variables that may or may not be antecedent to attributions. In this sense, he may have "overcontrolled" the relationship out of existence.
4. As noted in Table 3.4 above, in the 1986 ABC News/*Washington Post* survey only seven percent of blacks scored 0 on the 0-6 scale of perceived discrimination against blacks. Similarly, in the 1984 NBES 12 percent agreed that "Discrimination against blacks is no longer a problem in the U.S." (Survey Research Center, 1984).
5. Table 3.4 shows that, in the 1981 ABC News/*Washington Post* survey, fully 48 percent of whites scored 0 on the same 0-6 scale of perceived discrimination against blacks.
6. As with education, Bobo (1989) finds a significant bivariate age effect but none in his multivariate analysis. Again, the reason may be that age is a significant predictor of the attitudinal variables (stereotyping and ethnocentrism) for which he institutes statistical controls.
7. These scores do not "average out" to the overall scores for whites because we have created our hypothetical baseline, comfortable, and poverty-stricken persons using the mean scores for blacks on the socioeconomic variables and perceptions of discrimination. Using a single set of scores is necessary if we are to compare across races, but it also means that these scores do not approximate the overall white score as closely as they do for blacks.

7

Blacks' views of remedies for racial inequality

Although many blacks believe that progress is being made, they also perceive enduring inequalities and serious impediments to further progress. Most blacks – far more than the corresponding proportion of whites – attribute these persisting race-based socioeconomic disparities to situational constraints on blacks.

Having considered perceptions and explanations of racial inequality, we now turn to blacks' appraisals of some possible remedies for racial inequality. As before, we not only examine the views of blacks, but also compare their views with those held by whites. And to a greater extent than was possible in examining perceptions and explanations of inequality, we focus on how blacks' views have changed over the years.

For at least two reasons, divisive racial issues in the United States tend to be about means, not ends. First, after centuries of officially enforced, culturally endorsed subordination of racial and ethnic minorities in the United States, the legal structure of segregation has been largely dismantled and a broad consensus in support of the principle of equal opportunity has emerged. Second, as yet no sustained push on behalf of the more radically egalitarian principle of equality of reward has yet surfaced in this country. Most Americans are not especially distressed by social and economic inequality per se as long as the bases of such inequality seem fair by some reasonable standard (see, e.g., Alves and Rossi, 1978; Della Fave, 1980; Stolte, 1983). It is particularly noteworthy that black leaders share in this view. Indeed, when a national sample of black leaders was asked in 1976 to choose between the goals of "equality of opportunity: giving each person an equal chance for a good education and to develop his or her ability" and "equality of results: giving each person a relatively equal income regardless of his or her education and ability," 86 percent chose equality of opportunity and only seven percent expressed a preference for equality of results (Verba and Orren, 1985: 72).[1]

In examining attitudes toward policies intended to alleviate racial inequality, we highlight two dimensions. One is the desired outcome of the policy, and the second is the level of government involvement in reaching that goal. That these two dimensions can vary independently is easily grasped by juxtaposing two oft-reported survey findings. Almost all Americans, black or white, say they are in favor of school integration. However, "forced" integration of the schools (i.e., governmentally induced desegregation, as in school busing) is extremely controversial (Orfield, 1978; Taylor, 1986). Consensus on the goal of school integration has not fostered a corresponding consensus on the role government should play in achieving that goal.

Agreement with a fundamental political principle often does not translate into acceptance of concrete applications of the principle (McClosky, 1964; Prothro and Grigg, 1960; Stouffer, 1955), so it should come as no great surprise that public support for the abstract goal of school desegregation far outstrips support for busing, a particular means of achieving that goal. Desegregation that seems to occur "naturally," e.g., as a consequence of black social and residential mobility, evokes relatively little opposition from whites. But desegregation that occurs as a direct result of government action is much more controversial, because of resentment at the obtrusiveness of government itself (Taylor, 1986). Thus Schuman et al. (1985: ch. 3) find that even though whites have been increasingly supportive of the principle of racial integration, white support for government action aimed at achieving integration has stagnated or even declined.

The distinctiveness of white attitudes concerning the means and ends of desegregation has provoked some heated disputes about the extent to which whites really favor racial equality. Some scholars (Jackman, 1978, 1981; Kinder and Sears, 1981; McConahay, 1986; McConahay, Hardee, and Batts, 1981; Sears, 1988; Sears and Allen, 1984; Sears, Hensler, and Speer, 1979) argue that even though few whites now express prejudice against blacks by agreeing with overtly racist statements, white racism is still observable in the failure of whites to support government actions that would implement racial equality (see Kuklinski, 1990, for some interesting experiments on whites' racial attitudes).

However, several critics (e.g., Kuklinski and Parent, 1981; Lipset and Schneider, 1978; Margolis and Haque, 1981; Schuman et al., 1985; Taylor, 1986) dispute the contention that opposition to specific programs necessarily signals rejection of the general principle of racial equality. While conceding that whites' reluctance to endorse certain government actions might be an indication of racism, these critics hold out the possibility that this reluctance might also reflect an aversion to "big government" and to perceived federal coercion. Seen from this perspective, opposition to busing and other forms of direct government action may have less to do with racial attitudes than with ideas about the legitimate scope of government action.[2] In the words of Merriman and Carmines, "Racial policies such as busing and affirmative action . . . go beyond this narrow view of fairness as equality of rights and treatment and, consequently, run afoul of classical liberal values. Such policies are regarded by many citizens as illegitimate and illiberal invasions of the rights of some citizens in the interest of others, exactly the sort of activity that tolerance is supposed to prevent" (1988: 51; see also Schuman and Bobo, 1988). Taylor (1986) argues that most Americans believe government is right to declare discrimination illegal, but not to force desegregation. Thus he interprets the public as supporting voluntary compliance because of the conviction that government intervention brings about undesirable consequences for neighborhoods and schools.

Then, too, questions have been raised about whether there really is as little connection as has sometimes been claimed between support for the general principle of racial equality and for concrete policies aimed at achieving equality. Sniderman et al. (1984: 90), for example, conclude that whites' policy preferences are "grounded in principle in the case of race. The person favoring racial equality at an abstract level is . . . ready to back efforts to realize it."

In light of this controversy, it should be especially instructive to explore the extent to which blacks draw a distinction between the goals they want to achieve and the role they want government to play in achieving these goals. If the same gap exists among blacks as among whites, it would be difficult to cite racial discrimination as the sole or primary explanation for the means-ends gap. We shall begin by examining attitudes toward school integration and the means of achieving it, then turn to attitudes toward remedies for job-related and educational discrimination, and finally consider attitudes toward programs designed to eliminate poverty and raise living standards among both blacks and whites.

School integration

Support for school integration is virtually universal among blacks, as it has been at least since the early 1970s (Figure 7.1). More than nine whites in every ten now feel the same way, a dramatic turnaround from the massive opposition that prevailed during the 1950s, when only about half of white adults nationwide were willing to concede that black and white students should attend the same schools. In the current atmosphere of calm biracial consensus concerning the goal of school integration, it is jarring to recall

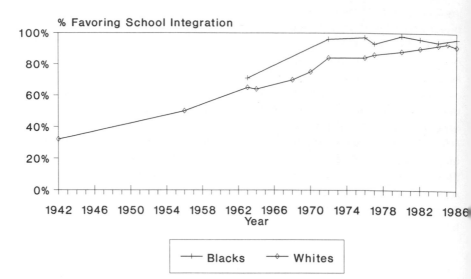

Figure 7.1. Support for school integration, blacks and whites, 1942–1986
Sources: Black data for 1963 are from *Newsweek* (July 29, 1963). All other data are from NORC surveys summarized by Schuman et al. (1985: 74–5 and 144–5), or, for 1984 and 1986, calculated by the authors from the GSS codebook (Davis and Smith, 1987). Question wording: NORC (1942, 1956, 1963 whites, 1968–86): "Do you think white students and black students should go to the same schools or to separate schools?" *Newsweek* (1963 blacks): "Would you like to see all Negro children in your family go to school with white children or not?"

how little time has passed since this was a goal over which Americans argued, demonstrated, marched, fought, and died.

Overall, some progress has been made toward integrating schools. Between 1968 and 1980, the proportion of black students in schools with 90 to 100 percent minority enrollment declined from 64 percent to 33 percent. However, 63 percent of all blacks still attended schools where minorities predominated (Orfield, 1983: 4).

The current biracial consensus on the desirability of school integration breaks down as soon as the discussion turns specific. For one thing, while most whites would register no objections to sending their children to a school with a few black students, there is still widespread opposition to the idea of sending one's children to a school with a majority of black students (see, e.g., Smith, 1981a, 1981b, 1982; Stanley and Niemi, 1988: 328; Taylor, 1986), and that opposition has declined only slightly over the past quarter-century. Another point of intense controversy relates to the means of implementing desegregation. The most persistent and widespread school segregation is found in big city schools. These are districts where housing patterns make integrated neighborhood schools difficult or impossible to achieve, so the busing of schoolchildren across neighborhood boundaries must be considered. When it is, consensus tends quickly to dissipate into bitter antagonism.

That opposition to busing is widespread among whites should surprise no one, but it is less well known that blacks, too, are uneasy about busing. In fact, only about half the blacks who have been queried about the issue since the early 1960s have expressed support for busing to achieve racial integration.[3] In 1963, 51 percent of black respondents favored busing and another 20 percent indicated uncertainty in a *Newsweek* survey ("The Negro in America," 1963) in which the following question was asked: "Of course, because of where they live today, Negro children go to all Negro schools and whites to white schools. Would you like to see children in your family be picked up in buses every day so they could go to another part of town to go to school with white children or would that be too hard on the children?" The stability of black opinion on busing can be gauged by comparing these responses to those from a question in the ABC News/ *Washington Post* Poll 23 years later. This question ("Thinking of school busing, would you say you favor or oppose the busing of black and white students as a last resort for school integration?") evoked approval of busing from 55 percent of blacks, with about 10 percent registering no opinion.[4]

Of the two major polls in which questions about busing have repeatedly been asked, the American National Election Study (ANES) and the GSS, the former has often uncovered somewhat less support for busing among blacks (see Figure 7.2). In the ANES, where respondents are asked whether school integration is so important that it justifies busing children to schools out of their neighborhoods, somewhat less than half of the black sample has typically supported busing. In the GSS, black support for busing has generally fallen into the 50 to 60 percent range. The intersurvey differential may occur because the GSS item does not invoke the potent symbol of neighborhoods but simply asks whether respondents "favor or oppose the busing of black and white school children from one school district to another." Moreover, the ANES question contains a neutral, middle alternative while the GSS question does not, and the availability of such an alternative should have a depressing effect on opinionation. Indeed, when support for busing is recalculated as a percentage of those who express an opinion one way or the other rather than as a percentage of all respondents, the ANES support range closely approximates that of the GSS.[5]

In contrast to the relative stability of blacks' views concerning busing, there has been a slight increase over time in approval among whites. Ac-

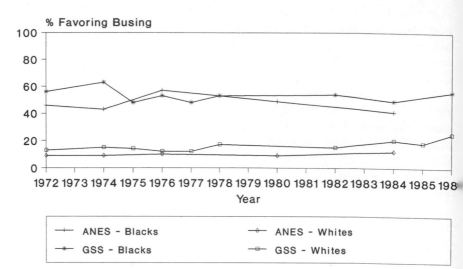

Figure 7.2. Support for busing, blacks and whites, 1972–1986
Sources: Data through 1980 are from the summary in Schuman et al. (1985: 88 and 144–7). Data from 1982–7 are taken directly from the American National Election Study and General Social Survey datasets. We combined data from the 1983 and 1984 General Social Survey datasets, and from 1985 and 1986, to achieve larger black sample sizes. Question wording: American National Election Study: "There is much discussion about the best way to deal with racial problems. Some people think achieving racial integration of schools is so important that it justifies busing children to schools out of their own neighborhoods. Others think letting children go to their neighborhood school is so important that they oppose busing. Where would you place yourself on this scale, or haven't you thought much about this?" Answers are on a 1–7 point scale, with 1–4 designating support and 5–7 opposition; the figure is based on the percentage choosing responses 1 through 4. General Social Survey: "In general, do you favor or oppose the busing of black and white school children from one school district to another?" The figure is based on the percentage answering "favor."

cording to the GSS, white support for busing rose from 13 percent in 1972 to 25 percent in 1986.[6]

   Unfortunately, other means of achieving school integration, such as establishing magnet schools and redrawing school boundaries, are rarely asked about in national surveys. However, between 1964 and 1978 ANES respondents were asked the more general question of whether "government should see to it that white and black children are allowed to go to the same schools." While this question may at first glance seem simply to gauge support for the broad principle of integration, the referent ("government should see to it") is of special interest. We noted above that for some time support for the general principle of integration has been virtually universal among blacks and whites. In this context, it is especially striking that between the mid-1960s and the late 1970s agreement with this ANES question declined among both blacks and whites, from a high of almost 90 percent for blacks in 1968 to a low of 60 percent in 1978, and from a high of around 50 percent for whites in 1966 to a low of 30 percent in 1978 (Schuman et al., 1985: 149).

Why did this shift occur? It is hard to believe that racism per se increased from the mid-1960s to the late 1970s, and it is also difficult to see how a shift that occurred in tandem for whites and blacks could be interpreted as an indication of growing prejudice against blacks. The shift is probably attributable to two factors. One is the changing nature of the policies under consideration. In the 1960s there was widespread support for federal action to outlaw the de jure segregation, including school segregation, that was so common in parts of the South. By the 1970s the focus had shifted away from Civil Rights laws abolishing "legal" segregation to the elimination of de facto segregation, such as that brought about by housing patterns. Then white attitudes supportive of voluntary compliance and against federal mandates came into play (Taylor, 1986). Thus the shift in focus led to a downturn in support for government action.

Moreover, attitudes toward government itself were changing. In the mid-1960s, confidence in government's ability to solve basic social problems ran high, but by the late 1970s this soaring optimism had given way to what President Carter proclaimed as a "crisis of confidence" in government (see, e.g., Lipset and Schneider, 1983). Growing more cynical about government, the public, both black and white, also became more skeptical about the capacity of government to produce results through the policies it was pursuing.

Consistent with these interpretations, the 1970s witnessed a sharp dropoff among blacks as well as whites in support for federal efforts to assist blacks and other minorities. In response to an ANES question that began by asserting that "Some people feel that the government in Washington should make every possible effort to improve the social and economic position of blacks and other minority groups" while "Others feel that the government should not make any special effort to help minorities because they should help themselves," 78 percent of the black respondents in 1970 embraced the former position. But by 1982 endorsement of this position by blacks dwindled to only 49 percent (Schuman et al., 1985: 144–5).

More generally, what can we conclude about public support for school integration? The basic point is that advocacy of the general principle of integrated education is not matched, among either blacks or whites, by equally widespread advocacy of specific policies intended to facilitate integration. Approximately 70 percent of the whites who favor school integration do not favor busing to achieve it. Among blacks the gap is smaller but still dramatic: 40 percent or more of the blacks who favor school integration do not favor busing to achieve it, and when asked directly 79 percent of the respondents in the 1984 NBES agreed that it is more important to improve schools in black neighborhoods than to bus to achieve racial integration; only 12 percent disagreed.

Why is opposition to busing and other governmentally imposed means of achieving school integration so widespread? Many explanations have been offered. For some whites, opposition to busing and other "coercive" measures may mask racism, or may at least bespeak a lack of genuine commitment to racial integration. But racism cannot be the whole answer, since opposition to busing and other specific measures is also widespread among blacks, whose aversion to busing stems from several sources. In at least one community (Detroit), blacks and whites have criticized busing for diverting attention from the more important need to maintain quality schools, for being inconvenient, for being unsafe, for depriving people of freedom of choice, and for contravening the principle of neighborhood schools. Whites are more likely (by 19 to 9 percent) to voice concern about freedom of choice and less likely (by 18 to 32 percent) to see busing as a diversion from the real issue of quality education (Schuman et al., 1985: 155). Others have argued that busing poor black children to middle class white schools deprives black children of the support and encouragement of black teachers and subjects them to racism and middle-class expectations. All of this lowers their self-esteem and may contribute to poor performance (Epps, 1975; Hochschild, 1984: 163–7). Moreover, the operation of second-generation discrimination means that blacks are more likely to end up in classes for the educable mentally retarded, to be routed into noncollege bound tracks, to be disciplined or suspended, and to suffer other kinds of discriminatory treatment in majority white schools (Bullock and Stewart, 1978, 1979; England and Meier, 1985; Jaynes and Williams, 1989: 82–3; Meier et. al., 1989). Thus many blacks have good reason to suspect that busing to integrate may harm their children.

Jobs, education, and affirmative action

Prior to the passage of the Civil Rights Act, job discrimination was the type of discrimination blacks resented most. In 1963, more blacks (30 percent) listed employment discrimination as affecting them than mentioned any other form of discrimination, with educational discrimination (11 percent) placing a distant second. Well over half believed their pay was lower than a white doing the same work would receive (Brink and Harris, 1964: 194). In another 1963 survey, 58 percent of blacks cited equal job opportunity as the highest priority for immediate government action; voting rights and school desegregation finished far behind, at 13 percent each, while only three percent mentioned integration of public accommodations (Schwartz, 1967). And in yet another 1963 survey, blacks rated the right to hold the same jobs as whites highest among "rights wanted by almost all Negroes" (Schwartz, 1967).

The Civil Rights Act outlawed discrimination in employment, but as we saw in Chapter 2, a quarter of a century after the passage of that landmark legislation blacks continue to lag in occupational status and pay. Although many potential solutions to this problem have been proposed, there still is no consensus about how to overcome job-related discrimination. There is, among both blacks and whites, a consensus that "Negroes should have as good a chance as white people to get any kind of job"; indeed, by the early 1970s agreement with this question had become so nearly unanimous that pollsters simply stopped asking it. Although this question now seems quite innocuous, as late as 1964 most whites actually disagreed with it, explicitly rejecting the principle of equal employment opportunity (Schuman et al., 1985: 74–5). Today the issue is not whether blacks deserve an equal chance, but how equal job opportunities are to be won.

On the question of means – of specific programs for integrating the workplace – consensus splinters. Indeed, affirmative action, a general label for a variety of procedures intended to open up job opportunities to minorities, women, and the physically handicapped, ranks alongside busing and abortions as one of the most heated public policy issues of our times. Many affirmative action procedures, such as the requirements that job vacancies be openly listed and that criteria for employment be related to the job skills needed, are not especially controversial, although numerous controversies have arisen about their application in particular circumstances. Other aspects of affirmative action have sparked great controversy. The use of numerical hiring goals has led to charges that "quota systems" are being established, and the implementation of hiring plans has fueled apprehension about "reverse discrimination" against white males.

Are blacks highly supportive of affirmative action? At least one scholar (Jacobson, 1983) has concluded that they are, but we recommend proceeding with great caution when analyzing public opinion on a topic as multifaceted as affirmative action. It is a truism that "what the public thinks" about a particular issue depends on how the issue is framed, and that truism has never been more apt than in the case of affirmative action, where so much depends on the specific aspect of the policy respondents are asked to consider and the precise phrasing of the question. Depending on the question asked and on the specific language used, one could truthfully say that as many as 96 percent of all blacks and 76 percent of all whites are in favor of affirmative action. But equally correctly one could say that as few as 23 percent of all blacks and 9 percent of all whites support affirmative action. These dramatic differences stem from the great diversity of questions asked in opinion surveys, diversity that makes trend analyses of support for affirmative action nearly impossible.

Even within a single survey, opinions vary greatly depending on question wording. In the 1984 NBES, for example, 57 percent of a sample of 1,150 blacks agreed and 38 percent disagreed that "Minorities should be given special consideration when decisions are made about hiring applicants for jobs." Three questions later, 72 percent agreed that "Job applicants should be judged solely on the basis of test scores and other individual qualities." Admittedly, the phrase "and other individual qualities" is ambiguous, but it does seem clear that blacks, like whites, believe in merit as the major criterion in hiring while also wanting to make opportunities more available to minorities.

In Table 7.1 we catalogue responses to an array of survey questions concerning affirmative action that have been asked since the late 1970s. Wide variability is evident in these responses, but some patterns are evident amid that variability. First, the aspects of affirmative action that blacks see as most desirable also win the greatest approval among whites, and the aspects blacks like least are rejected most often by whites. Although the black-white differential in agreement with these items ranges from 5 to 40 percentage points, blacks and whites rank these options in much the same order; in fact, across the thirteen items the correlation between the percentage of blacks agreeing and the percentage of whites agreeing is almost perfect.

In general, blacks appraise affirmative action most positively when responding to questions that either specifically mention that no quotas are involved or are worded in a vague, nonthreatening manner (e.g., the items about giving minorities and women a "chance" and allowing them to "get ahead," neither of which alludes to quotas or preferential treatment). Most blacks also look favorably upon training programs. Responding to questions like these, upwards of 75 percent of blacks say they support affirmative action. Responding to the same questions, whites are also highly supportive; in fact, on each of the first six questions more than 60 percent of white respondents express support for affirmative action.

On the other hand, affirmative action finds few supporters, black or white, when the idea of giving minorities special treatment to make up for

Table 7.1. *Support for affirmative action in employment, blacks and whites, 1977–1988*
(in %)

	Blacks	Whites
Affirmative action programs that help blacks get ahead should be supported (1980-G)	96	76
Agree that after years of discrimination only fair to set up special programs to ensure that women and minorities are given every chance to have equal opportunities in employment and education (1978-H)	91	71
Favor affirmative action programs in employment for blacks, provided there are no rigid quotas		
(1978-H)	89	67
(1988-H)	78	73
Approve of requiring large companies to set up special training programs for members of minority groups (1977-NYT)	88	63
Favor affirmative action programs in employment for blacks, provided there are no rigid quotas (1988-H)	78	73
As long as no quotas, makes sense to give special training and advice to women and minorities so they can perform better on the job (1978-H)	77	70
Employers should set aside places to hire qualified blacks and other minorities (1980-G)	73	51
Approve of requiring businesses to hire a certain number of minority workers (1977-NYT)	64	35
Approve of requiring some corporations to practice affirmative action, sometimes requiring special preference to minorities or women when hiring (1978-C)	58	35[a]
Approve Supreme Court decision allowing employer to set up a special training and promotion program for minorities and women (1978-H)	56	36
Support Court ruling allowing employers to favor women and minorities in hiring over better qualified men and whites (1987-G)	56	25
Support giving blacks preference in getting jobs over equally qualified whites because of past discrimination against blacks (1984-GJ)	49	9
To make up for past discrimination, women and minorities should be given preferential treatment in getting jobs and places in college as opposed to mainly considering ability as determined by test scores (1985J, 1984G)	23	10[a]

Notes: The correlation between the percentage of blacks supporting a given policy and the corresponding percentage of whites is .92.

[a] The survey is of the entire public, not just whites. *Sources:* H = Louis Harris and Associates. G = Gallup Poll. NYT = *New York Times*. C = Cambridge Survey Research, summarized by Lipset and Schneider (1978). J = Lawrence Johnson and Associates and Metro Research Services, summarized by Lichter (1985). GJ = Gallup Joint Center Poll.

past discrimination is directly contrasted with hiring solely on the basis of merit (see also Bolce and Gray, 1979; Lipset and Schneider, 1978; Sackett, 1980). Presented with such a choice, only about one black in four supports special treatment, and not even one white in ten does so.

Thus, most blacks agree with most whites on eight of the thirteen items in Table 7.1 – the first six and the last two. On all eight of these questions, blacks are more supportive of affirmative action than whites are, but there is no fundamental disagreement between blacks and whites about what is most acceptable and what least so.

On the seventh item in Table 7.1, which concerns the idea that employers should reserve positions for hiring qualified blacks, three blacks in four and a bare majority of whites agree. This contrasts with the response pattern on the next item, where most blacks support but most whites oppose requiring businesses to hire a certain number of minority workers. The disparity in responses evoked by the seventh and eighth items may seem odd, given the overlapping content of the two items, but the seventh question merely suggests that employers "should" set aside places for minorities, while the eighth inquires about "requiring" businesses to do so. Moreover, the seventh question also refers to hiring "qualified" blacks, but the eighth makes no mention of qualifications. Together, these wording differences seem sizable enough to account for the observed disparity in responses.

There is substantial black-white disagreement on three other items. The differential is greatest (40 percentage points) on a 1984 item asking whether because of past discrimination, blacks should be given job preference over "equally qualified whites" – an idea endorsed by about half of black respondents but only one white in ten. There is also racial discord on a question concerning a Supreme Court decision allowing employers to set up special training and promotion programs for minorities and women. Ordinarily, we suppose that most people would assent to this sort of "soft" scenario "allowing" employers to set up training and promotion programs. However, not only is the wording of the question quite lengthy and complex,[7] but the question points out that critics of the Court ruling alleged that whites and males were victims of reverse discrimination and that seniority rights would be violated. These cues seem to have triggered negative responses among whites.

A third item over which there is great disagreement between blacks and whites concerns a 1987 Supreme Court ruling that it is permissible for an employer to hire a woman instead of a man who scored slightly higher on a screening test. Unfortunately for the sake of gauging support for the Court's decision, the Gallup Poll oversimplified the issue by asking whether employers should be able to favor women and minorities in hiring over "better

Table 7.2. *Support for affirmative action in education, blacks and whites, 1976–1980* (in %)

	Blacks	Whites
Favor affirmative action programs in higher education for blacks, provided there are no rigid quotas (1978-H)	91	68
Colleges and universities should set aside a certain number of positions to admit qualified blacks and other minorities (1980-KS)	84	60
Approve of a college giving special consideration to best minority applicants to help more get admitted (1977-CBS/NYT)	64	35
Approve of a school reserving a certain number of places for qualified minority applicants even if some qualified white applicants wouldn't be admitted (1977-CBS/NYT)	46	32
Choose black applicant for last opening to law school in a case where a white student has better college record but both black and white meet qualifications (1976-H)	42	14
Approve of medical school lowering its standards to enroll black medical student who may not have the right qualifications but who shows real promise (1976-H)	37	10

Sources: H = Louis Harris and Associates. KS = Kluegel and Smith. CBS/NYT = CBS News/ *New York Times*.

qualified" men and whites. Unless a screening test were extraordinarily reliable, a difference of only a few points would presumably say virtually nothing about the relative qualifications of two job applicants. Nonetheless, even though it does not fairly represent the substance of the Court's holding, this item taps into respondents' reactions to preferential treatment, and we learn from it that many Americans find the idea of bypassing a "better qualified" applicant repugnant; just over half of blacks and only a quarter of whites are willing to say that the "better qualified" applicant should not get the job.[8]

The general patterns we have observed in blacks' attitudes toward affirmative action in employment are echoed in their attitudes toward affirmative action in education, shown in Table 7.2. On three of these six items, blacks are strongly supportive of affirmative action, while on the other three most blacks oppose affirmative action practices. Again, the specific wording of the items greatly influences support. Blacks overwhelmingly favor affirmative action when no quotas are involved (the first item), when black applicants are qualified and no mention is made of qualified whites being turned away (the second item), and when only vague reference is made to "special consideration to the best minority students" (the third item). Most blacks reject affirmative action when it is specifically noted that qualified whites would be turned away (the fourth and fifth items) and when it is assumed that the black applicant is unqualified (the sixth item). Even under the latter conditions, however, a sizable minority of blacks still supports affirmative action.

Again, whites are less supportive of these affirmative action practices, though most do support affirmative action as described in the first and second questions. Only about one white in three endorses giving "special consideration to the best minority applicants" or reserving places for qualified minorities when some qualified whites must be turned away. Even fewer whites favor the affirmative action procedures pinpointed in the last two items: choosing a black over a better qualified white and lowering standards for unqualified blacks. On these items, as on the earlier questions on affirmative action in the workplace, blacks are 20 to 30 percent more supportive of affirmative action than are whites.

Explaining attitudes on affirmative action

The key to understanding public opinion on affirmative action has been said to lie in the distinction between compensatory action and preferential treatment (Lipset and Schneider, 1980). Thus understood, compensatory action involves "measures to help disadvantaged groups catch up to the standards of competition set by the larger society," while preferential treatment involves "suspending those standards and admitting or hiring members of disadvantaged groups who do not meet the same standards as white males" (41). Relatively few whites, Lipset and Schneider argue, object to compensatory action, but most renounce policies involving preferential treatment. In other words, most whites are said to be willing "to provide minorities with a starting point on the inside lane" but still believe that "ultimately the race must go to the swift" (Sackett, 1980: 22).

We doubt that the distinction between compensatory action and preferential treatment holds the key to understanding attitudes toward affirmative action, especially since compensatory action is a form of preferential treatment and preferential treatment is a type of compensatory action. The picture that emerges from our data is much more complex than Lipset and Schneider's distinction. The main elements in this picture are as follows.

First, both whites and blacks support programs designed to allow minorities to "get ahead," to deliver training, to provide equal opportunities, and to extend affirmative action as long as no quotas are involved. Second, blacks but not whites favor general "affirmative action" strategies even when quotas are not explicitly disavowed. Third, blacks tend to be divided and whites to be negative about affirmative action policies that pass over

Table 7.3. *Perceptions of the consequences of affirmative action, blacks and whites, 1978 and 1980 (in %)*

	Blacks	Whites
Without affirmative action blacks would not get a fair shake		
Agree	74	26
Without quotas there will be a slowing of hiring of blacks		
Agree	75	45
Unsure	11	13
Without affirmative action, women and minorities will fail to get their fair share of jobs and education		
Agree	73	42
Unsure	16	19
Affirmative action is bound to lead to reverse discrimination against white men		
Agree	20	40
Unsure	20	15
Preferential treatment (setting aside places to hire qualified blacks) is fair		
Agree	42	35

Notes and Sources: Question wordings and sources (in order): "Unless quotas are used, blacks and other minorities just won't get a fair shake" (Harris, 1978). "In business and education, without set quotas there will be a slowing down in the hiring of blacks and other minorities" (Harris, 1978). "If there are no affirmative action programs helping women and minorities in employment and education, then these groups will continue to fail to get their share of jobs and higher education, thereby continuing past discrimination in the future" (Harris, 1978). "Once affirmative action programs for women and minorities are started, the result is bound to be reverse discrimination against white men" (Harris, 1978). "Do you personally feel that such preferential treatment [for blacks] is/would be: fair, unfair" (Kluegel and Smith, 1980).

equally or more qualified whites. Finally, most members of both races oppose preferential hiring when such preferences run afoul of the principle of merit.

More generally, supporters of affirmative action consider it necessary in order to make up for past racism and to ensure that blacks have a fair chance at jobs and higher educational opportunities. Opponents argue that because affirmative action inappropriately focuses on group characteristics rather than individual qualifications, it may lead to people being admitted to college or being hired even though they are less qualified than others who are passed over. These rationales for supporting or opposing affirmative action are reflected in Table 7.3, which summarizes what blacks and whites think would happen in the absence of affirmative action.

Three blacks in four say that affirmative action is needed to ensure that blacks get "a fair shake" and, more concretely, to forestall a dropoff in black access to jobs and education. Only one black in five sees affirmative action as inevitably leading to reverse discrimination against white males.

Only 42 percent of blacks consider preferential treatment – the aspect of affirmative action whites find most objectionable – fair. The enthusiasm blacks display for affirmative action, then, is clearly not premised on endorsement of preferential treatment. This enthusiasm, in fact, can be said to hold in spite of blacks' qualms about the principle of preferential treatment. Obviously, for most blacks affirmative action is not a synonym for preferential treatment.

In stark contrast to most blacks, most whites do not agree that without affirmative action blacks would be denied a "fair shake" or that blacks' opportunities for schooling and jobs would be adversely affected. This view is, of course, quite consistent with the widespread perception among whites, which we initially encountered in Chapter 3, that racial discrimination is not really much of a problem in this country. Beyond this, many whites consider affirmative action undesirable as well as unnecessary: 40 percent of whites believe that it leads to reverse discrimination, twice as high as the black proportion, and most whites, like most blacks, do not believe that preferential treatment is fair.

On the other hand, when we add to the whites who support affirmative action on the first three items in Table 7.3 the fairly substantial number who are uncertain, we see that most whites at least are open to the possibility that progress toward racial equality would be slower in the absence of affirmative action.

These data suggest that in addition to assessing the effects of affirmative action differently, many blacks and whites actually define affirmative action differently. Most blacks concede that preferential treatment is unfair, but still support the other components of affirmative action. Most whites also consider preferential treatment unfair, but whites are more likely than blacks to regard preferential treatment as a central component of affirmative action. Large minorities of whites support affirmative action only when they are assured that no quota system or preferential treatment is involved.

Many whites simply do not see any need for affirmative action since they do not perceive that much racial discrimination exists. This denial, compounded by the tendency to view themselves as potential victims of "reverse discrimination," goes far toward explaining why so many whites bitterly oppose affirmative action. On the other hand, blacks, most of whom have personally experienced discrimination, are more likely to consider affirmative action a necessary tool for black advancement.

Improving blacks' living standards

The incidence of poverty is much higher among blacks than whites. As recently as 1960, more than half of all black Americans were living below the poverty line. In the early 1960s, large proportions of blacks did not have in their homes such basic amenities as a washing machine (39 percent), a telephone (29 percent), hot water (14 percent), or an inside toilet (11 percent). Among southern rural blacks, fewer than 60 percent had indoor plumbing or central heat (Brink and Harris, 1964).

Blacks' living standards have improved markedly since the early 1960s, but for many blacks poverty is a current reality or a living memory, not merely an abstract social issue. Thus, improving the standard of living of poor people in general and of blacks in particular is an especially salient goal for blacks.

Two distinct types of survey questions can help us understand how blacks assess programs designed to raise people out of poverty. One type focuses on programs specifically for blacks, and the other on programs for poor people in general.

Programs for blacks

Although questions about affirmative action typically describe a particular program that might give blacks an extra boost in hiring or college admissions, another set of questions taps into affect for the generic idea of special help for blacks. By their very nature, such questions are inexplicit about exactly what is being proposed. For example, an ABC News/*Washington Post* item asks whether "because of past discrimination, blacks who need it should get some help from the government that white people in similar economic circumstances don't get." What does "some help" mean? Job training programs? Income supplements? Job quotas? Nothing concrete is specified.

Similarly, ANES respondents are asked whether "government in Washington should make every possible effort to improve the social and economic position of blacks and other minority groups, even if it means giving them preferential treatment." Here again, the exact programs that would help blacks are not mentioned. A final example comes from the GSS, in which, after being told that the nation faces many problems, none of which can be solved easily or inexpensively, respondents are asked whether too much money, too little, or about the right amount is currently being spent in several different areas, including "improving the condition of blacks."

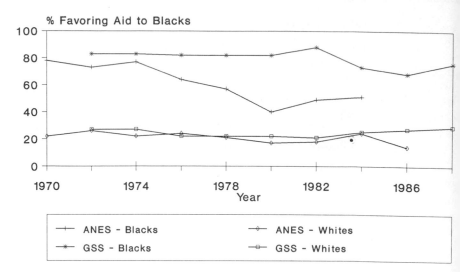

Figure 7.3. Support for aid to blacks, blacks and whites, 1970–1987.
Sources: American National Election Study and General Social Survey datasets.

How are blacks aligned on the general issue of programs intended expressly for the betterment of blacks? The answer might seem obvious, since for many blacks these questions involve a considerable element of self-interest. Moreover, even in cases where immediate, personal self-interest does not come into play, as it may not among middle-class blacks, responses to questions like these seem likely to tap into the general dimensions of racial identification and affect toward blacks. On the other hand, all these questions call for government action of one kind or another. To the extent that blacks, like many whites, are uncertain about or opposed to governmental intervention into "market" processes, we should anticipate hesitancy about these programs. The "ethic of self-reliance" holds sway in a large segment of American society (see, e.g., Sniderman and Brody, 1977). In Chapter 5 we found indications that whites are more steeped in this ethic than blacks are, but it is still true that many blacks view people as masters of their own fate and have real qualms about government "interference."

Indeed, as Figures 7.3 and 7.4 show, blacks are divided on the general issue of government programs for blacks. For example, only about half agree that government should make every effort to improve the social and economic position of blacks. There is an even closer balance between support and opposition on the issue of whether blacks should get help that

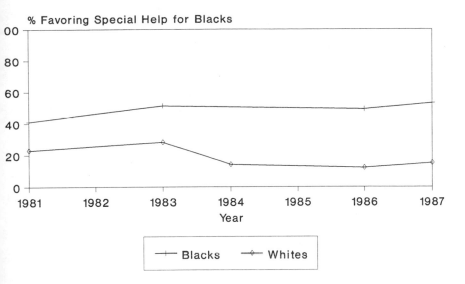

Figure 7.4. Support for special help for blacks, 1981–1987
Sources: February–March 1981 ABC News/*Washington Post* nationwide survey and January 1986 ABC News/*Washington Post* nationwide survey of blacks; August 1983 ABC News/*Washington Post* nationwide survey, summarized by Bunzel (1986: 48). Question wording: "I am going to read you a few statements and for each I'd like you to tell me whether you tend to agree to disagree with it, or if perhaps you have no opinion about the statement . . . 'Because of past discrimination, blacks who need it should get some help from the government that white people in similar economic circumstances don't get.' "

would not be available to whites in similar economic circumstances.[9] But again, slight changes in question wording can dramatically affect responses. For example, in the preelection wave of the 1984 NBES, 59 percent of the black respondents weighed in on the "should" side of a seven-point scale asking: "Some feel that government in Washington should make every possible effort to improve the social and economic position of blacks and other minority groups . . . Others feel that the government should not make any special effort to help minorities. And of course other people have opinions somewhere in between. Where would you place yourself on the scale or haven't you thought much about it?" Fourteen percent were at the neutral point and 26 percent on the side of "minority groups should help themselves," with 2 percent undecided. This item yielded a clear majority, but not a consensus, in favor of special government help. But in the postelection wave of the survey, when only four responses were provided for the statement that "The government in Washington should make every possible effort to improve the social and economic position of blacks and other minority groups," 85 percent agreed and only 12 percent disagreed. Moments later, 24 percent agreed that "The government should not make any special effort to help blacks and other minorities because they should help themselves."

Despite these anomalies, it appears that support for these general initiatives has eroded among blacks since the early 1970s, when three-quarters or more favored such programs. Perhaps the attitudes of the early 1970s still reflected the context established by the civil rights struggles of the 1960s, when federal intervention was crucial to securing equal rights. By contrast, the declining significance of racial issues in the minds of many Americans, the "crisis of confidence" in political leadership, and the so-called Reagan revolution have apparently combined to diminish belief in the need for and efficacy of government programs in general, and especially programs targeted for blacks. Among blacks in particular, the inability of government to erase de facto segregation and the anti-civil rights position of the Reagan administration seem to have shaken faith in the benificence of the federal government.

Another variant of the question about government aid to blacks also evokes majority support from blacks. Throughout the 1970s, more than eight blacks in ten told GSS interviewers that too little was being spent to improve the condition of blacks, broadly paralleling the trend documented in the ANES question on government aid for minorities. This support has declined in recent years, but a clear majority of blacks still accepts the general proposition that not enough is being done to help blacks.

What, then, can we conclude about blacks' commitment to the concept of special government programs for blacks? For one thing, this commitment seems to have declined since the 1970s. In addition, acceptance of the concept of special assistance for blacks is less widespread among blacks than support for some specific affirmative action policies. This pattern of lesser agreement on generalities than on specifics reverses the classic pattern to which we referred earlier, but it is not all that difficult to understand. Given the vagueness of the survey items we have just considered, there is ample room for different respondents to interpret a given question differently. For example, "making every effort to improve the condition of blacks" could, for one respondent, suggest a job training program, while for another respondent it conjures up images of job quotas or special preferences. Over time, the meanings that respondents read into such questions probably have changed, accounting for the apparent decline in commitment to special government programs for blacks. Early on, general questions about government involvement may have been interpreted as focusing on civil rights legislation, while more recently the connotation of such questions may have shifted to the more controversial aspects of affirmative action programs.

As can also be seen in Figure 7.3, white support for specially targeted programs for blacks predictably falls well below the black support line. It is also true that white opinion varies less from question to question. No matter how a question is phrased, about one white in four favors increased spending or special help for blacks. Unlike blacks, whose responses to these questions have undergone change over the last fifteen years, whites' attitudes have been stable. Few whites favored such programs in the early 1970s and few whites favor them today. However, because of the downturn in black support, the black-white differential in these opinions is now substantially narrower than it was during the early and mid-1970s.

Programs for the poor

The other pertinent type of question focuses on government assistance to the poor, without reference to race or ethnicity. Americans hold notoriously negative attitudes toward welfare and welfare recipients (see, e.g., Feagin, 1975), and over the years welfare has been the one program area for which the general public has consistently said that too much is being spent. However, relatively little is known about blacks' attitudes toward welfare and other programs for the poor. It seems logical to expect blacks to be less negative toward welfare programs than whites are, but is this actually the case?

GSS respondents have regularly been asked whether too little, too much, or about the right amount is being spent on welfare.[10] Blacks are divided on this issue, with only about half responding "too little" (see Figure 7.5). No real trend toward either greater or lesser support for welfare spending is evident among blacks, though support appeared to peak twice, first in the early 1970s and again in the early 1980s. The small number of blacks in most of these surveys means that yearly fluctuations must be interpreted cautiously, but the stability evident in these estimates suggests that about half of blacks continue to believe that more should be spent on welfare programs. Relatively few blacks, around 20 percent, believe that too much is being spent on welfare.

Whites' attitudes toward welfare spending are altogether different. Only about 15 percent agree that too little is being spent, and about half consider the opposite to be the case. In recent years, however, the latter proportion has fallen to the mid-40 percent range.

Thus, blacks are much more likely to favor increased welfare spending, and whites to advocate welfare cuts. Even so, the black-white difference

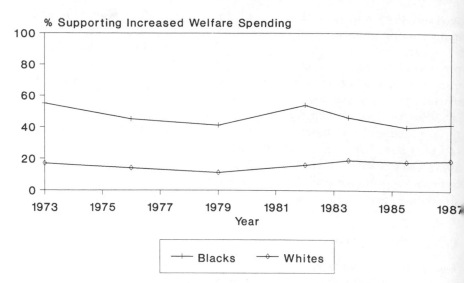

Figure 7.5. Support for welfare spending, blacks and whites, 1972–1987
Sources: General Social Surveys, 1982–7; Welch and Combs (1985). Except for 1982, when the GSS oversampled blacks, we combined data for various years in order to increase the stability of these estimates. Question wording: "We are faced with many problems in this country, none of which can be solved easily or inexpensively. I'm going to name some of these problems, and for each one I'd like you to tell me whether you think we're spending too much money on it, too little money, or about the right amount." ". . . Welfare . . ."

should not be overstated. For one thing, some blacks are critical of welfare spending, and some whites consider current welfare spending levels insufficient. Moreover, even within the black community, where support for welfare spending is relatively high, only about half favor spending more.

Why are blacks more supportive than whites of welfare spending? An obvious possibility is that this difference reflects a more widespread belief among blacks that welfare programs produce positive results. However, this is not true, for in Table 7.4 we see that blacks and whites hold similar views about the consequences of welfare. Large majorities of both races believe that being on welfare provides a disincentive for working, and most blacks and whites maintain that welfare encourages young women to have babies before they are married.[11] Most whites, but fewer blacks, also believe that welfare discourages women from marrying the fathers of their children. Although whites are somewhat more likely than blacks to hold each of these negative views about the consequences of welfare, this difference is far too small to account for the black-white gap in support for welfare spending.

Table 7.4. *Beliefs in negative features of welfare, blacks and whites, 1986*

	Percentage accepting belief	
	Blacks	Whites
Believes that welfare encourages people to work less	71	86
Believes welfare encourages young women to have babies before they are married	51	61
Believes welfare mainly discourages people from improving themselves[a]	47	
Believes welfare discourages women from marrying the father of their children	44	59
Disagrees that welfare helps keep people's marriages together	42	40
Disagrees that welfare helps people get on their feet	14	17

Notes and Sources: [a] This item is from the January 1986 ABC News/ *Washington Post* nationwide survey of blacks. The item wording is: "Do you think government welfare programs mainly discourage people from improving themselves, or do you think they mainly help people until they begin to stand on their own?" The remainder of the items are from the 1986 GSS. The question reads: "Here are some opinions other people have expressed about welfare. For each of the following statements, please tell me whether you strongly agree, agree, disagree, or strongly disagree with it: 1. Makes people work less than they would if there wasn't a welfare system; 2. Helps people get on their feet when facing difficult situations such as unemployment, a divorce or a death in the family; 3. Encourages young women to have babies before marriage; 4. Helps keep people's marriages together in times of financial problems; 5. Helps to prevent hunger and starvation; 6. Discourages young women who get pregnant from marrying the father of the child."

So, even though blacks and whites hold reasonably similar views of the consequences of welfare, blacks are more supportive of welfare spending. Another possible reason for the racial gap in support for welfare is that in the minds of many whites, welfare is a program for blacks. Black-white differences in support for welfare, in this context, can be understood in part as reflections of differential sympathy for the plight of blacks. Another relevant consideration, we suspect, is that whites are even more steeped in the ethic of self-reliance than blacks are, and welfare programs are sometimes seen as a direct affront by those who believe that people arise from poverty only by pulling themselves up by their bootstraps. Finally, it bears repeating that a much larger proportion of blacks than whites falls below the poverty line and must therefore rely on welfare. In this context, it seems especially important to probe the socioeconomic bases of welfare attitudes, as we shall do in Chapter 8.

The preceding questions focus on the "welfare" program. We have already seen that in soliciting attitudes about controversial policies and programs, question wording is key, and the area of social services is certainly no exception. Support is much greater for "helping the poor" than it is for increased spending on welfare (T. Smith, 1987). Since 1984, the GSS has asked not only about welfare spending but also about "assistance to the poor." When the latter wording is used, an overwhelming majority of blacks (80 to 86 percent in four surveys) and a substantial majority of whites (57 to 62 percent) agree that too little is being spent; only a small minority (a mere trace among blacks and 10 percent of whites) give the "too much" response.

In considering this whole set of responses to questions about spending to improve the living conditions of those who are poor and/or black, we see that blacks are only slightly more unified in their beliefs than are whites. Blacks are less likely to favor cutting back welfare programs and more likely to support programs for improving the living conditions of blacks, but they are far from unanimous in these views. The extent to which these differences reflect social, economic, and demographic cleavages within the black community is an issue to be addressed in the next chapter.

Conclusion

Blacks are by no means homogeneous in their views of appropriate policy choices. If we stereotype blacks as overwhelmingly favoring busing, welfare, and special help for blacks, we greatly exaggerate the degree of consensus that prevails within the black community. Blacks, like whites, are sharply divided on these issues.

The attitudes of blacks and whites are similar in another way as well, since both are much more united in their support of the goal of racial equality than of specific means of achieving this goal. For example, almost every black wants integrated schools, but only about half favor busing. Almost all blacks favor equality of job opportunities, but blacks are sharply divided over affirmative action. And, although it seems likely that almost all blacks want everyone to have an adequate standard of living, there is fairly widespread opposition to increasing government spending to help improve the living conditions of blacks or to increase welfare benefits. Thus, just as is true of whites, among blacks there is a disjuncture between support for general goals and support for government actions to achieve these goals.

A further point of similarity between blacks' and whites' policy views can be seen in opinion changes over the past twenty years. Like whites, blacks have become less enthusiastic about some kinds of government activism in pursuance of the goals of equality, though they have become more committed to the policy goals per se.

Although we have been emphasizing similarities between blacks and whites, we should not lose sight of the differences that still divide the races on policy issues. Blacks, though varied in their attitudes toward busing, are more supportive than whites are. Blacks, though opposing some aspects of affirmative action, are generally more favorable than whites are. And blacks, though far from unanimous in their support for special aid for blacks and increased welfare spending, are more supportive of these strategies than whites are. In general, on issues where government action is contemplated, blacks as a group are more activist than whites. This greater activism is quite consistent with the differences between blacks and whites sketched in Chapter 5. That is, blacks are considerably more likely than whites to believe that a major reason why blacks have unequal standing in American society is white racism and discrimination. Given these attributions, it is not surprising that blacks are more favorably disposed to government action. If racial inequality is caused in large part by societal forces external to and beyond the control of the black community, then government action is necessary.

We have now sketched the broad outlines of blacks' policy attitudes and highlighted the foremost changes in these attitudes that have developed over the last quarter century. But to complete our picture of black attitudes we need to understand the forces that shape opinion differences within the black community. Accordingly, in Chapter 8 we seek to determine whether disagreements among blacks on policy matters stem from social and economic cleavages and from differing conceptions of racial inequality and its sources.

Notes

1. To be sure, when asked whether a fairer economic system would be one in which "people with more ability would earn higher salaries" or one in which "all people would earn about the same," the black leaders proved to be less supportive than any other group of basing earnings on ability (Verba and Orren, 1985: 72). However, there was only a small margin between the black leaders and the leaders of feminist and college student organizations; because these were three of the four most liberal groups surveyed, it would seem that what distinguished the black leaders on this question was primarily liberalism rather than race. Indeed, the black leaders were notably inegalitarian with regard to income redistribution; their satisfaction with the current occupational distribution of income was matched only by that of the two most conservative groups sampled, business leaders and leaders of the Republican Party (Verba and Orren, 1985: 163).
2. There is considerable overlap between these issues and those raised in the debate over "symbolic racism." As Sniderman and Tetlock (1986a: 184) note, "Symbolic racism may take precisely the form of supporting the principle of equality, but resisting implementation of it."

3. Of course, in the days of legalized school segregation, many black children were bused away from nearby schools to those farther away in order to maintain segregation.
4. The trend line has fluctuated from around 40 percent to 60 percent over the years. This probably reflects some true opinion change intermixed with question wording differences, different modes of administering surveys (for example, by telephone or in person), and sampling error (which looms large as a consequence of the small number of black respondents in general population surveys).
5. With no middle-response alternative offered, the 1984 NBES showed blacks evenly split, with 48 percent agreeing and 48 percent disagreeing that "Racial integration of schools is so important that it justifies busing children outside of their neighborhoods."
6. In 1980 Gallup, whose question (which inquires whether respondents favor or oppose "busing children to achieve a better racial balance in the schools") is similar to the GSS item, achieved a similar reading to those the GSS was obtaining at the time: roughly 17 percent white support for busing. Over the same period, the ANES tracked little or no change, from 9 percent in 1972 to 12 percent in 1984.
7. The stem of this question actually contains 101 words, upholding the tradition that survey questions about the Supreme Court's affirmative action decisions are generally complex. Harris polls in particular tend to ask long, complicated questions describing a case and laying out the issues. Providing background information may seem useful, since most people know little or nothing about a given Supreme Court decision. However, long, complicated questions tend to confuse respondents (see Converse and Presser, 1986: 11–13; 24–5).

   Another extremely complicated Harris item on affirmative action related to the Court's 1978 *Bakke* decision (Louis Harris and Associates, 1978). The 171-word stem of this item informed respondents that the Court had held against quotas and in favor of special consideration for members of disadvantaged races: "Recently, the U.S. Supreme Court handed down a decision in the Bakke case. A white man, Alan Bakke, claimed that he was refused admission to a University of California medical school because the school automatically set aside 16 out of 100 places in the freshman class for non-whites, even if on their tests the non-whites scored below whites who applied. The Supreme Court decided that Bakke had been the victim of reverse discrimination and should be admitted to the medical school. The Court also decided that such rigid quotas as setting aside 16 out of 100 places for non-whites are not proper or legal. At the same time, the Court made clear that students from less advantaged races may be given special consideration on racial grounds. In effect, then, the Supreme Court decided that strict quotas are out, and affirmative action could be used to make up for past discrimination against racial minorities. All in all, do you personally favor or oppose the U.S. Supreme Court decision in the Bakke case?"

   Seventy-seven percent of the white respondents and 29 percent of the black respondents said they favored the decision, with 23 percent of the blacks and 11 percent of the whites indicating uncertainty. Unfortunately, it is not apparent which aspect of the Bakke decision, as summarized in the Harris question, would have struck a particular respondent as more salient – the Court's rejection of strict quotas or its general endorsement of affirmative action. In light of the other evidence we have analyzed on whites' attitudes toward affirmative action, it seems likely that whites were indicating support for the overturning of quotas. However, black support for quotas has never been strong, so it is difficult to know the basis of the overwhelmingly negative black reaction to the question.
8. In the facts of the specific case, it appeared that the white woman candidate had a lower test score than the leading white male candidate only because of a more subjective oral interview conducted by a panel of men who had never hired a woman for a professional position. We doubt that this can be translated into a more general rule about hiring the "less qualified" under other circumstances.
9. The same ambivalence surfaced in the 1984 NBES, in which 59 percent of the respondents used the supportive end of a seven-point scale (points 1, 2, or 3) and 26 percent the nonsupportive end (points 5, 6, or 7) to answer the same question about government programs for blacks.

10. In the sequence of items using this stem ("We are faced with many problems in this country, none of which can be solved easily or inexpensively. I am going to name some of these problems and for each one I'd like you to tell me whether you think we're spending too much money on it, too little money, or about the right amount."), the item on blacks is eighth and welfare is eleventh.

11. Although the notion that welfare encourages young unmarried women to have babies is fairly popular (Murray, 1984), it does not actually appear to be accurate (see, e.g., Ellwood and Bane, 1984; Placek and Hendershot, 1974; Polgar and Hiday, 1974; Presser and Salsberg, 1975). There is, however, some evidence that welfare increases the probability that teen-age mothers will form their own households (Ellwood and Bane, 1984).

8

The sources of blacks' views of remedies for racial inequality

Although blacks are far from unanimous in their policy views, they are more supportive than whites are of policies aimed at helping minorities and the poor. In this chapter we try to isolate factors that lead some blacks to support these policies and others to oppose them. We test the expectation that those who are least able to fend for themselves are the most likely to advocate government help. Our analyses go well beyond this, however. No previous work, to our knowledge, has tested models of blacks' policy preferences based not only on their social and economic characteristics but also on their perceptions of and explanations for racial inequality.[1] These perceptions and attributions play central roles in our attempt to understand differing policy preferences.

Predicting policy views

The predictive model employed in Chapter 6, which includes indicators of socioeconomic status, gender, age, and interracial friendship, along with perceptions of discrimination, is now augmented to include explanations of racial inequality as determinants of more favorable orientations toward remedial action by government. We know of no prior research bearing directly on this topic, yet it seems only logical to suppose that before one would advocate government programs to deal with some problem one would have to perceive that a serious problem exists.

We also expect causal attributions to affect policy views. Blacks who attribute racial inequality to shortcomings of blacks themselves, that is, to lack of willpower, effort, ability, or motivation, are expected to be unenthusiastic about affirmative action and special government programs for blacks. By the same token, we expect those who attribute inequality to situational factors such as white racism or the lack of educational opportunity to favor affirmative action and other forms of special help for blacks.

Although we know of no prior research linking blacks' explanations of either poverty or racial inequality to their policy preferences, evidence on whites is available. For Bay Area whites, Apostle et al. (1983) identify patterns close to those we have just outlined. Whites who attribute racial inequality to blacks' dispositional traits, such as not trying hard enough or genetic inferiority, are much less supportive of affirmative action and other compensatory programs than are those who attribute racial inequality to white racism. Bay Area whites who attribute racial inequality to situational factors, such as the legacy of slavery, approve of 1960s-type civil rights policies, though even they are not favorably disposed toward affirmative action. Similar findings have been reported by Sniderman with Hagen (1985), who observe that whites who consider blacks primarily responsible for their own problems are less supportive of aid to minorities and guaranteed jobs than are whites who consider blacks victims of current white racism or historical discrimination. Also consistent with these findings is Kluegel and Smith's (1983) multivariate analysis of national survey data, which reveals a link between whites' perceptions of the opportunities open to blacks and their views of affirmative action.[2]

These findings are based on whites alone. But we have no reason to doubt that while blacks are more likely than whites to attribute racial inequalities to discrimination and racism, the same link between such perceptions and support for ameliorative action that exists for whites exists also for blacks. Those who attribute racial inequality to the failures of blacks should be unlikely to favor government action to remedy that inequality. Those who attribute racial inequality to forces over which blacks have little or no control, on the other hand, should have greater cause to favor government action to help solve the problem. Consistent with this idea, Fine (1990) shows that among both blacks and whites, individualistic values are associated with opposition to government programs that could aid many blacks. Commitment to the norms of equal opportunity increases support for such programs.

We hold parallel expectations concerning support for policies aimed not at blacks in particular but more generally at the poor. Blacks are more likely than whites to agree with the idea that society has a responsibility to help people succeed (Jaynes and Williams, 1989: 212–13; Kendrick, 1988), presumably because blacks have a different, more situational, understanding of the sources of poverty.

More generally, the individualistic ethic of hard work, competition, and individual responsibility for failure promotes anti-welfare sentiments. Welfare recipients are widely viewed as immoral: unwilling to work, lazy, sexually promiscuous, dishonest, and wasteful (Feagin, 1975: 119).

We expect these relationships to run in the same direction for whites as for blacks, but even more strongly. If we are correct, even those blacks who see racial inequality as in large measure the fault of blacks should be more sympathetic to providing special help for blacks than are whites with similar attributional mindsets. Accordingly, we expect support for such programs to vary more among whites, and to be more closely tied to explanations of why racial inequality continues to exist. Highly suggestive in this regard are findings reported by Merriman and Parent (1982), who observe that among whites, being wedded to the market mentality leads to far lower levels of support for policies like fair job treatment, school integration, busing, and aid to minorities.

Data and analysis

As in Chapters 4 and 6, we test these expectations using data from the 1981 and 1986 ABC News/*Washington Post* surveys. However, these surveys contain too few policy opinion items to meet our needs. In fact, the 1981 survey includes only one relevant policy item, which asked whether, because of past discrimination, blacks who need it should get some help from the government that whites do not receive. In this chapter, we analyze whites' responses to this item and blacks' responses to its exact counterpart in the 1986 survey. Respondents in the 1986 survey were also asked whether they favored school busing and whether welfare programs mainly discourage people from improving themselves or are of benefit to recipients.[3] This is the sum and substance of the pertinent policy items in the ABC News/*Washington Post* polls.

To supplement these items, we introduce several policy questions from the GSS (Davis and Smith, 1987). These items expand the range of policy opinions we are able to explore, but their utility is limited by the rather small number of black respondents and by the absence from the GSS interviews of questions about interracial friendship, receipt of government aid, and perceptions of racism.[4] Moreover, some of the GSS policy questions were asked only of half-samples in certain years and were not asked at all in others.

We employ GSS data only from 1985 and 1986, since in recent years the items tapping explanations of racial inequality, which are central to our analysis, have been asked only in those two surveys. Unfortunately, when GSS drew a black oversample in 1987, the questions concerning explanations for racial inequality were not asked.

One GSS policy item concerns blacks in particular, focusing on government spending to improve the standard of living of blacks. Two other items measure support for helping the poor, including spending for welfare and spending to provide assistance to the poor.[5]

Table 8.1. *Predictors used in analyses based on the 1985–1986 GSS*

Predictor	Description
Demographic characteristics	
Gender	0 = male, 1 = female.
Age, in years	Number of years since year of birth.
Interracial friendship	No measure available.
Socioeconomic status	
Family income, in thousands	In which of these groups did your total family income, from all sources, fall last year before taxes?
Homeowner	Do you own your (home/apartment), pay rent, or what? 1 = own, 0 = other.
Subjective middle-class member	If you were asked to use one of four names for your social class, which would you say you belong in: the lower class, the working class, the middle class, or the upper class? 0 = working or lower, 1 = middle or upper.
Unemployed	Last week were you working full time, part time, going to school, keeping house, or what? 1 = unemployed, laid off, or looking for work, 0 = other.
Government aid recipient	No measure available for both years.
Perceived economic pressure	We are interested in how people are getting along financially these days. So far as you and your family are concerned, would you say that you are pretty well satisfied with your present financial situation [1], more or less satisfied [2], or not satisfied at all [3]?
Years of education	What is the highest grade in elementary school or high school you finished and got credit for? Did you complete one or more years of college for credit – not including schooling such as business college, technical or vocational school? Responses coded in years.
Perceptions of racism	No measures available.
Explanations of racial inequality	On average, blacks have worse jobs, income and housing than white people. Do you think these differences are . . . mainly due to discrimination? Because most blacks don't have the chance for education that it takes to rise out of poverty? Because most blacks have less inborn ability to learn? Because most blacks just don't have the motivation or willpower to pull themselves up out of poverty? Each item was coded 0 = no, 1 = yes. Based on these four items, two additive scales were created, the first to measure situational attributions, the second to measure dispositional attributions.

The GSS-based measures of demographic characteristics, socioeconomic status, perceived racism, and explanations of racial inequality are summarized in Table 8.1. Although no indicators of interracial friendship, receipt of government assistance, or perceptions of racism are available in these

surveys, the full range of measures of demographic characteristics, socioeconomic standing, and attributions for inequality are available for the
years in question.

We will first examine views of policies intended to improve the condition
of blacks, and then views of policies providing assistance to the poor,
irrespective of race.

Policies toward blacks

Patterns among blacks

Does the considerable disagreement among blacks over busing conform to
socioeconomic differences or other identifiable cleavages? Table 8.2 summarizes our analyses of the sources of support for busing among blacks,
based on a question asking whether busing is acceptable as a last resort to
achieve school integration. Not a single socioeconomic variable significantly affects blacks' views of busing. Thus, the great variety in blacks'
opinions about busing is not aligned according to socioeconomic status.

Table 8.2. *Projected probability of supporting busing and special aid to blacks, blacks,
1986*

Personal characteristics	Projected probability	
	Busing	Aid
Baseline	.57	.61
Male	.68	
Not a homeowner		.48
Self-discrimination = 0	.53	
Self-discrimination = 4	.69	
Black discrimination = 0	.71	.49
Black discrimination = 6	.49	.67
Dispositional attributions = 0		.52
Dispositional attributions = 3		.76
Situational attributions = 0		.29
Situational attributions = 3		.76
In poverty	.50	.54
Comfortable	.59	.47

Notes: N = 484 and 467, respectively. These projections are based on Table A.8.
Source: January 1986 ABC News/*Washington Post* nationwide survey of blacks.

Blacks' support for busing is significantly related to three of the predictors in the model. One of these is gender, with women being less likely than men to favor busing. This effect translates into a difference of 11 percentage points between probability that the "baseline" black – a woman – would express support for busing and the probability of support by her exact male counterpart.[6] While this difference may appear to be part of a broader gender gap on policy issues, in fact it is the only instance of a significant male-female difference on policy issues we will observe among blacks. How, then, can we account for this difference? Our answer must be speculative, but perhaps women, who are main providers of care and nurturance to children, are more inclined to think of the potential danger and discomfort to small children of busing them considerable distances to achieve a broad policy goal. Moreover, to the extent that busing to enroll black children in middle class white schools erodes black children's sense of self-esteem (see Chapter 7), women may be more sensitive than men to this negative impact.

The remaining significant predictors of blacks' support for busing are perceptions of discrimination against oneself and against blacks as a group. Blacks who perceive greater discrimination against themselves are more likely to favor busing, but those who perceive more widespread discrimination against blacks in general are less likely to favor busing. A black with all the "baseline" characteristics except a minimum score (0) on perceived discrimination against herself has a score 16 points lower than an otherwise-identical black who perceives maximum discrimination (4) against herself. The difference based on perceptions of discrimination against blacks is even greater. A "baseline" black who perceives no discrimination at all against blacks (who would, as we conceded in Chapter 6, be fairly unusual) would have a 71 percent likelihood of supporting busing, compared to a 49 percent likelihood if the same black perceived a maximum amount of discrimination.

Contrary to our expectations, then, perceived discrimination against oneself and against blacks in general work against one another in their effects on support for school busing. Perceptions of greater discrimination against oneself enhance support for busing, but perceptions of more widespread discrimination against blacks as a group diminish such support. It is not obvious why the latter effect occurs, but we suspect that part of the reason may be that blacks who perceive pervasive white prejudice and discrimination see busing as serving no useful purpose and, even worse, as forcing vulnerable black children into direct confrontations with hostile whites.

Because blacks' support for busing is not significantly linked to any measure of socioeconomic status, we would not anticipate a very broad gap between poverty-stricken and more economically comfortable blacks in support for busing. According to our projections, socioeconomic factors do have a perceptible cumulative effect, with more affluent blacks being more supportive of busing. This difference is too large to be casually dismissed, but it is certainly not so large that socioeconomic status would be viewed as a fundamental determinant of blacks' opinions about busing.

We now turn from support for the specific policy of busing to more generic support for government aid for blacks. Respondents in the ABC News/*Washington Post* survey were asked whether government should give special aid to blacks for the purpose of raising their living standards. This item says little about support for specific policies, but it does tap one's general orientation toward government aid to blacks.

Socioeconomic differences are, with a single exception, unrelated to blacks' views of government aid to blacks. The exception is that home owners are significantly more likely to favor such aid.

Blacks who perceive more widespread discrimination against blacks as a group are more supportive of special government aid to blacks. For an otherwise typical black who perceives no discrimination at all against blacks, the projected probability of favoring special government help is 18 points less than the probability for an identical black who perceives discrimination as pervasive. This is hardly unexpected, nor is it surprising that those who attribute racial inequality to discrimination and other situational factors are likely to endorse government aid for blacks. The chances are less than three in ten that a black with the lowest score on the situational attribution scale would favor special aid for blacks, but more than three in four that a black with the highest score on the same scale would do so.

More surprisingly, the belief that racial inequality is caused by failures of blacks themselves is also associated with support for special government assistance to blacks. Being willing to place the blame for racial inequality, even on blacks themselves, leads to greater support for government aid to blacks. So high scores on both the dispositional and the situational attribution scales are associated with support for special government aid to blacks, though presumably for different reasons. Those who accept situational explanations of inequality probably view special government assistance for blacks as a means of restructuring the situation, while those who espouse dispositional explanations presumably see special assistance as necessary if blacks are to overcome their purported lack of motivation or ability.[7] The sizable magnitude of these attribution-based differences testifies to the importance of attributions in understanding blacks' policy preferences.

Overall, then, blacks' perceptions of racial discrimination and their attributions for racial inequality appear to have a powerful effect on their opinions about school busing and government aid to blacks. It follows that in order to understand where blacks stand on policy issues that directly affect them, we need to take into account their perceptions of how widespread racial discrimination is and their understandings of why racial inequality continues to exist in this country.

On the other hand, socioeconomic differences provide only an indirect basis for understanding blacks' differing preferences on these issues, a finding that lends support to earlier failures to isolate strong links between socioeconomic status and blacks' support for policies to aid blacks (Seltzer and Smith, 1985; Welch and Combs, 1985; Welch and Foster, 1987). Only occasionally, we have seen, do status variables directly influence blacks' opinions on these policies. But we must also recognize that to the extent that status affects perceptions of, and attributions for, discrimination, it indirectly affects policy opinions as well. And, as we saw in Chapter 6, more educated blacks and those not receiving government aid are less likely to accept dispositional explanations of racial inequality. Thus education and welfare status have indirect positive effects on some aspects of support for government aid to blacks.

Patterns among whites

How do these patterns compare with those for whites? On busing, whites' opinions are somewhat more likely to be directly shaped by socioeconomic status than are those of blacks (see Table 8.3), though here we should be careful about precise black-white comparisons because of the slightly different wording of the ABC News/*Washington Post* and GSS busing questions. Education and home ownership both significantly affect whites' opinions, with those who completed more years of school and who own their own homes being less supportive of busing. However, these differences are not large. A white with characteristics identical to those of the baseline black is projected to have only a 24 percent probability of expressing support for busing, but the probability for an identical white who does not own her own home is only slightly higher (29 percent). Similarly, the difference based on a six-year differential in schooling works out to only ten percentage points.

Overall, a white who fits the profile of a poverty-stricken black would be about twice as likely to support busing as a white who matches the profile of the more economically comfortable black. This finding does not gibe with reports that more educated people are more tolerant and presumably more positively disposed toward policies favorable to blacks and civil rights (Quinley and Glock, 1979; Stouffer, 1955; Prothro and Grigg, 1960). It is,

Table 8.3. *Projected probability of supporting busing and special aid to blacks, whites, 1981 and 1985–1986*

	Projected probability	
Personal characteristics	Busing	Aid
Baseline	.24	.32
25 years old	.29	
65 years old	.15	
$10,000 income		.28
$50,000 income		.40
Not a homeowner	.29	.46
10 years of education	.27	.37
16 years of education	.17	.24
Black discrimination = 0		.23
Black discrimination = 6		.38
Dispositional attributions = 0		.28
Dispositional attributions = 3 (2 for GSS)		.43
Situational attributions = 0	.11	.24
Situational attributions = 3 (2 for GSS)	.29	.37
In poverty	.41	.40
Comfortable	.20	.34

Notes: N = 2,118 and 764, respectively, These projections are based on Table A.9.
Sources: NORC GSS, 1985 and 1986; February–March 1981 ABC News/*Washington Post* nationwide survey.

however, consistent with reports that middle-class whites are more negative than lower-class whites about social welfare policies in general, and with the view that education promotes individualistic values (Jackman and Muha, 1984).

We also considered whites' support for special government aid to blacks. Upper-income whites are more likely than their lower-income counterparts to favor government aid to blacks, as are white homeowners. However, controlling for the other predictors in the model, better educated whites are less likely to support special government aid to blacks. Because education largely cancels out the effects of income and home ownership, we project an overall differential in policy support based on socioeconomic status of only six percentage points. This marginal direct effect is echoed in the possible indirect effects of socioeconomic status. Education among whites is negatively linked to a tendency to accept dispositional explanations, but as we are about to see, dispositional attributions have little bearing on whites' policy views. The socioeconomic basis of situational attributions among whites is fairly weak, but it is whites of higher socioeconomic status who offer more situational explanations. It follows that more affluent whites are more supportive of policies directed at ameliorating the condition of blacks. These indirect effects, while not precisely measured in our probit analyses, must be fairly weak because of the minimal status-attribution link.

The foremost influence on whites' opinions about special policies for blacks is their understanding of the causes of racial inequality. Those who accept all three situational explanations of racial inequality are 13 percentage points more likely to favor special aid for blacks than are those who reject all three situational explanations. Moreover, whites who accept all three dispositional explanations of inequality are 15 percentage points more likely to favor special government aid than are those who disagree with all three dispositional explanations.

Overall, then, causal attributions have a great bearing on whites' opinions about special government aid to blacks. The link we have noted between whites' support for government aid and their belief that blacks are held back by situational constraints closely parallels the pattern that stands out for blacks. Among whites, like blacks, support for special government aid to blacks is also positively associated with the tendency to hold blacks responsible for their inferior socioeconomic status.

Policies toward the poor

Patterns among blacks

The 1985 and 1986 GSS solicited opinions about antipoverty programs in two ways. Half of the GSS respondents were asked whether too much, too little, or about the right amount was being spent for "welfare," while the other half were asked the same question about "assistance to the poor." In the 1986 ABC News/*Washington Post* survey, a single question was asked concerning aid to the poor. The subject of this question was whether "government welfare programs mainly discourage people from improving themselves, or . . . mainly help people until they begin to stand on their own."

Neither of the GSS questions evoked responses from blacks that are highly structured according to demographic or socioeconomic lines, or, for that matter, according to perceptions of or attributions for racial inequality. There are, however, some not entirely consistent indications of a modest socioeconomic effect. On the issue of whether more should be spent to "assist the poor," income differences are not apparent, but

Table 8.4. *Projected probability of supporting welfare and aid to the poor, blacks, 1985–1986*

	Projected probability	
Personal characteristics	Welfare	Aid
Baseline	.36	.76
$10,000 income	.52	
$50,000 income	.28	
In poverty	.38	.90
Comfortable	.34	.71

Notes: N = 238. These projections are based on Table A.10.
Sources: GSS 1985 and 1986.

Table 8.5. *Projected probability of supporting welfare programs, blacks, 1986*

Personal characteristics	Projected probability
Baseline	.51
Not a homeowner	.37
Economic pressure = 0	.46
Economic pressure = 4	.62
10 years of education	.57
16 years of education	.39
In poverty	.55
Comfortable	.23

Notes: N = 461. These projections are based on Table A.11.
Source: January 1986 ABC News/*Washington Post* nationwide survey of blacks.

higher-income blacks are considerably less likely to support welfare spending (see Tables 8.4 and 8.5).

The only other indicator of socioeconomic status that predicts in the expected fashion is level of education. Whereas the probability is 51 percent that a typical black would agree with the idea that welfare programs help people, the counterpart probabilities for an otherwise typical black who graduated from college or who only completed tenth grade would be 39 percent and 57 percent, respectively. However, in spite of its negative effect on the perceived efficacy of welfare programs, education has no significant bearing on support for government spending on welfare or assistance to the poor.

Unexpectedly, home ownership displays a significant positive impact on the belief that welfare helps rather than discourages people. That is, other things being equal, black homeowners arc more sympathetic to welfare than other blacks are. This gap is not especially large – eleven percentage points for otherwise-typical blacks – nor does it recur for the two other items, making it somewhat anomalous. It is worth noting, however, that we observed earlier that black homeowners are more positively disposed to government aid for blacks than other blacks are, leaving us to wonder whether the support black homeowners express for welfare is really anomalous or is part of a somewhat broader phenomenon.

Overall, the composite poverty-level and economically better off blacks differ consistently on these items, ranging from a small gap of 6 percent in support for welfare to gaps of 19 and 24 percent on spending to aid the poor and 32 percent on assessments of the consequences of welfare. In each of these cases, those who are poverty-stricken are more supportive of spending for welfare and for the poor.

A final point of interest is that while blacks' perceptions of and explanations for racial inequality strongly influence their appraisals of government programs designed to help blacks (see Table 8.2), they have little to do with their evaluations of programs to assist poor people irrespective of race; opinions about welfare and aid to the poor are unaffected by perceptions of racial discrimination and causal understandings of black-white inequality. It seems fair to say that these perceptions and attributions do not carry over from blacks' evaluations of special programs for blacks to their evaluations of generic programs for the poor. This may seem so predictable that it hardly merits comment, but as we shall soon see, the same is not true for whites.

Patterns among whites

Income shapes whites' views of welfare and poverty programs, but so do other factors. As Table 8.6 shows, situational attributions guide whites' thinking on both questions about government aid for the poor. Those who attribute the black-white socioeconomic gap largely to discrimination and lack of opportunities are, in general, more sympathetic to welfare spending than are those who blame the gap largely on blacks. The projected differences in policy opinions between whites who score at the highest and lowest levels of the situational attribution scale range from 9 percentage points on support for welfare spending to 18 on support for government spending to assist the poor. This pattern contrasts with that observed

Table 8.6. *Projected probability of supporting aid to improve the standard of living and welfare, whites, 1985–1986*

Personal characteristics	Projected probability	
	Aid	Welfare
Baseline	.35	.19
Male	.31	
$10,000 income	.39	.24
$50,000 income	.33	.17
Economic pressure = 1	.30	
Economic pressure = 3	.38	
10 years of education	.40	
16 years of education	.30	
Dispositional attributions = 0	.37	
Dispositional attributions = 2	.29	
Situational attributions = 0	.25	.13
Situational attributions = 2	.38	.22
In poverty	.39	.30
Comfortable	.21	.16

Notes: N = 1,020 and 1,026 respectively. These projections are based on Table A.12.
Sources: GSS 1985 and 1986.

among blacks, whose explanations of racial inequality are unconnected to their evaluations of antipoverty programs. In this sense, it would seem, whites view poverty as a black problem. Many whites apparently translate "assistance to the poor" into "assistance to blacks," or at least "assistance to the black poor."[8]

As expected, economically comfortable whites are less sympathetic to government spending for the poor than are their lower-income counterparts. Both income and education undermine support for poverty spending, and perceived economic pressure adds to this effect on aid to improve standards of living. Various indicators of socioeconomic status are less closely related to attitudes toward spending on "welfare" than to attitudes toward spending on "the poor." Only income is significantly related to support for welfare, while three socioeconomic indicators are related to support for the other item. Although the impact of each socioeconomic factor taken one at a time is not especially large, their cumulative impact is impressive. A white who matches the profile of the composite poverty-stricken black would be 18 percentage points more likely than her economically comfortable counterpart to support spending for the poor, and

14 percentage points more likely to favor welfare spending; in relative terms, an economically comfortable white would be only about half as likely as a poverty-stricken white to support these programs. Thus, while each individual component of socioeconomic status has a modest effect on attitudes toward assistance for the poor, together these components go a long way toward helping us understand who within the white community favors such aid. On the whole, these status differences are comparable to those observed between poverty-stricken and better-off blacks, even though the absolute level of support for government aid is higher among blacks.

Conclusions

Before we highlight the elements of our model that display the most pronounced impacts on opinions concerning programs for blacks and the poor, we should pause briefly to mention the factors that seem to have little or no effect. Among blacks, there is no gender gap on these issues, nor are age and interracial friendship relevant factors. We expected perceptions of discrimination to be positively related to support for these government programs, but the impact of these perceptions proved to be surprisingly inconsistent.

The views of both blacks and whites concerning special aid to blacks are predominantly shaped by causal understandings of the inferior socioeconomic status of blacks in American society. Those who tend to attribute such status to situational constraints are much more supportive of special aid for blacks than those who do not. For whites, attributing racial inequality to dispositional factors also significantly affects support for aid to blacks, but blacks' policy preferences are unaffected by these dispositional attributions.[9] These findings bear out earlier indications of a link between explanations of racial inequality and policy opinions among whites (Apostel et al., 1983; Kluegel and Smith, 1983; Sniderman with Hagen, 1985) and greatly expand what has previously been known about the policy preferences of blacks.

Whites' attributions carry over into their views of antipoverty programs, a pattern indicative, we think, of a link in the minds of whites between being poor and being black. In this sense, poverty and welfare are seen, in part, as black problems. On the other hand, blacks' explanations of racial inequality do not carry over into their opinions concerning assistance for the poor. Blacks apparently see "the poor" and ways to help them as distinct from "blacks" and curing the effects of racism.

The impact of socioeconomic status on blacks' policy views is mixed. These differences have little bearing on support for government aid to blacks or busing, but a noticeable impact on blacks' views of programs for the poor. These conclusions reinforce the dominant pattern reported in prior studies (e.g., Parent and Stekler, 1985; Welch and Combs, 1985; Welch and Foster, 1987).

In Chapters 4 and 6, we considered the ambiguous relationship between education and the racial outlooks of both blacks and whites. Here we observe that education has little independent impact on blacks' policy views. It modestly affects support for aid to blacks, through its effect on the acceptance of situational attributions. But independent of that, more highly educated blacks are neither more nor less likely to support aid for the poor and for blacks than are less educated blacks. Higher levels of education are clearly not associated with greater conservatism among blacks.

Among whites, too, education is not consistently related to attitudes toward government programs for blacks, but it does tend to be negatively related to support for government aid to the poor. This effect is balanced, in part, by the negative effect of education on acceptance of dispositional attributions. Rejection of dispositional attributions, in turn, sometimes promotes positive opinions about government spending for the poor. Education also indirectly promotes acceptance of government programs designed to aid blacks, but only to a very limited extent. Aside from these small indirect effects, just as with other socioeconomic indicators, the higher the educational level, the less supportive a white person is likely to be toward providing public funds to the less fortunate members of society. Thus, whereas increasing education may diminish prejudice among whites, it does not do much to promote support for government programs for problems associated with racism and poverty, a finding entirely consistent with the more general observation that "education may build support for the value of equality without at the same time increasing support for policies designed to realize it" (Sniderman et al., 1984: 75).

This completes our analyses of blacks' perceptions and explanations of racial inequality and opinions about policies to remedy such inequality. In Chapter 9, we ponder the meanings and implications of these findings and consider the past and future directions of black thinking about these issues.

Notes

1. · Even Jaynes and Williams, who present a fairly lengthy survey of black attitudes, mention only briefly their attributions for inequality, and do not link them to policy preferences (1989: chs. 3 and 5, esp. 150–1, 211–13).

2. Sniderman et al. (1986), in an analysis of the link between explanations of racial inequality and racial policy preferences among whites, suggest that the causal flow between attributions and policy choices is not as simple as we have proposed. They argue that some people (1) support or oppose policies designed to promote racial equality largely because of their own affect toward blacks, and then (2) reason backwards from their policy views to their explanations of racial inequality. People who feel positively toward blacks, for example, decide to support policies to promote racial equality. They then rationalize this support by agreeing that blacks' problems are largely due to discrimination. Similarly, those who feel negatively toward blacks oppose policies promoting racial equality and rationalize their opposition by arguing that blacks are responsible for most of their own problems. Although it is plausible that some people arrive at their opinions and beliefs in this way, and although causality among beliefs and attitudes is hardly ever straightforward, we do not consider Sniderman et al.'s evidence on this point compelling.

Sniderman et al. use two nonrecursive models to estimate the link between attributions and policy preferences. In one, they eliminate the causal link between affect towards blacks and attributions for racial inequality (421), a link earlier shown to be highly significant (418). The combination of discarding this link and using attribution as a dependent variable permits policy preferences to capture some of the variance in attribution that otherwise would be captured by affect, thus inflating the impact of policy preferences on attribution. In the other model, two-way causation is observed only among the college-educated, but the causal chain is complicated by the addition of a poverty attribution variable. The complication stems from ignoring the potential direct link between poverty attribution and affect toward blacks, an omission that affects the estimates for other paths as well. Later in this chapter we show that such a link is probable.

Even though this reverse causality may be valid for some whites, such as the more educated, it is hard to extend it to many blacks, among whom the key concept of affect toward blacks would presumably vary relatively little and would therefore be less likely to affect policy preferences.

3. These questions are worded as follows:

Thinking of school busing, would you say you favor or oppose the busing of black and white students as a last resort for school integration? (0=oppose, 1=favor)

I am going to read you a few statements and for each I'd like you to tell me whether you tend to agree or disagree with it, or if perhaps you have no opinion about the statement . . . "Because of past discrimination, blacks who need it should get some help from the government that white people in similar circumstances don't get." (0=disagree, 1=agree)

Do you think government welfare programs mainly discourage people from improving themselves, or do you think they mainly help people until they begin to stand on their own? (0=mainly discourage people, 1=mainly help people)

4. We eliminated a few other pertinent GSS policy items because the N fell below 200. The absence of indicators of interracial friendship and receipt of government assistance is less serious than it might initially seem, because (as reported below) analyses of the ABC News/*Washington Post* data indicate that these factors have little bearing on blacks' policy preferences. The omission of perceptions of racial discrimination is, of course, more problematic.

5. These dependent variables were worded as follows:

We are faced with many problems in this country, none of which can be solved easily or inexpensively. I'm going to name some of these problems, and for each one I'd like you to tell me whether you think we're spending too much money on it, too little, or about the right amount on . . . Welfare [asked of half-samples in 1985–6]; Assistance to blacks; Assistance to the poor [both asked of half-samples in 1985–6].

Some people think that blacks have been discriminated against for so long that the government has a special obligation to help improve their living standards. Others believe that the government should not be giving special treatment to blacks. Where would you place yourself on this scale, or haven't you made up your mind on this? [Coded from one to five, 1986].

Because of past discrimination, blacks who need it should get some help from the government that white people in similar economic circumstances don't get [ABC News/ *Washington Post*].

6. The "baseline" black is defined as in Chapters 4 and 6, except that to those definitions are now added two new elements: average scores on the scales of dispositional and situational attributions for racial inequality (that is, a score of 1 on the former and 2 on the latter). In projecting probabilities for respondents in the GSS surveys, we use the same attributes, but with a few modifications. In place of the ABC News/*Washington Post* items indicating receipt of government assistance and difficulty in meeting the family's monthly expenses, we substitute one on whether the individual is satisfied with her financial status. For that item, the mean is "more or less satisfied" (that is, a score of 2). On each of the attribution scales, on which scores range from 0 through 2, the baseline GSS respondent is assigned a score of 1.

7. The low reliability of the dispositional attribution scale for blacks should also be mentioned at this point. The effect of random measurement error is to depress statistical relationships, so presumably the impact of dispositional attributions would have been greater had we been able to devise a more reliable measure.

8. Referring back to the Sniderman et al. (1986) study discussed in note 2 above, the fact that many whites seem to link poverty and blacks suggests the potential utility of testing the link between affect toward blacks and attributions for poverty.

   Skocpol (1988) argues that most people viewed the Great Society poverty programs of the 1960s are primarily aid to blacks, and that this contributed to the unpopularity of the programs. This is plausible but not demonstrated. However, the linkage of welfare and black aid in the public mind probably precedes the 1960s, even though then and now most recipients of AFDC are white.

9. Once again, let us issue a caveat concerning the unreliability of the dispositional attribution scale for blacks. We simply do not know whether dispositional attributions would be a poor predictor of blacks' policy preferences if a more reliable measure of dispositional attributions were available.

9

What has happened to the dream deferred?

We began this book by noting that studies of black attitudes about race are very rare. Theory is underdeveloped and measurement primitive, compared to much other research on opinion and perception. Had black racial attitudes been a subject of intense scholarly interest through the years, we would presumably possess much more refined measures of blacks' perceptions of discrimination, rather than the few coarse measures available to us. At the very least, future studies of black perceptions of discrimination must devise more imaginative and more comprehensive indicators of perceived discrimination against blacks in their roles as consumers and students, in their interactions with public agencies, and in their participation as members of community groups and organizations, supplementing the measures of perceived discrimination in housing, education, and employment used here. The same holds, of course, for future research on racial stereotypes, racial identification, explanations of racial inequality and progress, and opinions concerning pertinent policy issues.

If this were a more developed research area, we would also be able to make fairly precise comparisons of changes in black attitudes over time, much as Schuman et al. (1985) have done for whites' racial attitudes. As it is, we have pieced together the evidence that now exists, but have little comparable data with which to assess change.

Because this is a relatively unexplored set of issues, theory is not far advanced, either. Accordingly, we have attempted to pull together a wide array of relevant considerations from the literatures of sociology, political science, economics, and psychology, to develop and test a simple model of perceptions, attributions, and policy preferences.

We hope our work will spark greater interest in the topic of black racial attitudes. We believe that we have provided some descriptive guideposts and some explanatory paths that can be followed in future work on this vital set of issues. Researchers examining black attitudes a decade hence should have not only better measures but also a temporal benchmark by which to gauge their findings.

In the course of this book, we have tried to determine how widespread blacks perceive racial discrimination to be, how much progress they think has been made in the past in race relations and how optimistic they are about the future, how they explain racial inequality, and what paths they would choose to try to remedy the remaining problems of racial discrimination and inequality.

The analyses reported in Chapters 3 through 8 have reaffirmed our initial premise that one cannot meaningfully discuss racial attitudes in the United States by referring only to whites. Blacks' and whites' racial perceptions, beliefs, and opinions differ, but they are not simply mirror images of one another. In some cases, the ideas that prevail among blacks are diametrically opposed to those that predominate among whites, but in other cases they are quite similar. Only by devoting careful attention to the views of blacks as well as whites can we reach accurate conclusions about Americans' racial attitudes.

In this concluding chapter, we summarize what and how Americans think about racial discrimination and inequality. We will emphasize the recurring themes that have surfaced throughout this book and then place our findings in the broader perspective of stability and change in the attitudes of blacks.

Two separate but overlapping world views

Two decades ago, the Kerner Commission concluded that "Our nation is moving toward two societies, one black, one white – separate and unequal" (U.S. National Advisory Committee on Civil Disorders, 1968: 1). Since then, race relations in the United States have undergone massive change in many respects, but even now blacks and whites inhabit two different worlds in their thinking about race and inequality. These worlds are not completely separate, but they are distinct enough for us to say that the predominant view of race relations among blacks differs markedly from that held by most whites.

Blacks inhabit a world characterized by perceptions of discrimination against themselves personally and, even more commonly, against blacks in general. Most blacks report having experienced discrimination in education, housing, getting a job, or being paid fairly, although most also say they have been discriminated against in "only" one or two of these ways. Nearly half believe that in their local area there is discrimination in housing and access to unskilled jobs, and two-thirds perceive discrimination in wages and access to skilled and managerial jobs. Only in education do most blacks believe that blacks today are not victims of discrimination.

Not only do most blacks perceive widespread racial discrimination. They also believe that such discrimination is the major reason why blacks continue to have trouble finding good jobs, adequate housing, and other forms of social and economic security. Although most blacks acknowledge that blacks are partially responsible for the problems they face, they blame primarily white discrimination. For most blacks, discrimination is an everyday fact of life that retards the progress blacks make in American society.

Consistent with the primacy of white discrimination in their conceptions of their place in American society, most blacks want government to play an active role in the search for racial equality. Although support for affirmative action varies greatly as a function of the specific affirmative action scenario that is presented to them, most blacks approve of programs that improve their chances for jobs and higher education, as long as these programs do not run roughshod over the principle of merit. Moreover, although many blacks are critical of the current welfare system, most support government aid to raise the standard of living of blacks, and most favor government assistance to the poor.

In sum, according to the world view of the typical black, significant racial discrimination persists and largely accounts for where blacks as a group stand today. As a remedy, government action is necessary, even though blacks themselves are seen (as noted in Chapter 5) as having gone a long way in helping their own cause.

The prevailing white view of race relations differs dramatically. In the first place, most whites simply do not perceive significant discrimination against blacks. Only about one white in ten, for example, believes that blacks encounter discrimination in getting unskilled jobs or fair wages, and the odds are little better than fifty-fifty that a white person can think of even one type of discrimination from which blacks in their area suffer.

Because most whites perceive racial discrimination as rare, it is only logical that they are less likely than blacks to attribute socioeconomic differences between blacks and whites to situational factors. Blacks' and whites' explanations of racial inequality coincide largely in their mutual agreement that blacks have not had a sufficient chance for the education that it takes to rise out of poverty and their overwhelming mutual rejection of the idea that blacks are by nature inferior.

In light of prevailing views among whites that racial discrimination is relatively rare and that such discrimination is not a main source of the black-white socioeconomic gap, it is hardly surprising that most whites oppose special government help for blacks. Most whites see little reason for government intervention in the form of affirmative action or spending programs. Though they are more supportive of the general idea of helping the poor without regard to race, they also tend to oppose spending on welfare and antipoverty programs, which they seem to view as "black" problems. When asked in the 1988 Louis Harris poll whether "the next administration in Washington should do more to help disadvantaged blacks and other minorities," only 43 percent of whites, compared to 85 percent of blacks, advocated doing more.

Though whites largely reside in a perceptual world apart from that of blacks, some similarities do exist. It is presumably in these overlapping perceptions, attributions, and policy preferences that some black-white consensus might eventually emerge.[1]

Many members of both races accept responsibility for racial inequality. Although most whites do not acknowledge racial discrimination as a major factor, many – 46 percent in the 1989 ABC News/*Washington Post* survey – do concede that discrimination plays some role in relegating blacks to lower economic levels. Most blacks, for their part, put some of the blame on blacks, even though discrimination is viewed as the primary explanation for their lower socioeconomic status. This recognition of problems within the black community predates the more widely publicized concerns black leaders have expressed about the growth of the black underclass and the erosion of the black family (Wilson, 1987).

In their views of public policy issues, most blacks and whites concur about the ultimate objective of equality of opportunity. For example, almost everyone, white as well as black, approves of school integration and equal employment opportunity (see also Jackman, 1978; Schuman et al., 1985; Taylor et al., 1978). On other specific race-related policies there is also common ground among many blacks and whites. For example, majorities of both races favor certain types of affirmative action programs, as long as these do not involve quotas. And most members of both races oppose affirmative action programs that clearly violate the principle of merit. The white majority does not disapprove of all government programs promoting equality, nor does the black majority favor every potential program designed to aid blacks. When they are confronted with general questions concerning busing and government aid for blacks, blacks tend to split nearly evenly, while most whites answer negatively. Most blacks do not advocate greater government spending on welfare, though the percentage of blacks favoring increased welfare spending is about twice as high as the percentage of whites.

On the whole, then, though cleavages in policy attitudes are not entirely along racial lines, the dominant policy view among blacks is more activist than is the majority view among whites. In light of the historical legacy of slavery, racism, and segregation, it is understandable that blacks today are more likely than whites to see government as a solution and to distrust the unfettered operation of the market economy. As Charles Hamilton (1982: 119–20) has written, "The private sector-oriented capitalist economy has always had a fundamentally different meaning for black Americans than for most of their fellow citizens. White Americans came to this country and could proceed to struggle to own private property. Black Americans came to this country and had to struggle to cease being owned as private property." Even long after they have ceased being regarded as property, blacks have had enormous hurdles to overcome, and in their struggle have enlisted the federal government as a powerful ally.

Differences within the black community

This brings us to the question of how to account for differences within the black community, and, for that matter, within the white community as well. Are the blacks who share some of the perspectives that prevail among whites, and the whites who share some of the perspectives that prevail among blacks, distinguishable in terms of their socioeconomic status or other visible traits? Are those who perceive discrimination in a certain way more likely to explain racial inequality in a certain way, and do these perceptions and attributions have consistent effects on preferences for racial policy?

Our answer, based on the analyses reported in Chapters 4, 6, and 8, is a qualified "yes." The weight of the evidence indicates that among blacks, those of higher socioeconomic status, variously defined by education, income, home ownership, and freedom from pressing economic concerns, are less likely to perceive racial discrimination, more likely to emphasize black shortcomings in assessing the reasons for racial inequality, and less likely to favor government spending programs for welfare and the poor. In these respects, blacks of higher socioeconomic status have perceptions and opinions that fall closer to the predominant white viewpoint than do the dominant perceptions and opinions of lower-status blacks. However, let us not overstate this contrast, for in most of these perceptions and opinions, better-off blacks have much more in common with lower-status blacks than they do with lower-status or better-off whites. Although some socioeconomic differences are obvious in blacks' racial perceptions, attributions, and opinions, these tend to be fairly limited and inconsistent.

Blacks who perceive antiblack discrimination as widespread are much more likely to attribute black-white socioeconomic inequality to situational factors than are those who perceive less discrimination. In turn, the primary determinant of how blacks assess government aid to blacks is causal understandings of racial inequality. Those who attribute black problems largely to racial discrimination are much more supportive of remedial legislation and programs than are other blacks.

Some prominent recent interpretations of the impact of race in American society are incongruent with these findings. For example, "the declining significance of race" (Wilson, 1978) has been a common theme among neoconservative analysts (see also Sowell, 1975; 1984). According to this argument, the unequal position of blacks and whites is largely due not to contemporary racial discrimination but to the inability of blacks to compete in the economic marketplace. Wilson argues that well educated blacks are moving ahead economically at rates similar to those of well educated whites, while other blacks are held back by their lack of education and job experience, factors that, combined with the changing nature of the American economy, have created a black underclass (see also Wilson, 1987).

Our findings temper these generalizations. First, racial discrimination is reported by blacks of all socioeconomic levels. To the respondents in the surveys we have examined, racial discrimination is not just an historical phenomenon or an abstract idea. It is experienced by almost every black in one form or another.

Thus, while the economically comfortable perceive less discrimination against themselves and against blacks as a group than do poverty-level blacks, these data do not fit the view that members of the black middle class, let alone poverty-stricken blacks, are largely immune from direct racial discrimination. But neither do our findings fit the most pessimistic view. We have seen that most blacks do not report discrimination in every aspect of their lives, but in one or two areas. And based on the evidence we have examined, the amount of discrimination reported by blacks seems to have declined. Blacks also report less discrimination against themselves than against "blacks as a group," which may indicate that personal experience with racism is on the decline. And according to the 1984 NBES, most blacks say that being black is not something they think about very often. This could mean that they are simply resigned to discrimination, but it could also mean that racial discrimination is not an omnipresent part of their lives.

It is possible that many blacks will not admit to being discriminated against even when they are. Victims of discrimination may find it demeaning to make that admission to an outsider or, indeed, to themselves. Or they may find discrimination so much a part of life that they do not even think about it when it occurs.

Thus, these findings are no cause for celebration. Over twenty-five years after the passage of major civil rights legislation, it is discouraging to find racial discrimination so widespread. And membership in the middle class does not seem to protect blacks against such discrimination.

Socioeconomic differences in whites' racial views are even less predictable than is true of blacks. White homeowners are consistently less likely than other whites to perceive discrimination against blacks and to support policies designed to ameliorate the conditions besetting blacks. Somewhat surprisingly, more educated whites are also less likely to perceive racial discrimination as widespread, but there is no consistent education-based differential on policy issues. Income, a prime indicator of socioeconomic status, performs poorly as a predictor of whites' policy views, although wealthier whites are less supportive of welfare spending. For whites as for blacks, perceptions of how widespread racial discrimination is spill over into understandings of the causes of blacks' inferior socioeconomic status, which in turn shape opinions about policies to aid blacks. Whites who blame blacks for their own problems and who deny that racial discrimination has much to do with these problems are much more likely than other whites to withhold support for such policies. These attributional tendencies also affect whites' opinions concerning antipoverty and welfare programs, a tendency not observable among blacks.

In sum, the whites who are most sympathetic to programs for blacks and the poor are those who share with most blacks the belief that racial discrimination is largely responsible for the current status of blacks.[2] The whites who are least sympathetic to such policies tend to reject such situational explanations.

Black attitudes and American society

The patterns of black and white perceptions, attributions, and opinions that we have traced here obviously did not originate, full-blown, when the first ABC News/*Washington Post* race relations survey was conducted in 1981. Instead, they are products of the historical experiences of black people and white people in this country. Let us, then, briefly reexamine these experiences as a means of illuminating blacks' attitudes today and projecting these attitudes into the future.

Since the nation's founding, race has been a central issue in American society. For example, in 1835 Tocqueville predicted that the end of slavery would not spell the end of America's racial struggles. Nearly seventy years later, W. E. B. DuBois, the black leader of his era, forecast in *The Souls of Black Folk* that the "color line" would be the primary political problem of the twentieth century. Ray Stannard Baker, a Northern journalist survey-ing race relations in the South only a few years after *The Souls of Black Folk* was published, documented his new understanding of Southern pre-occupation with the question of race: "The Negro in the south is both the labor problem and the servant question, he [sic] is preeminently the politi-cal issue, and his place, socially, is of daily and hourly conversation" (1964: 26). This observation was echoed by V. O. Key (1949) in his classic study of Southern politics in the 1940s, and by Gunnar Myrdal (1944), who labeled the problem of race relations, and especially the yawning gap between democratic ideals and the treatment of blacks, an "American dilemma."

For the nearly four hundred years since whites brought blacks to this country in chains of slavery, blacks and whites have been chained together. Despite mutual hostilities, distrust, and even hatred toward one another, members of both races have had to work out arrangements whereby they could live together without destroying one another or the society both helped to build. Despite the sporadic attempts of both black and white organizations to transport blacks to Africa,[3] the black American, as Ken-neth Clark (1968: 219) has commented, "is American. His [sic] destiny is one with the destiny of America. His culture is the culture of America." Or, in the terms of the National Research Council study (Jaynes and Wil-liams, 1988), blacks and whites in America have "a common destiny."

The arrangements through which blacks and whites have coexisted have evolved over the years, and this evolution has shaped the major turning points of American history. The race issue hung heavily over the Constitu-tional Convention. As the central issue underlying the debates over states' rights and slavery, it was a contributing factor in the Civil War. After the Reconstruction era, the system of legalized segregation imposed by South-ern whites and acceded to by Northerners dominated Southern society, and the race issue shaped national party cleavages and political alignments. The Republicans were the party of Lincoln, the emancipators of the slaves. White Southerners flocked to the Democratic Party, making the "Solid South" a Democractic bastion in a Republican-dominated era. Blacks of-fered an allegiance to the Republicans that lasted until Franklin Delano Roosevelt and the New Deal. For many blacks, Republican loyalties per-sisted until the 1950s. And the evolutionary processes by which the barriers of legal segregation were dismantled have helped define the politics of the post-World War II United States (see Carmines and Stimson, 1989).

During the past two decades, the rate of change in race relations has slowed, and the issue has become less central on the mainstream political agenda. Nonetheless, the unease with which most Americans view the lower economic status of blacks relative to whites undergirds considerations of innumerable issues, ranging from welfare to the draft. Problems of racial inequality continue to haunt the body politic.

Stability and change in black attitudes

It would be fascinating to trace in detail black and white attitudes during these changing historical eras. But the attitudes of whites and especially of blacks over most of American history can only be inferred from impressionistic evidence. We have broad descriptive accounts by commentators like Tocqueville and Baker, diaries and private papers, essays by black leaders, compilations from the black press, and slave reminiscences compiled and published during the WPA era (see, e.g., Aptheker, 1966; Dann, 1971; Meltzer, 1964, 1965, 1967; Rawick, 1972). Although such documentary evidence has been put to good use by historians and others (e.g., Johnson and Roark, 1984), only in the last forty years has systematic evidence become available on black and white racial perceptions, beliefs, and opinions. This evidence is much more comprehensive for whites, for whom we have survey data extending back to the 1940s, than it is for blacks, who were largely ignored in opinion surveys prior to the 1960s.

Still, even though we lack precise public opinion data, we can offer some perspective on how black attitudes have changed over the past few decades. For one thing, blacks' perceptions of and opinions about whites seem to have remained remarkably stable. Skepticism toward whites is pervasive. Three-fourths of all blacks, for example, still agree that many whites do not want blacks to get ahead. Given the more than three-century history of slavery and suppression, it would be remarkable if most blacks were not still suspicious of whites. Blacks' skepticism, too, is a recognition that although many whites acknowledge racial equality in principle, they are unwilling to sacrifice other values to achieve racial equality in practice. As Lewis Killian (1968: 27) has argued, blacks in the United States have "always had the moral support of a significant minority of white Americans," but that moral support has never assumed a place of primacy in the white American value system. Nor for most white Americans has it become a rallying point for political action.

Blacks' ideas about the role of the federal government have changed somewhat over the years. Until the early and middle 1960s, blacks believed that new civil rights laws barring discrimination in voting, employment, housing, and public accommodations were desperately needed.[4] The passage of these laws ushered in some tremendous changes, but also revealed that legislation would not be sufficient to correct the massive problems blacks continued to face. Perhaps because of the slowness with which barriers in housing, employment, and other key areas have fallen and the ineffectiveness of government in knocking them down, blacks are less likely today than they were in the early 1960s to view the federal government as a strong ally. In 1963, an overwhelming 88 percent of blacks saw the Kennedy administration as helpful, and almost as many said the same about the U.S. Supreme Court (Brink and Harris, 1964). Black attitudes toward the federal government shifted significantly during the late 1960s (see Killian, 1968), when the limits of legal change began to be recognized and when the Black Power movement began to stress black autonomy from white institutions and control (Carmichael and Hamilton, 1967). The sagging national economy of the 1970s and early 1980s and the negative civil rights posture of the Reagan administration further undermined blacks' confidence in the federal government's ability to improve their lives. Nonetheless, as we noted in Chapter 5, about three-fourths of all blacks give the federal government at least some credit for improving the status of blacks over the years.

Both stability and change are also evident in blacks' specific policy preferences. Recognition of the limits of the civil rights laws of the 1960s probably accounts for the somewhat sagging enthusiasm for government programs. In particular, as we noted in Chapter 7, federal programs specifically targeted on blacks are less warmly received today than they were during the 1960s. Although support for government assistance to blacks is still more widespread among blacks than whites, the trend line is pointing downward for both races. Blacks are ambivalent about affirmative action, though they are generally more supportive of it than whites are. It is interesting to note that, in the 1989 ABC News/*Washington Post* survey, only a small minority of either race (and more blacks than whites, 23 percent to 14 percent) thought that black progress had come at the expense of whites.

Consistent with the idea that economic remedies, not more civil rights laws, are what is needed, blacks remain highly supportive of government assistance to the poor, but are divided on the merits of the welfare system. Overall, government action is no longer seen as the panacea of the 1950s and 1960s, when national legislation was desperately needed to expunge state-sanctioned segregation. Still, blacks have retained some faith in government's ability to help solve their problems, and most credit the federal government with fostering racial progress.

Along with the need for government assistance, the self-help motif has long been a prominent strain in black thinking, among both conservative and liberal leaders. For example, as different as their views were, both Booker T. Washington and W. E. B. DuBois believed that blacks could and must help themselves; Washington emphasized education and hard work as means of getting ahead, while DuBois also urged organizational mobilization by blacks and their allies (Fullinwider, 1969; Meier, 1968). Later generations of black leaders, from Marcus Garvey to A. Philip Randolph and from Martin Luther King to Bayard Rustin, have stressed that blacks working together can promote great change. And today the message of self-help – getting an education, spurning drugs, and working to overcome obstacles induced by poverty and racism – is a central theme in the rhetoric of Jesse Jackson.

The message of self-help has always had a receptive audience in the black public, which has never concealed its approval of black efforts at organizing and working to ameliorate racial inequality. This was apparent in the 1950s and 1960s in the participation of black Southerners in the sit-in protests (Matthews and Prothro, 1966) and the overwhelming support of blacks nationwide for black organizational leaders (Aberbach and Walker, 1973; Brink and Harris, 1964; Sears and McConahay, 1973), and it continues to be apparent in the widespread beliefs among blacks that the civil rights movement improved their lives (Jackson and Gurin, 1987) and that the key to racial progress has been the efforts of blacks themselves, though not necessarily the unaided efforts of blacks, in light of the credit also accorded to the federal government.

It is appropriate to close our consideration of stability and change in black attitudes by recognizing one of the most persistent strains in these attitudes: optimism. Despite their perceptions of deep and abiding racism and discrimination in this country, and despite their belief that blacks continue to be held down by such discrimination, most blacks remain optimistic about the future. Table 9.1 displays some pertinent data drawn from surveys conducted over the past twenty-five years (see also Figure 3.6 above). Shortly after World War II, three out of four blacks expressed confidence that their children's opportunities for success would be better than their own had been. Two decades later, at the height of the struggles of the 1960s, most blacks believed that the progress they were then experiencing would continue. Almost three-quarters of a national sample of blacks believed that whites would have more favorable attitudes toward blacks five years hence, and about two-thirds agreed that they themselves would probably be better off as far as work, housing, and pay were concerned (Brink and Harris, 1964: 268; the latter data are not shown in Table 9.1). By 1986, as blacks were voting and being elected to public office in record numbers (L. Williams, 1987),[5] optimism was widespread that life for black Americans would be better in the future, and only one black in seven believed that the future for blacks would be worse.

However, the optimism of blacks may be declining. The proportion giving optimistic responses in the 1970s and 1980s declined somewhat below

Table 9.1. *Optimism about the future, blacks, 1942–1986*

	Percent agreeing
Do you think your son's opportunities to succeed will be better than, or not as good as, those you have had? (national, 1942 [McAdam, 1982]).	75
Your son's opportunities to succeed will be better than those you have had (national, 1947 [Erskine, 1969]).	75
Whites will have a better attitude in five years (national, 1963 [Brink and Harris, 1966]).	73
Blacks will be better off in five years (Buffalo [Cataldo et al., 1970]).	65
If a young [Negro] works hard enough, he or she can get ahead in this country despite discrimination and prejudice (15-city study, 1968 [Schuman and Hatchett, 1974: 81]).	77
In twenty years there will be less discrimination than now (national, 1979 [Jackson and Gurin, 1987]).	58
Life will be better in the future for blacks in this country (national, 1986 [ABC News/*Washington Post*]).	57
Will blacks in this country *ever* achieve full social and economic equality? (national, 1984 [Survey Research Center, 1984]).	46

the levels of the 1950s and 1960s. Perhaps this is a small blip in larger cyclical upturns and downturns, but it seems likely that declining optimism is due to the economic setbacks experienced by many blacks and by a large portion of the white population. During the last decade poverty rates have risen as the real wages of American workers have fallen and as government has cut back on social programs for the poor (Berry, 1988; Harrison and Bluestone, 1988; Levy, 1987; Rich, 1986). After a quarter century of fairly steady economic gains for average American families, in 1973 the real dollar income of the average family began to stagnate. But the "average" disguises some very separate realities. The richest 10 percent of all Americans gained over 37 percent in real income between 1977 and 1988, but the poorest tenth lost 10.5 percent of its income. Meanwhile, the middle 40 percent stayed about even with inflation.

The only way these families have stayed even is by having two wage earners, or even three. Blacks, being disproportionately found in one-parent, one-earner families, are increasingly economically disadvantaged. As we saw in Chapter 2, black income has actually declined since 1973. Even in times of low unemployment, most single-earner families cannot escape from poverty. For example, even when Massachusetts had an unemployment rate near the "full" employment level and even when only 2.5

percent of all two-earner families in the state were poor, over a quarter of all female-headed families still remained poor (Levy, 1987). The economic boom did not touch a significant portion of the public. Thus, despite the successes of the Civil Rights Acts, harsh economic conditions for America's bottom half have brought disillusionment to more and more blacks. And there are growing signs that this disillusionment is carrying over into the political realm, in the form of declining turnout and disaffection from the parties (see, e.g., Kinder, Mendelberg, Dawson, Sanders, Rosenstone, Sargent, and Cohen, 1989).

Despite the increasing pessimism, there is still an underlying optimistic core among blacks. Some might say that this optimism bespeaks a great capacity for self-delusion. However, despite their optimism, the vast majority of blacks do not shy away from acknowledging that whites in general harbor at least a fair amount of prejudice against them (see Chapter 3 above). Others might consider blacks' optimism amply justified, in light of the great strides that have been made in race relations and blacks' living conditions during the postwar era. In any event, it seems highly unlikely, in light of their history in this nation and the continuing obliviousness of most whites to the nature, extent, and effects of racial discrimination, that blacks' optimism about the future is based on a perception that new opportunities will simply be handed to them without a struggle. Martin Luther King (1963) wrote in his *Letter from a Birmingham Jail* "We know through painful experience that justice is never voluntarily given by the oppressor. It must be demanded by the oppressed." By demanding that "the dream deferred" of equality and justice become reality, and by remaining optimistic about their future in America, blacks have been a major force in narrowing the gap between the values Americans profess and those they practice.

Notes

1. For now-outdated but still useful expansions on the idea of similarity and difference in the attitudes of blacks and whites, see Broom and Glenn (1966), Glenn (1974–5), and Schwartz and Schwartz (1976).
2. A parallel finding was reported by Matthews and Prothro (1966: 353), who showed that the most prointegrationist Southern whites were the ones who most accurately perceived blacks' preferences for racial equality. Prosegregationist whites were the most ignorant of how blacks really felt about race relations.
3. These attempts persisted at least for a century and a half. In 1777, a Virginia legislative committee chaired by Thomas Jefferson set forth a plan of gradual emancipation and exportation (Franklin, 1966: 238). In the early part of the nineteenth century, Paul Cuffe, a black shipbuilder and owner, took thirty-eight blacks to Africa at his own expense. Later in that century, until the Civil War, several organized attempts were made to establish colonies of American blacks in Liberia and other parts of Africa. Reportedly, about 12,000 blacks left the U.S. in these ventures. And of course, an important theme in the twentieth-century Garveyite movement (briefly discussed in Chapter 2) was to return to

Africa and liberate it from white rule (Essien-Udom, 1967). But most black Americans, then and now, would no more think of moving to Africa than Italian Americans would think of moving to Italy (see Herskovits, 1958, for a discussion of the influence of Africa on the culture of American blacks).

4. Early in this century, black activists worked for federal action to prevent lynchings. During the World War II era, they pushed for federal action to ensure blacks' access to jobs. And the civil rights agenda of housing, voting, education, and jobs did not spring up out of nowhere in the 1960s; it had been pushed by black leaders for many decades.

5. Blacks now participate in national elections at a rate about five to eight percentage points below that of whites, although their participation in some local races with visible and active black candidates is much higher than in national elections. The number of black officials soared from less than 300 in 1965 to nearly 7,000 in 1988 (*Ebony,* 1966; Joint Center for Political Studies, annual). These aggregate figures include officials at all levels of government, ranging from tiny towns to large cities. In terms of major offices, by 1989 there were nearly thirty black mayors of cities of 50,000 or more. Blacks hold or have held the mayor's office in most of the largest U.S. cities, including New York, Chicago, Los Angeles, Philadelphia, Detroit, Atlanta, Baltimore, Washington D.C., and many cities in which blacks were far from a majority, such as Seattle and Charlotte. The growth in Southern black officials from 1968 to 1988 includes an increase of from 23 to 184 state legislators. The first black governor was elected in 1989 in Virginia.

Appendix
Factor Analysis and Probit Summary Tables

Table A.1. *Factor analysis of perceptions of discrimination, blacks, 1986, and whites, 1981*

	Blacks, 1986: factor					Whites, 1981: factor	
Perceptual item	I	II	III	IV	V	I	II
Discrimination against blacks							
Education	.72	.30	−.58	−.19	.07	.85	.38
Housing	.72	.27	−.56	.33	.15	.87	.24
Unskilled jobs	.65	.29	−.35	.28	.42	.86	.24
Skilled jobs	.86	.13	−.37	.19	.13	.93	.23
Managerial jobs	.87	.14	−.32	.14	.15	.88	.16
Wages	.77	.27	−.32	.23	.39	.88	.24
Discrimination against self							
Education	.30	.19	−.78	.13	.01		
Housing	.40	.26	−.83	.34	.13		
Job	.40	.22	−.79	.22	.31		
Wages	.49	.34	−.76	.31	.26		
Trend in antiblack feeling							
National	.16	.91	−.18	.21	.22	.16	.86
Local	.22	.91	−.28	.20	.26	.20	.86
Trend in living conditions							
Blacks	.24	.21	−.24	.85	.12	.37	.32
Self	.16	.19	−.21	.86	.17		
Prevalence of Klanlike attitudes	.19	.22	−.10	.22	.84	.43	.55
Prevalence of white prejudice	.28	.30	−.28	.11	.77		
Eigenvalue	5.64	1.70	1.41	1.21	1.05	5.10	1.63
Proportion of total variance accounted for by factor	.35	.11	.09	.08	.07	.51	.16
Factor correlation matrix:							
	I	II	III	IV	V	I	II
I		.24	.45	.24	.24		.30
II			−.28	.23	.26		
III				−.26	−.15		
IV					.18		

Table A.1. *(cont.)*

Note: The table shows structure coefficients, i.e., the correlations between each item and each factor, based on a principal components analysis with oblique rotation.
Source: January 1986 ABC News/*Washington Post* nationwide survey of blacks and February–March 1981 ABC News/*Washington Post* nationwide survey.

Table A.2. *Probit analyses of the sources of perceived discrimination against oneself and against blacks, blacks, 1986*

Predictor	Discrimination against oneself		Discrimination against blacks	
	Max. likelihood estimate	t–ratio	Max. likelihood estimate	t–ratio
Demographic characteristics				
Gender	−.17	−2.08[a]	−.13	1.51
Age, in years	.01	2.71[b]	.01	1.83
Friendship with a white person	−.03	−.36	−.08	−.87
Socioeconomic status				
Family income, in thousands	.004	1.60	.001	.24
Homeowner	−.08	−.94	−.20	−2.22[a]
Subjective middle-class member	−.18	−2.14[a]	.03	.27
Unemployed	.07	.57	−.05	−.31
Government aid recipient	.23	2.49[a]	−.02	−.18
Perceived economic pressure	.20	5.06[c]	.18	3.98[c]
Years of education	.04	2.57[a]	.02	1.12
Constant	−.72	−2.85[b]	.85	2.89[b]
Chi-square/df	35.87/10[c]		38.72/10[c]	

Note: N = 750 and 636, respectively. All *t*-tests are two-tailed. Projections based on this table are shown in Table 4.2.
[a]$p < .05$
[b]$p < .01$
[c]$p < .001$
Source: January 1986 ABC News/*Washington Post* nationwide survey of blacks.

Table A.3. *Probit analyses of the sources of the perceived trend in antiblack feelings, blacks, 1986*

Predictor	Max. likelihood estimate	*t*-ratio
Demographic characteristics		
Gender	.08	1.05
Age, in years	.01	1.83
Friend of a white person	−.15	−1.61
Socioeconomic status		
Family income, in thousands	.001	.56
Homeowner	.01	.09
Subjective middle-class member	−.16	−1.75
Unemployed	.12	.99
Government aid recipient	.02	.26
Perceived economic pressure	.05	1.05
Years of education	.03	1.89
Constant	.05	.19
Chi-square/df	19.08/10[a]	

Note: N = 758. All *t*-tests are two-tailed. Projections based on this table are shown in Table 4.3.
[a]*p* < .05
Source: January 1986 ABC News/*Washington Post* nationwide survey of blacks.

Table A.4. *Probit analyses of the sources of perceived discrimination against blacks and the trend in antiblack feelings, whites, 1981*

Predictor	Discrimination against blacks		Trend in antiblack feelings	
	Max. likelihood estimate	t-ratio	Max. likelihood estimate	t-ratio
Demographic characteristics				
Gender	−.08	−1.14	.01	.11
Age, in years	−.01	−2.66[a]	.002	.80
Friend of a white person	−.04	−.54	−.14	−2.18[b]
Socioeconomic status				
Family income, in thousands	.004	1.59	.002	1.03
Homeowner	−.35	−3.91[c]	−.12	−1.69
Subjective middle-class member	.13	1.54	.05	.77
Unemployed	−.02	−.17	−.02	−.12
Years of education	−.03	−2.03[b]	−.05	−4.13[c]
Constant	.42	2.14[b]	1.19	6.02[c]
Chi-square/df	38.77/8[c]		0.80/8	

Note: N = 933 and 1,071, respectively. All *t*-tests are two-tailed. Projections based on this table are shown in Table 4.4.
[a] $p < .01$
[b] $p < .05$
[c] $p < .001$
Source: February–March 1981 ABC News/*Washington Post* nationwide survey.

Table A.5. *Factor analysis of explanations of racial inequality and progress, blacks, 1986, and whites, 1981*

	Blacks, 1986		Whites, 1981	
Explanation	Factor I	Factor II	Factor I	Factor II
A. Explanations for black–white inequality				
Lack of educational opportunity	.79	−.02	.79	−.21
Opposition from whites	.74	.06	.81	−.10
Discrimination	.74	−.22	.83	−.20
Lack of in-born ability to learn	.23	.70	.14	.84
Lack of motivation or willpower	−.11	.87	−.48	.84
Blacks bring problems on selves	−.25	.56	−.51	.70
Eigenvalue	1.88	1.57	2.79	1.44
Proportion of total variance accounted for by factor	.31	.26	.47	.24
Factor correlation matrix:				
I	−.06	−.21		
B. Explanations for black progress				
Decline in white prejudice	.60			
Federal laws and court decisions	.71			
Younger blacks' assertiveness	.66			
Government financial assistance	.69			
Increase in black education	.75			
Hard work and determination	.67			
Eigenvalue	2.78			
Proportion of total variance accounted for by factor	.46			

Note: The table shows structure coefficients, i.e., the correlations between each item and each factor, based on a principal components analysis with oblique rotation.
Source: January 1986 ABC News/*Washington Post* nationwide survey of blacks, and February–March 1981 ABC News/*Washington Post* nationwide survey.

Table A.6. *Probit analyses of the sources of dispositional and situational racial inequality attributions, blacks, 1986*

Predictor	Dispositional attributions		Situational attributions	
	Max. likelihood estimate	*t- ratio*	Max. likelihood estimate	*t- ratio*
Demographic characteristics				
Gender	−.03	−.29	.15	1.49
Age, in years	−.001	−.43	.001	.16
Friend of a white person	−.07	−.60	−.13	−1.17
Socioeconomic status				
Family income, in thousands	−.003	−.93	.004	1.48
Homeowner	.14	1.31	.04	.34
Subjective middle-class member	.06	.53	−.15	−1.43
Unemployed	.10	.73	.24	1.50
Government aid recipient	.25	2.19[a]	−.13	−1.10
Perceived economic pressure	−.02	−.44	.07	1.42
Years of education	−.07	−3.50[b]	−.03	−1.27
Discrimination against self	−.06	−1.61	.02	.47
Discrimination against blacks	−.002	−.07	.23	8.49[b]
Constant	1.55	4.37[b]	.95	2.63[c]
Chi-square/df	25.58/12[a]		95.32/12[b]	

Note: N = 532 and 561, respectively. All *t*-tests are two-tailed. Projections based on this table are shown in Table 6.1.
[a] $p < .05$
[b] $p < .001$
[c] $p < .01$
Source: January 1986 ABC News/*Washington Post* nationwide survey of blacks.

Table A.7. *Probit analyses of the sources of dispositional and situational racial inequality attributions, whites, 1981*

Predictor	Dispositional attributions		Situational attributions	
	Max. likelihood estimate	*t-ratio*	Max. likelihood estimate	*t-ratio*
Demographic characteristics				
Gender	−.03	−.41	.03	.38
Age, in years	.01	6.11[a]	−.003	−1.26
Friend of a black person	−.04	−.53	−.14	−1.93
Socioeconomic status				
Family income, in thousands	−.0002	−.06	−.003	−1.19
Homeowner	.11	1.24	−.007	−.08
Subjective middle-class member	−.18	−2.42[b]	.15	1.77
Unemployed	−.02	−1.00	−.40	−3.01[c]
Years of education	−.05	−3.97[a]	.01	.70
Discrimination against blacks	−.02	−1.00	.32	12.70[a]
Constant	1.30	6.02[a]	.53	2.41[b]
Chi-square/df	83.53/9[c]		175.02/9[a]	

Note: N = 841 and 857, respectively. All t-tests are two-tailed. Projections based on this table are shown in Table 6.2.
[a] $p < .001$
[b] $p < .05$
[c] $p < .01$
Source: February–March 1981 ABC News/*Washington Post* nationwide survey.

Table A.8. *Probit analyses of the sources of support for busing and special aid to blacks, blacks, 1986*

	Busing		Special aid	
Predictor	Max. likelihood estimate	*t-ratio*	Max. likelihood estimate	*t-ratio*
Demographic characteristics				
Gender	−.29	−2.37[a]	−.08	−.64
Age, in years	−.03	−.59	−.00	−.30
Friend of a white person	.16	1.14	.05	.36
Socioeconomic status				
Family income, in thousands	.00	.51	−.00	−.34
Homeowner	.15	1.12	.32	2.40[a]
Subjective middle-class member	.08	.62	−.03	−.24
Unemployed	−.04	−.21	−.04	−.18
Government aid recipient	−.05	−.35	−.11	−.74
Perceived economic pressure	.04	.56	.10	1.43
Years of education	−.01	−.39	−.05	−1.75
Perceived discrimination against oneself	.11	2.21[a]	.01	.10
Perceived discrimination against blacks	−.09	−2.37[a]	.08	2.00[a]
Dispositional inequality attributions	−.04	−.66	.21	3.00[b]
Situational inequality attributions	.02	.22	.42	5.63[a]
Constant	.54	1.10	−.97	−1.86
Chi-square/df	18.5/14		77.9/14[c]	

Note: N = 484 and 467, respectively. All t-tests are two-tailed. Projections based on this table are shown in Table 8.2.
[a] *p* < .05
[b] *p* < .01
[c] *p* < .001
Source: January 1986 ABC News/*Washington Post* nationwide survey of blacks.

Table A.9. *Probit analyses of the sources of support for busing and special aid to blacks, whites, 1985–1986 and 1981*

Predictor	Busing		Special Aid	
	Max. likelihood estimate	t-ratio	Max. likelihood estimate	t-ratio
Demographic characteristics				
Gender	.06	.92	.08	.75
Age, in years	−.01	5.69[a]	.00	.44
Friend of a black person			.16	1.55
Socioeconomic status				
Family income	−.01	−1.70	.01	2.26[b]
Homeowner	−.16	−2.21[b]	−.34	−2.82[a]
Subjective middle-class member	.05	.65	.08	.72
Unemployed	.19	.90	−.14	−.66
Perceived economic pressure	−.09	−1.87		
Years of education	−.05	−3.78[a]	−.06	2.97[a]
Perceived discrimination against blacks			.07	2.02[b]
Dispositional inequality attributions	−.08	−1.56	.14	2.38[b]
Situational inequality attributions	.35	8.22[c]	.13	2.35[b]
Constant	−1.49	−4.42[a]	−.55	−1.53
Chi-square/df	159.8/10[c]		28.5/11[c]	

Note: N = 2,118 and 764, respectively. All t-tests are two-tailed. Projections based on this table are shown in Table 8.3.
[a] $p < .01$
[b] $p < .05$
[c] $p < .001$
Sources: 1985 and 1986 NORC GSS and February–March 1981 ABC News/*Washington Post* nationwide survey.

Table A.10. *Probit analyses of the sources of support for welfare and aid to the poor, blacks,*
1985–1986

Predictor	Government spending for welfare		Government spending to assist poor	
	Max. likelihood estimate	t-ratio	Max. likelihood estimate	t-ratio
Demographic characteristics				
Gender	.16	.63	−.25	−.73
Age, in years	.01	.71	.00	.02
Socioeconomic status				
Family income	−.06	−2.38[a]	−.01	−.21
Homeowner	.38	1.54	−.46	−1.47
Subjective middle-class member	.46	1.92	−.06	−.18
Unemployed	−.43	−.76	NA[b]	NA[b]
Perceived economic pressure	.15	.92	.12	.62
Years of education	−.03	−.65	.02	.30
Dispositional inequality attributions	−.26	−1.63	−.26	−1.21
Situational inequality attributions	.01	.04	−.03	−.11
Constant	1.20	1.02	−.39	−.27
Chi-square/df	18.0/10		6.4/9	

Note: N = 238. All t-tests are two-tailed. Projections based on this table are shown in Table
8.4.
[a] $p < .05$
[b] The model would not converge until this variable was dropped.
Sources: 1985 and 1986 GSS. N = 238.

Table A.11. *Probit analyses of the sources of support for welfare programs, blacks, 1986*

Predictor	Welfare helps		Government should help the poor	
	Max. likelihood estimate	*t-ratio*	Max. likelihood estimate	*t-ratio*
Demographic characteristics				
Gender	−.13	−1.01	.07	.29
Age, in years	−.00	−.53	.01	.94
Friend of a white person	−.23	−1.60	NA	NA
Socioeconomic status				
Family income, in thousands	−.01	−1.69	−.05	−2.05[a]
Homeowner	.36	2.69[b]	.10	.47
Subjective middle-class member	−.15	−1.11	.16	.69
Unemployed	−.19	−.98	−.40	−.87
Government aid recipient	.11	.77	NA	NA
Perceived economic pressure	.13	1.99[a]	.15	1.06
Years of education	−.08	−3.08[b]	−.01	−.35
Perceived discrimination against oneself	.04	.74	NA	NA
Perceived discrimination against blacks	−.04	−1.00	NA	NA
Dispositional inequality attributions	−.12	−1.69	−.11	−.80
Situational inequality attributions	.06	.78	.17	1.10
Constant	1.05	2.07[a]	.32	.31
Chi-square/df	41.2/14[c]		14.8/10	

Note: N = 461. All t-tests are two-tailed. Projections based on this table are shown in Table 8.5.
[a] $p < .05$
[b] $p < .01$
[c] $p < .001$
Sources: January 1986 ABC News/*Washington Post* nationwide survey of blacks.

Table A.12. *Probit analyses of the sources of support for aid to the poor and welfare, whites, 1985–1986*

Predictor	Favor aid to improve standard of living		Favor spending to assist poor	
	Max. likelihood estimate	*t-ratio*	Max. likelihood estimate	*t-ratio*
Demographic characteristics				
Gender	*.14*	2.11[a]	.05	.62
Age, in years	−.00	1.83	−.00	−.67
Socioeconomic status				
Family income	−.02	−2.21[a]	−.03	−2.79[b]
Homeowner	.06	.71	−.16	−1.91
Subjective middle-class member	−.07	−.97	−.05	−.68
Unemployed	−.21	−.83	.00	.00
Perceived economic pressure	.12	2.35[a]	.09	1.65
Years of education	−.03	−2.19[a]	.02	1.66
Dispositional inequality attributions	−.11	−2.18[a]	−.08	−1.34
Situational inequality attributions	.19	4.16[c]	.17	3.51[c]
Constant	.44	1.21	.65	1.63
Chi-square/df		76.3/10[c]		65.3/10[c]

Note: N = 1,020 and 1,026, respectively. All t-tests are two-tailed. Projections based on this table are shown in Table 8.6.

[a] $p < .05$
[b] $p < .01$
[c] $p < .001$

Sources: 1985 and 1986 GSS.

References

Aberbach, Joel, and Jack Walker. 1973. *Race in the City*. Boston: Little, Brown.
Adorno, T. W., Else Frenkel-Brunswik, Daniel J. Levinson, and R. Nevitt Sanford. 1950. *The Authoritarian Personality*. New York: Harper & Row.
Allen, Richard L., Michael C. Dawson, and Ronald E. Brown. 1989. "A Heuristic and Schema Approach to Modeling an African American Racial Belief System." *American Political Science Review* 83:421–2.
Allport, Gordon W. 1954. *The Nature of Prejudice*. New York: Addison Wesley.
Altschuler, Glenn. 1982. *Race, Ethnicity and Class in American Social Thought, 1865–1919*. Arlington Heights, Il: Harlan Davidson.
Alves, Wayne M., and Peter H. Rossi. 1978. "Who Should Get What? Fairness Judgments of the Distribution of Earnings." *American Journal of Sociology* 84:541–64.
Alwin, Dwaine, and Arland Thornton. 1984. "Family Origins and the Schooling Process: Early Versus Late Influence of Parental Characteristics." *American Sociological Review* 49:784–802.
Anderson, Barbara A., Brian D. Silver, and Paul R. Abramson. 1988. "The Effects of the Race of the Interviewer on Race-Related Attitudes of Black Respondents in SRC/CPS National Election Studies." *Public Opinion Quarterly* 52:289–324.
Apostle, Richard A., Charles Y. Glock, Thomas Piazza, and Marijean Suezele. 1983. *The Anatomy of Racial Attitudes*. Berkeley: University of California Press.
Aptheker, Herbert, ed. 1966. *A Documentary History of the Negro People in the United States*. New York: Citadel.
Auletta, Ken. 1982. *The Underclass*. New York: Random House.
Baker, Ray Stannard. [1908] 1964. *Following the Color Line*. New York: Harper Torchbooks.
Bancroft, Hubert H. 1912. *Retrospection*. New York: Bancroft.
Barkin, Steve M., and Michael Gurevitch. 1987. "Out of Work and On the Air: Television News of Unemployment." *Critical Studies in Mass Communication* 4:1–20.
Bean, Robert B. 1906. "The Negro Brain." *Century Magazine* (September): 778–84.
Berry, John. 1988. "The Legacy of Reaganomics." *Washington Post National Weekly Edition* (December 19–25).
"Black & Hispanic College Enrollments Continue to Decline." 1990. *Lincoln* (Nebraska) *Star* (January 15).

Bobo, Lawrence. 1983. "White Opposition to Busing: Symbolic Racism or Realistic Group Conflict?" *Journal of Personality and Social Psychology* 45:1196–1210.
———. 1988. "Attitudes toward the Black Political Movement: Trends, Meaning, and Effects on Racial Policy Preferences." *Social Psychology Quarterly* 51:287–302.
———. 1989. "Worlds Apart: Blacks, Whites, and Explanations of Racial Inequality." Paper prepared for delivery at the annual meeting of the Midwest Political Science Association, Chicago.
Bolce, Louis H., III. 1985. "Reagan and the Reverse Gender Gap." *Public Opinion Quarterly* 15:372–85.
Bolce, Louis H., III, and Susan H. Gray. 1979. "Blacks, Whites, and 'Race Politics.' " *Public Interest* (Winter): 61–75.
Boston, Thomas. 1988. *Race, Class and Conservatism*. Boston: Unwin Hyman.
Bradley, Gifford W. 1978. "Self-Serving Biases in the Attribution Process: A Reexamination of the Fact or Fiction Question." *Journal of Personality and Social Psychology* 36:56–71.
Brady, Henry E., and Paul M. Sniderman. 1985. "Attitude Attribution: A Group Basis for Political Reasoning." *American Political Science Review* 79:1061–78.
Branch, Taylor. 1988. *Parting the Waters: America in the King Years 1954–1968*. New York: Simon and Schuster.
Brimmer, Andrew. 1966. "The Negro in the National Economy." In *The American Negro Reference Book*. Ed. John P. David. Englewood Cliffs, N.J.: Prentice Hall.
Brink, William, and Louis Harris. 1964. *The Negro Revolution in America*. New York: Simon and Schuster.
———. 1966. *Black and White: A Study of U.S. Racial Attitudes Today*. New York: Simon and Schuster.
Broman, Clifford L., Harold W. Neighbors, and James S. Jackson. 1988. "Racial Group Identification Among Black Adults." *Social Forces* 67:146–58.
Broom, Leonard, and Norval D. Glenn. 1966. "Negro–White Differences in Reported Attitudes and Behavior." *Sociology and Social Research* 50:187–200.
Brown, Ronald E., and James S. Jackson. 1986. "Church-Based Determinants of Black Campaign Participation." Paper prepared for delivery at the 1986 annual meeting of the American Political Science Association, Washington, D.C.
Bullock, Charles, and Joseph Stewart. 1978. "Second Generation Discrimination in American Schools." *Policy Studies Journal* 7:219–24.
———. 1979. "Incidence and Correlates of Second-Generation Discrimination." In *Race, Sex and Policy Problems*. Ed. Marian Palley and Michael Preston. Lexington, Mass.: Lexington Books.
Bunzel, John H. 1986. "Affirmative Re-Actions." *Public Opinion* (February/March): 45–9.
Campbell, Angus, and Howard Schuman. 1968. "Racial Attitudes in Fifteen American Cities." In *Supplemental Studies for the National Advisory Commission on Civil Disorders*. Washington, D.C.: U.S. Government Printing Office.
Caplan, Nathan, and Jeffrey Paige. 1968. "A Study of Ghetto Rioters." *Scientific American* 219:15–21.
Caplow, Theodore, and Howard M. Bahr. 1979. "Half a Century of Change in Adolescent Attitudes: Replication of a Middletown Survey by the Lynds." *Public Opinion Quarterly* 43:1–17.
Carmichael, Stokeley, and Charles V. Hamilton. 1967. *Black Power*. New York: Vintage.

Carmines, Edward G., and James A. Stimson. 1989. *Issue Evolution: Race and the Transformation of American Politics.* Princeton, N.J.: Princeton University Press.

Cartwright, Walter, and Thomas Burtis. 1969. "Race and Intelligence: Changing Opinions in Social Science." In *Blacks in the United States.* Ed. Norval Glenn and Charles Bonjean. San Francisco: Chandler Publishing.

Castells, Manuel. 1975. "Advanced Capitalism, Collective Consumption and Urban Contradictions: New Sources of Inequality and New Models for Change." In *Stress and Contradictions in Modern Capitalism.* Ed. Leon Lindberg. Lexington, Mass.: D. C. Heath.

Cataldo, Everett, Richard Johnson, and Lyman Kellstedt. 1970. "Political Attitudes of Urban Blacks and Whites." In *Black Conflict with White America.* Ed. Jack R. Van Der Slik. Columbus, Ohio: Charles E. Merrill.

Center on Budget and Policy Priorities. 1986. "Falling Behind: A Report on How Blacks Have Fared Under Reagan." *Journal of Black Studies* 17:148–72.

Christenson, James A., and Riley E. Dunlap. 1984. "Freedom and Equality in American Political Ideology: Race and Gender Differences." *Social Science Quarterly* 65:861–7.

Clark, Kenneth. 1968. *Dark Ghetto.* New York: Harper and Row.

Colasanto, Diane. 1988. "Black Attitudes." *Public Opinion* (January/February): 45–9.

Collins, Sharon M. 1983. "The Making of the Black Middle Class." *Social Problems* 30:369–82.

Condran, John G. 1979. "Changes in White Attitudes toward Blacks: 1963–1977." *Public Opinion Quarterly* 43:463–76.

Conover, Pamela Johnston. 1985. "The Impact of Group Economic Interests on Political Evaluations." *American Politics Quarterly* 13:139–66.

Conover, Pamela Johnston, and Stanley Feldman. 1981. "The Origins and Meaning of Liberal/Conservative Self-Identification." *American Journal of Political Science* 25:617–45.

Converse, Jean M., and Stanley Presser. 1986. *Survey Questions: Handcrafting the Standardized Questionnaire.* Sage University Paper series on Quantitative Applications in the Social Sciences, series no. 01–063. Beverly Hills, Calif.: Sage Publications.

Corbett, Michael. 1990. "Race, Religion, and Political Attitudes." Paper prepared for delivery at the annual meeting of the Midwest Political Science Association, Chicago.

Cotton, Jeremiah. 1989a. "The Declining Relative Economic Status of Black Families." *Review of Black Political Economy* 18:75–86.

Cotton, Jeremiah. 1989b. "Opening the Gap: The Decline in Black Economic Indicators in the 1980s." *Social Science Quarterly* 70:803–19.

Cronon, Edmund D. 1955. *Black Moses: The Story of Marcus Garvey and the United Negro Improvement Association.* Madison: University of Wisconsin Press.

Crosby, Faye J. 1982. *Relative Deprivation and Working Women.* New York: Oxford University Press.

Crosby, Faye J., Stephanie Bromley, and Leonard Saxe. 1980. "Recent Unobtrusive Studies of Black and White Discrimination and Prejudice: A Literature Review." *Psychological Bulletin* 87:546–63.

Dann, Martin, ed. 1971. *The Black Press.* New York: G. P. Putnam's.

Davis, James A., and Tom W. Smith. 1987. *General Social Surveys, 1972–1987: Cumulative Codebook.* Chicago: National Opinion Research Center.

de la Garza, Rodolfo O. 1987. *Ignored Voices: Public Opinion Polls and the Latino Community.* Austin: University of Texas, Center for Mexican American Studies.

Della Fave, L. Richard. 1980. "The Meek Shall Not Inherit the Earth: Self Evaluation and the Legitimacy of Stratification." *American Sociological Review* 45:955–72.

Deutsch, Morton, and Mary Collins. 1951. *Interracial Housing.* Minneapolis: University of Minnesota Press.

Dillingham, Gerald. 1981. "The Emerging Black Middle Class: Class Conscious or Race Conscious?" *Ethnic and Racial Studies* 4:432–47.

Dovidio, John F., and Samuel L. Gaertner. 1986. "Prejudice, Discrimination, and Racism: Historical Trends and Contemporary Approaches." In *Prejudice, Discrimination, and Racism.* Ed. John F. Dovidio and Samuel L. Gaertner. New York: Academic Press.

Dowden, Sue, and John P. Robinson. 1990. "Age Difference in American Racial Attitudes: The Generational Replacement Hypothesis Revisited." Paper delivered at the Conference on Prejudice, Politics and Race in America Today, University of California, Berkeley.

Dower, John. 1986. *War Without Mercy: Race & Power in the Pacific War.* New York: Pantheon.

Drake, St. Clair, and Horace R. Cayton. 1945. *Black Metropolis: A Study of Negro Life in a Northern City.* New York: Harper and Row.

DuBois, W. E. B. 1961. *The Souls of Black Folk.* Greenwich, Conn.: Fawcett.

Duncan, Otis D., David Featherman, and Beverly Duncan. 1972. *Socioeconomic Background and Achievement.* New York: Seminar Books.

Durant, Thomas J., and Joyce Louden. 1986. "The Black Middle Class in America: Historical and Contemporary Perspectives." *Phylon* 47:253–63.

Ebony. 1966. *The Negro Handbook.* Chicago: Johnson Publishing.

Edwards, Ozzie. 1972. "Intergenerational Variation in Racial Attitudes." *Sociology and Social Research* 57:22–31.

Eisenberg, Bernard. 1982. "Only for the Bourgeois? James Weldon Johnson and the NAACP, 1916–1930." *Phylon* 43:110–24.

Ellwood, David, and Mary Jo Bane. 1984. *The Impact of AFDC on Family Structure and Living Arrangements.* Report prepared for the U.S. Department of Health and Human Services. Cited by Wilson (1987:78).

England, Robert, and Kenneth J. Meier. 1985. "From Desegregation to Integration: Second-Generation Discrimination as an Institutional Impediment." *American Politics Quarterly* 13:227–47.

Epps, Edgar. 1975. "The Impact of School Desegregation on Aspirations, Self-Concepts and Other Aspects of Personality." *Law and Contemporary Problems* 39:300–13.

Erskine, Hazel G. 1969. "The Polls: Negro Philosophies of Life." *Public Opinion Quarterly* 33:147–58.

Essien-Udom, E. U. 1967. "Introduction" to *Philosophies and Opinions of Marcus Garvey.* New York: Frank Carr.

———. 1970. "Garvey and Garveyism." In *America's Black Past.* Ed. Eric Foner. New York: Harper and Row.

Farley, Reynolds. 1984. *Blacks and Whites: Narrowing the Gap?* Cambridge: Harvard University Press.

———. 1988. "After the Starting Line: Blacks and Women in an Uphill Race." *Demography* 25:477–96.

arley, Reynolds, and Walter Allen. 1987. *The Color Line and the Quality of Life in America.* New York: Russell Sage.

arley, Reynolds, Shirley Hatchett, and Howard Schuman. 1979. "A Note on Changes in Black Racial Attitudes in Detroit." *Social Indicators Research* 6:439–443.

eagin, Joe R. 1975. *Subordinating the Poor: Welfare and American Beliefs.* Englewood Cliffs, NJ: Prentice-Hall.

eather, N. T. 1974. "Explanations of Poverty in Australian and American Samples: The Person, Society, or Fate?" *Australian Journal of Psychology* 26:199–216.

eatherman, David, and Robert Hauser. 1978. *Opportunity and Change.* New York: Academic Press.

eldman, Stanley. 1983. "Economic Self-Interest and Mass Belief Systems." *American Journal of Political Science* 26:446–466.

———. 1988. "Structure and Consistency in Public Opinion: The Role of Core Beliefs and Values." *American Journal of Political Science* 32:416–40.

ine, Terri Susan. 1990. "Blacks, Whites and Individualism: How Commitment to Individualism Affects Opinion Toward Policies Targeting Blacks." Paper delivered at the annual meeting of the Southwestern Political Science Association, Fort Worth, Tex.

irebaugh, Glenn, and Kenneth E. Davis. 1988. "Trends in AntiBlack Prejudice, 1972–1984: Region and Cohort Effects." *American Journal of Sociology* 94:251–72.

ord, W. Scott. 1973. "Interracial Public Housing in a Border City." *American Journal of Sociology* 78:426–44.

orm, William H., and Claudine Hanson. 1985. "The Consistency of Stratal Beliefs." In *Research in Social Stratification and Mobility.* Ed. Robert V. Robinson. Greenwich, Conn.: JAI Press.

ranklin, John Hope. 1967. *From Slavery to Freedom,* 3rd ed. New York: Alfred Knopf.

razier, E. Franklin. 1939. *The Negro Family in the United States.* Chicago: University of Chicago Press.

———. 1957. *Black Bourgeoisie: The Rise of a New Middle Class in the United States.* New York: Free Press.

———. 1974. *The Negro Church in America.* New York: Schocken.

rederickson, George. 1971. *The Black Image in the White Mind.* New York: Harper and Row.

reeman, Richard. 1976. *Black Elite: The New Market for Highly Educated Black Americans.* New York: McGraw-Hill.

ullinwider, S. P. 1969. *The Mind and Mood of Black America.* Homewood, Ill.: Dorsey Press.

urnham, Adrian. 1982. "Why Are the Poor Always with Us? Explanations for Poverty in Britain." *British Journal of Social Psychology* 21:311–22.

arrow, David J. 1986. *Bearing the Cross: Martin Luther King, Jr., and the Southern Christian Leadership Conference.* New York: William Morrow.

ilder, George. 1981. *Wealth and Poverty.* New York: Basic Books.

iles, Micheal, and Arthur Evans. 1986. "The Power Approach to Intergroup Hostility." *Journal of Conflict Resolution* 30:469–86.

illiam, Franklin D., Jr., and Kenny J. Whitby. 1987. "Race, Class, and Attitudes toward Social Welfare Spending: An Ethclass Interpretation." *Social Science Quarterly* 70:88–100.

Glenn, Norval D. 1963. "Some Changes in the Relative Status of American Non-Whites, 1940–1960." *Phylon* 24:109–22.

———. 1974–5. "Recent Trends in White–NonWhite Attitudinal Differences." *Public Opinion Quarterly* 38:596–604.

Greeley, Andrew M., and Paul B. Sheatsley. 1971. "Attitudes toward Racial Integration." *Scientific American* 225:13–19.

Green, Donald P. 1988. "On the Dimensionality of Public Sentiment toward Partisan and Ideological Groups." *American Journal of Political Science* 32:758–80.

Gurin, Patricia, Gerald Gurin, Rosina C. Lao, and Muriel Beattie. 1968. "Internal-External Control in the Motivational Dynamics of Negro Youth." *Journal of Social Issues* 25:29–53.

Gurin, Patricia, Shirley Hatchett, and James Jackson. 1988. *Hope and Indifference. Blacks' Struggle in the Two Party System*. New York: Russell Sage.

Gwaltney, John L. 1981. *Drylongso*. New York: Random House.

Hall, Marcia L., Arlene F. Mays, and Walter R. Allen. 1984. "Dreams Deferred: Black Student Career Goals and Fields of Study in Graduate/Professional Schools." *Phylon* 45:271–83.

Haller, John. 1971. *Outcasts from Evolution*. Urbana: University of Illinois Press.

Hamilton, Charles V. 1976. "Public Policy and Some Political Consequences." In *Public Policy for the Black Community*. Ed. Marguerite Ross Barnett and James A. Hefner. New York: Alfred Publishing.

———. 1982. "Measuring Black Conservatism." In *The State of Black America*. Washington, D.C.: National Urban League.

Hare, Nathan. 1965. *The Black Anglo-Saxons*. New York: Marzoni and Mumsell.

Harris, Frederick C. 1989. "Religion among Blacks: A Political Mobilizer, Not 'Opiate.'" Paper prepared for delivery at the annual meeting of the Midwest Political Science Association, Chicago.

Harris, Louis and Associates, Inc. 1978. *A Study of Attitudes toward Racial and Religious Minorities and toward Women*. Study no. S2829–B, prepared for The National Conference of Christians and Jews (mimeo).

———. 1989. *The Unfinished Agenda on Race in America*. Vol. 1. Study no. 883006, 9, conducted for the NAACP Legal Defense and Educational Fund, Inc.

Harrison, Bennett, and Barry Bluestone. 1988. *The Great U-Turn*. New York: Basic Books.

Hauser, Robert M. 1990. "The Decline in College Entry among African Americans: Findings in Search of Explanations." Paper delivered at the Conference on Prejudice, Politics and Race in America Today, University of California, Berkeley.

Heider, Fritz. 1958. *The Psychology of Interpersonal Relations*. New York: Wiley.

Herring, Cedric. 1989. "Convergence, Polarization, or What? Racially Based Changes in Attitudes and Outlooks, 1964–1984." *Sociological Quarterly* 30:267–81.

Herrnstein, Richard J. 1990. "Still an American Dilemma." *Public Interest* 98 (Winter): 3–17.

Herskovits, Melville. 1958. *The Myth of the Negro Past*. New York: Beacon.

Hewstone, Miles, and J. M. F. Jaspars. 1982. "Intergroup Relations and Attribution Processes." In *Social Identity*. Ed. Henri Tajfel. Cambridge University Press.

Hill, Robert. 1981. *Economic Policies and Black Progress: Myths and Realities*. Washington, D.C.: National Urban League.

Hochschild, Jennifer. 1981. *What's Fair? American Beliefs about Distributive Justice*. Cambridge: Harvard University Press.

———. 1984. *The New American Dilemma*. New Haven, Conn.: Yale University Press.

———. "Disjunction and Ambivalence in Citizens' Political Thought." In *Reconsidering the Democratic Public*. Ed. George Marcus and John L. Sullivan. Chicago: University of Chicago Press. Forthcoming.

Hunt, Larry L., and Janet G. Hunt. 1977. "Black Religion as Both Opiate and Inspiration of Civil Rights Militance: Putting Marx's Data to the Test." *Social Forces* 56:1–14.

Hyman, Herbert H. 1972. *Secondary Analysis of Sample Surveys: Principles, Procedures and Potentialities*. New York: Wiley.

Hyman, Herbert H., and Paul B. Sheatsley. 1956. "Attitudes on Integration." *Scientific American* 195:35–9.

———. 1964. "Attitudes toward Desegregation." *Scientific American* 211:16–23.

Jackman, Mary R. 1978. "General and Applied Tolerance: Does Education Increase Commitment to Racial Equality?" *American Journal of Political Science* 22:302–24.

———. 1981. "Education and Policy Commitment to Racial Equality." *American Journal of Political Science* 25:256–69.

Jackman, Mary R., and Marie Crane. 1986. " 'Some of My Best Friends are Black. . .': Interracial Friendship and Whites' Racial Attitudes." *Public Opinion Quarterly* 50:459–86.

Jackman, Mary R., and Robert W. Jackman. 1983. *Class Awareness in the United States*. Berkeley: University of California Press.

Jackman, Mary R., and Michael J. Muha. 1984. "Education and Intergroup Attitudes: Moral Enlightenment, Superficial Democratic Commitment, or Ideological Refinement." *American Sociological Review* 49:751–69.

Jackman, Mary R., and Mary Scheuer Senter. 1980. "Images of Social Groups: Categorical or Qualified?" *Public Opinion Quarterly* 44:341–61.

———. 1983. "Different, Therefore Unequal: Beliefs About Trait Differences Between Groups of Unequal Status." *Research in Social Stratification and Mobility* 2:309–35.

Jackson, James S., and Gerald Gurin. 1987. *National Survey of Black Americans, 1979–1980*. Ann Arbor, Mich.: Inter-University Consortium for Political and Social Research.

Jackson, James S., M. Belinda Tucker, and Phillip J. Bowman. 1982. "Conceptual and Methodological Issues in Survey Research on Black Americans." In *Methodological Problems in Minority Research*. Ed. William T. Liu. Chicago: Pacific/Asian American Mental Health Center.

Jacobson, Cardell K. 1983. "Black Support for Affirmative Action Programs." Presented at the annual meeting of the American Association for Public Opinion Research.

Jaynes, Gerald D., and Robin M. Williams, Jr., eds. 1989. *A Common Destiny: Blacks and American Society*. Washington, DC: National Academy Press.

Jelen, Ted G. 1990. "The Impact of Home Ownership on Whites' Racial Attitudes." *American Politics Quarterly* 18:208–14.

Joe, Tom, and Peter Yu. 1984. "Black Men, Welfare and Jobs." *New York Times* (May 11): A31.

Johnson, Michael P., and James L. Roark. 1984. *Black Masters: A Free Family of Color in the Old South*. New York: W. W. Norton.

Johnson, Robert. 1957. "Negro Reactions to Minority Group Status." In *American Minorities*. Ed. Milton L. Barron. New York: Alfred A. Knopf.

Joint Center for Political Studies. Annually since 1970. *A National Roster of Black Elected Officials*. Washington, D.C.: Joint Center.

Jordan, Vernon. 1980. "Introduction." In *The State of Black America 1980*. Ed. James D. Williams. Washington, D.C.: National Urban League.

Jordan, Winthrop. 1968. *White Over Black: American Attitudes Toward the Negro, 1550–1812*. Baltimore: Penguin.

———. 1974. *The White Man's Burden*. New York: Oxford University Press.

Kelley, Jonathan. 1974. "The Politics of School Busing." *Public Opinion Quarterly* 38:23–39.

Kendrick, Ann. 1988. "The Core Economic Beliefs of Blacks and Whites." Paper prepared for the Committee on Status of Black Americans. Washington, D.C.: National Research Council.

Key, V. O., Jr. 1949. *Southern Politics in State and Nation*. New York: Alfred Knopf.

Kiecolt, K. Jill, and Laura E. Nathan. 1985. *Secondary Analysis of Survey Data*. Beverly Hills, Calif.: Sage Publications.

Killian, Lewis. 1968. *The Impossible Revolution?* New York: Random House.

Kinder, Donald R. 1986. "The Continuing American Dilemma: White Resistance to Racial Change 40 Years After Myrdal." *Journal of Social Issues* 42:151–71.

Kinder, Donald R., and D. Roderick Kiewiet. 1979. "Economic Grievances and Political Behavior: The Role of Personal Discontents and Symbolic Judgments in Congressional Voting." *American Journal of Political Science* 23:495–527.

Kinder, Donald R., Tali Mendelberg, Michael C. Dawson, Lynn M. Sanders, Steven J. Rosenstone, Jocelyn Sargent, and Cathy Cohen. 1989. "Race and the 1988 American Presidential Election." Paper prepared for delivery at the annual meeting of the American Political Science Association, Atlanta, Ga.

Kinder, Donald R., and David O. Sears. 1981. "Prejudice and Politics: Symbolic Racism Versus Racial Threats to the Good Life." *Journal of Personality and Social Psychology* 40:414–31.

King, Martin Luther, Jr. 1963. *Why We Can't Wait*. New York: Times-Mirror.

Kingston, Paul W., John L. P. Thompson, and Douglas M. Eichar. 1984. "The Politics of Homeownership." *American Politics Quarterly* 12:131–50.

Kluegel, James R. 1990. "Trends in Whites' Explanations of the Black White Gap in Socioeconomic Status, 1977–1989." *American Sociological Review*. Forthcoming.

Kluegel, James R., and Lawrence Bobo. 1990. "The Structure of Structuralism: Dimensions of Whites' Beliefs about the Black–White SES Gap." Paper delivered at the Conference on Prejudice, Politics and Race in America Today, University of California, Berkeley.

Kluegel, James R., and Eliot R. Smith. 1986. *Beliefs about Inequality: Americans' Views of What Is and What Ought to Be*. New York: Aldine de Gruyter.

Kluger, Richard. 1975. *Simple Justice: The History of Brown v. Board of Education and Black Americans' Struggle for Equality*. New York: Random House.

Kuklinski, James H. 1990. "Emotions, Images, and Political Ideology. An Experimental Survey Test of the Symbolic Racism Hypothesis." Paper prepared for delivery at the annual meeting of the Midwest Political Science Association, Chicago.

Kuklinski, James H., and Wayne Parent. 1981. "Race and Big Government: Contamination in Measuring Racial Attitudes." *Political Methodology* 8:131–59.

Landry, Bart. 1987. *The New Black Middle Class*. Berkeley: University of California Press.

Lane, Robert E. 1978. "Interpersonal Relations and Leadership in a 'Cold Society'." *Comparative Politics* 10:443–59.

Lazear, Edward. 1979. "The Narrowing of Black–White Wage Differentials Is Illusory." *American Economic Review* 69:553–64.

Lerner, Melvin J. 1975. "The Justice Motive in Social Behavior." *Journal of Social Issues* 31:1–20.

Levy, Frank. 1987. *Dollars and Dreams*. New York: W. W. Norton.

Lewis, I. A., and William Schneider. 1985. "Hard Times: The Public on Poverty." *Public Opinion* (June/July): 2–7, 59–60.

Lichter, Daniel T. 1988. "Racial Differences in Underemployment in American Cities." *American Journal of Sociology* 93:771–92.

Lichter, Linda S. 1985. "Who Speaks for Black America?" *Public Opinion* (August/ September): 41–4, 58.

Lipset, Seymour Martin, and Reinhard Bendix. 1959. *Social Mobility in Industrial Society*. Berkeley: University of California Press.

Lipset, Seymour Martin, and William Schneider. 1978. "The Bakke Case: How Would It Be Decided at the Bar of Public Opinion?" *Public Opinion* (March/ April): 38–44.

———. 1983. *The Confidence Gap: Business, Labor and Government in the Public Mind*. New York: Free Press.

Lynd, Robert S., and Helen M. Lynd. 1929. *Middletown: A Study in Contemporary American Culture*. New York: Harcourt, Brace.

Margolis, Michael, and Khondaker E. Haque. 1981. "Applied Tolerance or Fear of Government? An Alternative Interpretation of Jackman's Findings." *American Journal of Political Science* 25:241–55.

Marriott, Michael. 1990. "Intense College Recruiting Drives Black Enrollment to a Record." *New York Times* (April 15).

Marx, Gary T. 1967. *Protest and Prejudice: A Study of Belief in the Black Community*. New York: Harper and Row.

——— 1971. "Religion: Opiate or Inspiration of Civil Rights Militancy among Negroes?" In *Racial Conflict: Tension and Change in American Society*. Boston: Little, Brown.

Matthews, Donald, and James Prothro. 1966. *Negroes and the New Southern Politics*. New York: Harcourt Brace.

Mays, Benjamin, and Joseph Nicholson. 1969. *The Negro's Church*. New York: Arno Press.

McAdam, Doug. 1982. *Political Process and the Development of Black Insurgency 1930–1970*. Chicago: University of Chicago Press.

McBride, David, and Monroe Little. 1981. "The Afro American Elite, 1930–1940." *Phylon* 42:105–19.

McClendon, McKee J. 1985. "Racism, Rational Choice, and White Opposition to Racial Change: A Case Study of Busing." *Public Opinion Quarterly* 49:214–33.

McClosky, Herbert. 1964. "Consensus and Ideology in American Politics." *American Political Science Review* 58:361–82.

McClosky, Herbert, and John Zaller. 1984. *The American Ethos: Public Attitudes toward Capitalism and Democracy*. Cambridge: Harvard University Press.

McConahay, John B. 1982. "Is It the Buses or the Blacks? Self-Interest Versus Racial Attitudes as Correlates of Anti-Busing Attitudes in Louisville." *Journal of Politics* 44:692–720.

———. 1986. "Modern Racism, Ambivalence, and the Modern Racism Scale." In *Prejudice, Discrimination, and Racism: Theory and Research*. Ed. John F. Dovidio and Samuel L. Gaertner. New York: Academic Press.

McConahay, John B., Betty B. Hardee, and Valerie Batts. 1981. "Has Racism

Declined in America? It Depends on Who Is Asking and What Is Asked.' *Journal of Conflict Resolution* 25:563–79.

McConahay, John B., and Joseph C. Hough, Jr. 1976. "Symbolic Racism." *Journal of Social Issues* 32:23–45.

McCready, William C., with Andrew M. Greeley. 1976. *The Ultimate Values of the American Population.* Beverly Hills, Calif.: Sage Publications.

McCrone, Donald, and Richard Hardy. 1979. "Combating Dual Discrimination: The Impact of Civil Rights Policies on the Income Status of Black Women." In *Race, Sex, and Policy Problems.* Ed. Marian Lief Palley and Michael B. Preston. Lexington, Mass.: Lexington Books.

Meer, Bernard, and Edward Freedman. 1966. "The Impact of Negro Neighbors on White Homeowners." *Social Forces* 45:11–19.

Meier, August. 1962. "Negro Class Structure and Ideology in the Age of Booker T. Washington." *Phylon* 23:258–67.

———. 1968. *Negro Thought in America, 1880–1915.* Ann Arbor: University of Michigan Press.

Meier, August, and Elliot Rudwick. 1973. *CORE: A Study in the Civil Rights Movement: 1942–1968.* New York: Oxford University Press.

———. 1976. *Along the Color Line.* Urbana: University of Illinois Press.

Meier, Kenneth, Joseph Stewart, Jr., and Robert E. England. 1989. *Race, Class, and Education.* Madison: University of Wisconsin Press.

Meltzer, Milton, ed. 1964, 1965, 1967. *In Their Own Words.* 3 vols. New York: Thomas Y. Crowell.

Merriman, W. Richard, and Edward G. Carmines. 1988. "The Limits of Liberal Tolerance: The Case of Racial Policies." *Polity* 20:519–26.

Merriman, W. Richard, and T. Wayne Parent. 1983. "Sources of Citizen Attitudes toward Government Race Policy." *Polity* 16:30–47.

Miller, Arthur H., Patricia Gurin, Gerald Gurin, and Oksana Malanchuk. 1981. "Group Consciousness and Political Participation." *American Journal of Political Science* 25:494–511.

Miller, Dale T., and Michael Ross. 1975. "Self-Serving Biases in the Attribution of Causality: Fact or Fiction?" *Psychological Bulletin* 82:213–25.

Miller, Frederick D., Eliot R. Smith, and James Uleman. 1981. "Measurement and Interpretation of Situational and Dispositional Attributions." *Journal of Experimental Social Psychology* 17:80–95.

Miller, Warren E., Arthur Miller, Richard Brody, Jack Dennis, David Kovenock, and Merrill Shanks. 1975. *The CPS 1972 American National Election Study: Codebook, Volumes I and II.* Rev ed. Ann Arbor, Mich.: Inter-University Consortium for Political Research.

Mitchell, Robert C. 1984. "Rationality and Irrationality in the Public's Perception of Nuclear Power." In *Public Reactions to Nuclear Power: Are There Critical Masses?* Ed. William R. Freudenberg and Eugene A. Rose. Boulder, Colo.: Westview Press.

Morgan, John T. 1890. "The Race Question in the United States." *Arena* 2:385–98.

Morin, Richard. 1989. "The Answer May Depend on Who Asked the Question." *Washington Post National Weekly Edition* (November 6–12): 38.

Morin, Richard, and Dan Balz. 1989a. "Shifting Racial Climate: Blacks and Whites Have Greater Contact But Sharply Different Views, Poll Finds." *Washington Post* (October 25).

———. 1989b. "There's Still Room for Improvement in Racial Relations." *Washington Post National Weekly Edition* (October 30–November 5): 37.

Morris, Aldon D. 1984. *The Origins of the Civil Rights Movement.* New York: Free Press.

Moulton, Faye. 1988. "Student Financial Aid and Minority Enrollments in Higher Education." M.A. thesis, Department of Political Science, University of Nebraska, Lincoln.

Moynihan, Daniel P. 1972. "The Schism in Black America." *Public Interest* 27:3–24.

Murray, Charles. 1984. *Losing Ground.* New York: Basic Books.

Muthen, Bengt O. 1987. *LISCOMP: Analysis of Linear Structural Equations With a Comprehensive Measurement Model.* Mooresville, Ind.: Scientific Software, Inc.

Myrdal, Gunnar. 1944. *An American Dilemma: The Negro Problem and Modern Democracy.* New York: Random House.

National Journal. 1988. (July 30): 1994.

The Negro in America. 1963. *Newsweek* (July 29): 19–29.

Newby, Idus A., ed. 1968. *The Development of Segregationist Thought.* Homewood, Ill.: Dorsey Press.

New York Times Poll. 1987. *New York City Race Relations Survey: March 6–11, 1987.* Mimeo.

Nilson, Linda B. 1981. "Reconsidering Ideological Lines: Beliefs about Poverty in America." *Sociological Quarterly* 22:531–48.

Nunn, Clyde Z., Harry J. Crockett, Jr., and J. Allen Williams, Jr. 1978. *Tolerance for Nonconformity.* San Francisco: Jossey-Bass.

O'Brien, Robert M., and Pamela Homer. 1987. "Corrections for Coarsely Categorized Measures: LISREL's Polyserial and Polychoric Correlations." *Quality & Quantity* 21:349–60.

O'Gorman, Hubert J. 1975. "Pluralistic Ignorance and White Estimates of White Support for Racial Segregation." *Public Opinion Quarterly* 39:313–30.

———. 1979. "White and Black Perceptions of Racial Values." *Public Opinion Quarterly* 43:48–59.

———. 1988. "Pluralistic Ignorance and Reference Groups: The Case of Intergroup Ignorance." In *Surveying Social Life: Essays in Honor of Herbert H. Hyman.* Ed. Hubert J. O'Gorman. Middletown, Conn.: Wesleyan University Press.

O'Gorman, Hubert J., with Stephen L. Garry. 1976–7. "Pluralistic Ignorance – A Replication and Extension." *Public Opinion Quarterly* 40:449–58.

Oliver, Melvin L. and Mark A. Glick. 1982. "An Analysis of the New Orthodoxy on Black Mobility." *Social Problems* 29:511–23.

Oliver, Melvin L. and Thomas M. Shapiro. 1989. "Race and Wealth." *Review of Black Political Economy.* Forthcoming.

Olsson, Ulf. 1979. "Maximum Likelihood Estimation of the Polychoric Correlation Coefficient." *Psychometrika* 44:443–60.

"Opinion Roundup." 1982. *Public Opinion* (April/May): 21–32.

Orbell, John. 1967. "Protest Participation among Southern Negro College Students." *American Political Science Review* 61:446–56.

Orfield, Gary. 1978. *Must We Bus?* Washington, D.C.: Brookings Institution.

———. 1983. *Public School Desegregation in the United States, 1968–1980.* Washington, D.C.: Joint Center for Political Studies.

Paige, Jeffrey M. 1970. "Changing Patterns of Anti-White Attitudes among Blacks." *Journal of Social Issues* 26:69–86.

Parent, Wayne. 1985. "A Liberal Legacy: Blacks Blaming Themselves for Economic Failures." *Journal of Black Studies* 16:3–20.

Parent, Wayne, and Paul Stekler. 1985. "The Political Implications of Economic Stratification in the Black Community." *Western Political Quarterly* 38:521–37

Peterson, Christopher, and Martin E. P. Seligman. 1983. "Learned Helplessnes and Victimization." *Journal of Social Issues* 32:103–16.

Pettigrew, Thomas F. 1964. *A Profile of the Negro American.* Princeton, N.J.: Van Nostrand Company.

————. 1979. "The Ultimate Attribution Error: Extending Allport's Cognitive Analysis of Prejudice." *Personality and Social Psychology Bulletin* 5:461–76

Phillips, Ulrich B. [1918] 1966. *American Negro Slavery.* Baton Rouge: Louisiana State University Press.

Placek, Paul J., and Gerry E. Hendershot. 1974. "Public Welfare and Family Plan ning." *Social Problems* 21:658–73.

Polgar, Steven, and Virginia A. Hiday. 1974. "The Effect of an Additional Birth on Low-Income Urban Families." *Population Studies* 28:463–71.

Poole, Keith T., and L. Harmon Zeigler. 1985. *Women, Public Opinion and Politics.* New York: Longman.

Presser, Harriett B., and Linda S. Salsberg. 1975. "Public Assistance and Early Family Formation: Is There a Pronatalist Effect?" *Social Problems* 23:226–41

Prothro, James W., and Charles M. Grigg. 1960. "Fundamental Principles of Democ racy: Bases of Agreement and Disagreement." *Journal of Politics* 22:276–94

Pryor, Frederick. 1981. "The 'New Class': Analysis of the Concept, the Hypothesis and the Idea as a Research Tool." *American Journal of Economics and Sociol ogy* 40:367–80.

Quinley, Harold E., and Charles Y. Glock. 1979. *Anti-Semitism in America.* New York: Free Press.

Rawick, George P., ed. 1972–. *The American Slave: A Composite Autobiography.* 23 vols. Westport, Conn.: Greenwood Press.

Rhodes, James F. 1966. *History of the United States from the Compromise of 1850.* Abridged and edited by Allen Nevins. Chicago: University of Chicago Press

Rich, Spencer. 1986. "Are You Really Better Off Than You Were 13 Years Ago?' *Washington Post National Weekly Edition* (September 8): 20.

Roberts, Harry W. 1953. "The Impact of Military Service upon the Racial Attitudes of Negro Servicemen in World War II." *Social Problems* 1:65–9.

Robinson, Jerry, and James Preston. 1976. "Equal Status Contact and Modification of Racial Prejudice." *Social Forces* 54:900–24.

Robinson, Jo Ann Gibson. 1987. *The Montgomery Bus Boycott and the Women Who Made It Possible.* Knoxville: University of Tennessee Press.

Robinson, Robert V., and Wendell Bell. 1978. "Equality, Success, and Social Justice in England and the United States." *American Sociological Review* 43:125–43.

Rokeach, Milton. 1973. *The Nature of Human Values.* New York: Free Press.

————. 1979. *Understanding Human Values: Individual and Societal.* New York: Free Press.

Roper Center. 1982. *A Guide to Roper Center Resources for the Study of American Race Relations.* Williamstown, Mass.: Roper Center.

Ross, Arthur. 1967. "The Negro in the American Economy." In *Employment, Race, and Poverty.* Ed. Arthur Ross and Herbert Hill. New York: Harcourt Brace.

Ross, Lee. 1977. "The Intuitive Psychologist and His Shortcomings: Distortions in the Attribution Process." In *Advances in Experimental Social Psychology,* vol. 10. Ed. Leonard Berkowitz. New York: Academic Press.

Ross, Lee, and Craig A. Anderson. 1982. "Shortcomings in the Attribution Process: On the Origins and Maintenance of Erroneous Social Assessments." In *Judgment Under Uncertainty: Heuristics and Biases*. Ed. Daniel Kahneman, Paul Slovic, and Amos Tversky. Cambridge University Press.

Roth, Byron M. 1990. "Social Psychology's 'Racism.' " *Public Interest* 98 (Winter): 26–36.

Sackett, Victoria. 1980. "Ignoring the People." *Policy Review* 12:9–22.

Sarnoff, Irving. 1951. "Identification with the Aggressor: Some Personality Correlates of Anti-Semitism among Jews." *Journal of Personality* 20:199–218.

Scammon, Richard M., and Ben J. Wattenberg. 1973. "Black Progress and Liberal Rhetoric." *Commentary* 10:35–44.

Schneider, David J., Albert H. Hastorf, and Phoebe C. Ellsworth. 1979. *Person Perception*. 2d ed. Reading, Mass.: Addison-Wesley.

Schuman, Howard. 1975. "Free Will and Determination in Public Beliefs about Race." In *Majority and Minority: The Dynamics of Racial and Ethnic Relations*. Ed. Norman R. Yetman and C. Hoy Steele. Boston: Allyn and Bacon.

Schuman, Howard, and Lawrence Bobo. 1988. "Survey-Based Experiments on White Attitudes toward Residential Integration." *American Journal of Sociology* 94:272–99.

Schuman, Howard, and Shirley Hatchett. 1974. *Black Racial Attitudes: Trends and Complexities*. Ann Arbor: University of Michigan, Institute for Social Research.

Schuman, Howard, Charlotte Steeh, and Lawrence Bobo. 1985. *Racial Attitudes in America: Trends and Interpretations*. Cambridge: Harvard University Press.

Schwartz, Mildred. 1967. *Trends in White Attitudes toward Negroes*. Report no. 119. Chicago: University of Chicago, National Opinion Research Center.

Schwartz, Sandra K., and David C. Schwartz. 1976. "Convergence and Divergence in Political Orientations between Blacks and Whites: 1960–1973." *Journal of Social Issues* 32:153–68.

Sears, David O. 1988. "Symbolic Racism." In *Eliminating Racism: Means and Controversies*. Ed. Phyllis A. Katz and Dalmas A. Taylor. New York: Plenum Press.

Sears, David O., and Harris M. Allen, Jr. 1984. "The Trajectory of Local Desegregation Controversies and Whites' Opposition to Busing." In *Groups in Contact: The Psychology of Desegregation*. Ed. Norman Miller and Marilyn B. Brewer. New York: Academic Press.

Sears, David O., Carl P. Hensler, and Leslie K. Speer. 1979. "Whites' Opposition to 'Busing': Self-Interest or Symbolic Politics?" *American Political Science Review* 73:969–95.

Sears, David O., and Donald R. Kinder. 1985. "Whites' Opposition to Busing: On Conceptualizing and Operationalizing 'Group Conflict.' " *Journal of Personality and Social Psychology* 48:1141–7.

Sears, David O., and John McConahay. 1973. *The Politics of Violence*. Boston: Houghton Mifflin.

Seligman, Martin E. P. 1975. *Helplessness: On Depression, Development, and Death*. San Francisco: W. H. Freeman.

Seltzer, Richard, and Robert C. Smith. 1985. "Race and Ideology: A Research Note Measuring Liberalism and Conservatism in Black America." *Phylon* 46:98–105.

Selznick, Gertrude J., and Stephen Steinberg. 1969. *The Tenacity of Prejudice*. New York: Harper and Row.

Sewell, William, and Robert M. Hauser. 1975. *Occupation and Earnings: Achievement in the Early Career*. New York: Academic Press.

Shapiro, Robert Y., and Harpreet Mahajan. 1986. "Gender Differences in Policy

Preferences: A Summary of Trends from the 1960s to the 1980s." *Public Opinion Quarterly* 50:42–61.

Sheatsley, Paul B. 1966. "White Attitudes toward the Negro." *Daedalus* 95:217–38.

Shepelak, Norma J. 1987. "The Role of Self-Explanations and Self-Evaluations in Legitimating Inequality." *American Sociological Review* 52:495–503.

Shingles, Richard D. 1981. "Black Consciousness and Political Participation: The Missing Link." *American Political Science Review* 75:76–91.

———. 1986. "The Black Gender Gap: Double Jeopardy and Politicization." Presented at the annual meeting of the Midwest Political Science Association, Chicago.

Sigelman, Lee, James W. Shockey, and Carol K. Sigelman. 1990. "Ethnic Stereotyping: A Black–White Comparison." Paper delivered at the Conference on Prejudice, Politics and Race in America Today, University of California, Berkeley.

Simms, Margaret C. 1987. "Update on the Job Status of Blacks." *Focus* (April): 6–7.

Sites, Paul, and Elizabeth Mullins. 1985. "The American Black Elite: 1930–1978." *Phylon* 46:269–80.

Sitkoff, Harvard. 1981. *The Struggle for Black Equality, 1954–1980*. New York: Hill and Wang.

Skocpol, Theda. 1988. "The Limits of the New Deal System and the Roots of Contemporary Welfare Dilemmas." In *The Politics of Social Policy in the United States*. Ed. Margaret Weir, Ann Shola Orloff, and Theda Skocpol. Princeton, N.J.: Princeton University Press.

Smith, A. Wade. 1981a. "Racial Tolerance as a Function of Group Position." *American Sociological Review* 46:558–73.

———. 1981b. "Tolerance of School Desegregation, 1954–77." *Social Forces* 59:1256–74.

———. 1982. "White Attitudes toward School Desegregation, 1954–1980: An Update on Continuing Trends." *Pacific Sociological Review* 25:3–25.

———. 1987. "Problems and Progress in the Measurement of Black Public Opinion." *American Behavioral Scientist* 30:441–55.

Smith, James P., and Finis Welch. 1987. "Race and Poverty: A Forty-Year Record." *American Economic Review* 77:152–8.

———. 1989. "Black Economic Progress After Myrdal." *Journal of Economic Literature* 27:519–64.

Smith, Kevin B. 1985a. "I Made It Because of Me: Beliefs about the Causes of Wealth and Poverty." *Sociological Spectrum* 5:255–68.

———. 1985b. "Seeing Justice in Poverty: The Belief in a Just World and Ideas about Inequalities." *Sociological Spectrum* 5:17–30.

Smith, Kevin B. and Wayne C. Seelbach. 1987. "Education and Intergroup Attitudes: More on the Jackman and Muha Thesis." *Sociological Spectrum* 7:157–70.

Smith, Tom W. 1980. "America's Most Important Problem: A Trend Analysis, 1946–1976." *Public Opinion Quarterly* 44:164–80.

———. 1984. "The Polls: Gender and Attitudes toward Violence." *Public Opinion Quarterly* 48:384–6.

Smith, Tom W., and Paul B. Sheatsley. 1984. "American Attitudes toward Race Relations." *Public Opinion* (October/November): 14–15, 50–3.

Sniderman, Paul M., and Richard A. Brody. 1977. "Coping: The Ethic of Self-Reliance." *American Journal of Political Science* 21:501–21.

Sniderman, Paul M., Richard A. Brody, and James H. Kuklinski. 1984. "Policy Reasoning and Political Issues: The Case of Racial Equality." *American Journal of Political Science* 28:75–94.

Sniderman, Paul M., with Michael G. Hagen. 1985. *Race and Inequality: A Study in American Values*. Chatham, N.J.: Chatham House.

Sniderman, Paul M., Michael G. Hagen, Philip E. Tetlock, and Henry E. Brady. 1986. "Reasoning Chains: Causal Models of Policy Reasoning in Mass Publics." *British Journal of Political Science* 16:405–30.

Sniderman, Paul M., Thomas Piazza, Ada Finifter, and Philip E. Tetlock. 1989. "Black Tolerance." Paper prepared for delivery at the annual meeting of the Midwest Political Science Association, Chicago.

Sniderman, Paul M., and Philip E. Tetlock. 1986a. "Reflections on American Racism." *Journal of Social Issues* 42:173–87.

———. 1986b. "Symbolic Racism: Problems of Motive Attribution in Political Analysis." *Journal of Social Issues* 42:129–50.

Sowell, Thomas. 1975. *Race and Economics*. New York: David McKay.

———. 1984. *Civil Rights: Rhetoric or Reality?* New York: Morrow.

Stanley, Harold, and Richard Niemi, eds. 1988. *Vital Statistics on American Politics*. Washington, D.C.: CQ Press.

Stolte, John F. 1983. "The Legitimation of Structural Inequality: Reformulation and Test of the Self-Evaluation Argument." *American Sociological Review* 48:331–43.

Stouffer, Samuel A. 1955. *Communism, Conformity and Civil Liberties*. New York: Doubleday.

Survey Research Center. 1984. *National Black Election Study Codebook*. Ann Arbor: University of Michigan.

Swinton, David. 1987. "Economic Status of Blacks 1986." In *The State of Black America*. Ed. Janet Dewart. New York: National Urban League.

Taylor, D. Garth. 1986. *Public Opinion and Collective Action*. Chicago: University of Chicago Press.

Taylor D. Garth, Paul Sheatsley, and Andrew M. Greeley. 1978. "Attitudes toward Racial Integration." *Scientific American* 238:42–9.

Terrell, Henry S. 1971. "Wealth Accumulation of Black and White Families: The Empirical Evidence." *Journal of Finance* 26:363–77.

Tetlock, Philip E. 1985. "Toward an Intuitive Politician Model of Attribution Processes." In *The Self and Social Life*. Ed. Barry R. Schlenker. New York: McGraw-Hill.

Thomas, Gail. 1979. "The Influence of Ascription, Achievement, and Educational Expectations on Black–White Post Secondary Enrollment." *Sociological Quarterly* 20:209–22.

Tobin, Gary A., with Sharon L. Sassler. 1988. *Jewish Perceptions of Anti-Semitism*. New York: Plenum Press.

U. S. Bureau of the Census. 1955, 1965, 1973, 1987, 1988, 1989. *Statistical Abstract of the United States*. Washington, D.C.: U.S. Government Printing Office.

———. 1985. *Household and Family Characteristics March 1985*. Current Population Reports. Ser. P–20, no. 411. Washington, D.C.: U.S. Government Printing Office.

———. 1986a. *Characteristics of the Population Below the Poverty Level, 1984*. Current Population Reports. Ser. P–60, no. 152. Washington, D.C.: U.S. Government Printing Office.

———. 1986b. *Economic Characteristics of Households in the U.S. Fourth Quarter, 1984*. Current Population Reports. Ser P–70, no. 6. Washington, D.C.: U.S. Government Printing Office.

U.S. National Advisory Commission on Civil Disorders. 1968. *Report*. New York: Bantam.

Vanneman, Reeve, and Lynn Weber Cannon. 1987. *The American Perception of Class*. Philadelphia: Temple University Press.

Vaughn-Cooke, Denis. 1985. "No Recovery in the Economic Status of Black America." *Black Scholar* (September/October): 2–13.

Verba, Sidney, and Gary R. Orren. 1985. *Equality in America: The View from the Top*. Cambridge: Harvard University Press.

Vobejda, Barbara. 1989. "Class, Color and College." *Washington Post National Weekly Edition* (May 15–21): 6.

Walton, Hanes, Jr. 1985. *Invisible Politics: Black Political Behavior*. Albany: State University of New York Press.

Welch, Susan, and Michael Combs. 1985. "Intra-Racial Differences in Attitudes of Blacks: Class Cleavages or Consensus." *Phylon* 46:91–7.

Welch, Susan, and Lorn Foster. 1987. "Class and Conservatism in the Black Community." *American Politics Quarterly* 15:445–70.

Welch, Susan, and John Gruhl. 1990. "The Impact of Bakke on Black and Hispanic Enrollment in Medical and Law School." *Social Science Quarterly*. In press.

Welch, Susan, and Lee Sigelman. 1989. "A Black Gender Gap?" *Social Science Quarterly* 70:120–33.

Welch, Susan, and Fred Ullrich. 1984. *The Political Behavior of Jewish Women*. New York: Biblio Press.

Willhelm, Sidney. 1986. "The Economic Demise of Blacks in America: A Prelude to Genocide?" *Journal of Black Studies* 17:201–54.

Williams, Juan. 1987. *Eyes on the Prize: America's Civil Rights Years, 1954–1965*. New York: Viking Press.

Williams, Linda. 1987. "Black Political Progress in the 1980s: The Elective Arena." In *The New Black Politics*. Ed. Michael B. Preston, Lenneal J. Henderson, Jr., and Paul Puryear. New York: Longman.

Williamson, J. B. 1974. "Beliefs about Welfare Poor." *Sociology and Social Research* 58:163–75.

Wilner, Daniel, Rosebelle Walkley, and Stuart Cook. 1955. *Human Relations in Interracial Housing*. Minneapolis: University of Minnesota Press.

Wilson, William J. 1978. *The Declining Significance of Race*. New York: McGraw-Hill.

———. 1987. *The Truly Disadvantaged*. Chicago: University of Chicago Press.

Wingert, Pat. 1990. "Fewer Blacks on Campus." *Newsweek* (January 29): 75.

Wirls, Daniel. 1986. "Reinterpreting the Gender Gap." *Public Opinion Quarterly* 50:316–30.

Wolters, Raymond. 1970. *Negroes and the Great Depression*. Westport, Conn.: Greenwood Press.

Woodrum, Eric, and Arnold Bell. 1989. "Race, Politics, and Religion in Civil Religion Among Blacks." *Sociological Analysis* 49:353–67.

Woodward, C. Vann. 1974. *The Strange Career of Jim Crow*. 3rd rev. ed. New York: Oxford University Press.

Zaccaro, Stephen J., Christopher Peterson, and Steven Walker. 1987. "Self-Serving Attributions for Individual and Group Performance." *Social Psychology Quarterly* 50:257–63.

Zeitz, Gerald, and James R. Lincoln. 1981. "Individualism–Social Determinism: A Belief Component in the Formation of Socio-Political Attitudes." *Sociology and Social Research* 65:283–98.

Author index

205

Subject index

209